THE HEART OF OUR
Covenants

TEMPLE PRINCIPLES
that **DRAW US**
unto **CHRIST**

THE HEART OF OUR *Covenants*

TEMPLE PRINCIPLES *that* DRAW US *unto* CHRIST

VALIANT K. JONES

CFI
An imprint of Cedar Fort, Inc.
Springville, Utah

© 2025 Valiant Jones
All rights reserved.

No part of this book may be reproduced in any form whatsoever, whether by graphic, visual, electronic, film, microfilm, tape recording, or any other means, without prior written permission of the publisher, except in the case of brief passages embodied in critical reviews and articles.

This is not an official publication of The Church of Jesus Christ of Latter-day Saints. The opinions and views expressed herein belong solely to the author and do not necessarily represent the opinions or views of Cedar Fort, Inc. Permission for the use of sources, graphics, and photos is also solely the responsibility of the author.

Paperback ISBN 13: 978-1-4621-4941-4
eBook ISBN 13: 978-1-4621-4940-7

Published by CFI, an imprint of Cedar Fort, Inc.
2373 W. 700 S., Suite 100, Springville, UT 84663
Distributed by Cedar Fort, Inc., www.cedarfort.com

Library of Congress Cataloging Number: 2025930147

Cover design by Shawnda Craig
Cover design © 2025 Cedar Fort, Inc.
Edited and Typeset by Liz Kazandzhy

Printed in the United States of America

10 9 8 7 6 5 4 3 2 1

Printed on acid-free paper

To my wife, Lori, for her support, patience, and love. And to our children, Allyson, Bradley, Craig, Camilla, and Dallin, for providing me with a schoolground of growth and learning.

Contents

Acknowledgments................................... xi
Introduction....................................... xiii

1 Three Temple Insights............................ 1
    Clothed in Temple Garments 3
    The Signs and Tokens Pertaining to the Holy Priesthood .. 12
    The Covenants of Eternal Marriage................. 18
    The Temple Centers on Covenants and Jesus Christ 24

2 Understanding the Keys of Temple Work 27
    The Restoration of Priesthood Keys................. 28
    Who Was Elias? 31
    Elias and the Dispensation of the Gospel of Abraham..... 36
    Elias and the Restoration of All Things 39
    Work for the Dead Commenced After Christ's Death..... 42
    Elijah's Keys Seal All Ordinances for the Living 43

  Elijah's Keys Extend Exalting Ordinances to the Dead 46
  A Culmination of the Restoration 49
  Restored Keys Extend Christ's Atonement to All 53
  I Shall Love Thee Better After Death 56

3 Eternal Families and Same-Sex Marriage 59
  Be Fruitful and Multiply 60
  Literal Children of Heavenly Parents 61
  There Are Also Celestial Bodies 65
  Families in Heaven 70
  The Abrahamic Blessing of Posterity or Seed 74
  Complementary Natures 78
  Implication of Our Doctrine 81
  Our Doctrine on Gender and Sexuality 86
  A Look at Two Historical Changes 90
  Irrevocable Doctrine 93

4 Support for Sexual Minorities through the Doctrine of Christ . 97
  The Two Dimensions of the Doctrine of Christ 99
  Connections Strengthen SSA Saints 103
  Come unto Christ, the Light of the World 110
  A Three-Act Play 115
  Jesus Christ Will Be Our Judge 120
  Love and Law: Leave Not the Other Undone 126
  The Doctrine of Christ Leads to Exaltation 133

5 Sustaining the Lord's Imperfect Leaders 137
  Prophets Are Not Infallible 139
  Disagreeing without Being Disagreeable 144
  The Purpose of Prophets and Apostles 148
  How God Guides His Prophets and Apostles 152

Following Those with Priesthood Keys 155
Facing the Racial Policies of Past Leaders 160
Does God Change? 166
My Grandmother's Choice 170
Common Sticks That Mark a Safe Path 173

6 Armed with Power: The Many Powers of Christ's Atonement . 179
Christ in Gethsemane 180
The Redeeming Power of Christ's Atonement 183
My Experience with Christ's Redeeming Power 188
The Enabling Power of Christ's Atonement 192
Strengthened When Polio Struck Our Family 196
The Healing Power of Christ's Atonement 199
My Sister's Healing through Christ 203
The Transforming Power of Christ's Atonement 204
My Father's Transformation 208
The Holy Ghost and Christ's Atonement 213
From Pain to Joy 216

Afterword 221
About the Author 227

Acknowledgments

I am grateful to my wife, Lori Ransom Jones, who not only provided emotional support during the writing of this book but also provided tangible help with the manuscript through her literary and editorial skills. I am also grateful to our daughter, Allyson Jones Blanch, for her additional help with editing.

I also thank my siblings who reviewed early drafts of this project and gave helpful suggestions on content and organization. This includes two of my sisters, Sandra Name and Christine Cole, as well as two of my brothers, Creed Jones and Wesley Jones. Their critiques and encouragement were welcomed and helpful. My friend, BYU Professor in the School of Family Life, Dr. Nathan Leonhardt, also provided helpful input with chapters 3 and 4. I am also grateful to my cousin, Joel Kirk Wright, for sharing his family research, which was helpful for telling our grandmother's story in chapter 5.

Finally, I am grateful to Cedar Fort Publishing & Media for publishing this book including the help of editors Liz Kazandzhy and Kyle Lund, and the beautiful cover by Shawnda Craig.

Introduction

When we think of the New Testament, we think of that part of the Bible that is a compilation of first-century writings documenting the life and teachings of Jesus Christ and His Apostles. However, the title *New Testament* means *New Covenant,* which refers to the covenant all Christians have with God through Jesus Christ. It is labeled as *New* to distinguish it from the Old Testament, or the *Old Covenant,* which refers to the covenant the Israelite people had with God through Abraham. Of course, Latter-day Saints know that the old covenant was also through Jesus Christ, but we agree that it was revealed through the ancient patriarch Abraham and thus associated with him.

In the days of the *New Covenant,* Christ's Church was originally called *the Way.*[1] This title is believed to have come from Isaiah 40:3, which says, "Prepare ye the way of the Lord," and from John 14:6,

---

1. Ramesh De Silva, "Sect of 'The Way', 'The Nazarenes' & 'Christians': Names given to the Early Church," Bible Things in Bible Ways, Nov. 21, 2013, https://biblethingsinbibleways.wordpress.com/2013/11/21/sect-of-the-way-the-nazarenes-christians-names-given-to-the-early-church/; see also Wikipedia, "Christianity in the 1st century," https://en.wikipedia.org/wiki/Christianity_in_the_1st_century.

wherein Jesus said, "I am the way, the truth, and the life: no man cometh unto the Father, but by me." Thomas A. Wayment, Brigham Young University (BYU) professor of classical studies and ancient scripture, wrote, "The title *the Way* is the earliest known title describing believers in Christ before the title *Christian* was used."[2] Professor Wayment also noted, "*The Way* refers to Christianity, and the group of believers continued to be designated by this term for some time."[3]

The New Covenant and *the Way* are both descriptions of the Church that Christ established. If we combine the two, we get "the Way of the New Covenant" or "the New Covenant Way." And since *way* and *path* are synonyms, the Church in Christ's day could be called "the New Covenant Path."

President Russell M. Nelson has emphasized that Christ's Church in these latter days continues to administer the covenant path by which we can receive salvation and exaltation through Jesus Christ. By emphasizing this covenant path, President Nelson has returned us to our roots. He taught, "Adam and Eve . . . entered the covenant path [through baptism]. When you and I also enter that path, we have a new way of life. We thereby create a relationship with God that allows Him to bless and change us. The covenant path leads us back to Him."[4]

This covenant path begins for everyone with baptism, and males are further schooled by accepting the oath and covenant of the Melchizedek Priesthood. The covenant path is then expanded through the endowment with its five covenants, and the path culminates with the covenant of eternal marriage. However, merely making these covenants will not exalt and sanctify us. We must live true to our covenants in order for them to have their desired effect, which is to make us more like Jesus Christ.

Therein lies the biggest challenge of our day: understanding and living true to our covenants. This is especially difficult in our day

---

2. Thomas Wayment, "Acts 9:2," *The New Testament: A Translation for Latter-Day Saints* (Religious Studies Center and Deseret Book, 2018), 224, footnote; emphasis in original.
3. Wayment, "Acts 19:23," *The New Testament*, 245, footnote; emphasis in original.
4. Russell M. Nelson, "The Everlasting Covenant," *Liahona*, Oct. 2022.

when political, social, and spiritual turmoil swirls around us. We face spiritual complexities unseen in past generations. However, the covenants and ordinances of the temple serve as anchors to moor us securely to Jesus Christ. This book seeks to deepen our understanding of the doctrinal truths that lie at the foundation of these covenants and ordinances. These are truths that draw us nearer to Jesus Christ, for He is the heart of our covenants.

Chapter Summaries

This book contains a series of essays, each designed to bless members of The Church of Jesus Christ of Latter-day Saints by strengthening their understanding of and commitment to the doctrine, ordinances, and covenants of the temple. This volume reflects my own love for the Savior, for the temple, and for the restored doctrines that lay the foundation of the ceremonies and covenants practiced therein. The following abstracts summarize each chapter.

Chapter 1—Three Temple Insights

The story of Adam and Eve in the temple parallels the narrative structure called "the hero's journey," showing the storyline that we must all follow as we seek to return to our heavenly parents and become like them. The temple initiatory, endowment, and sealing ordinances fit into this saga, and insights into each can help us on our journey. The first insight reviews the purposes and blessings of wearing temple garments. The second suggests how we can understand what President Brigham Young called "the signs and tokens, pertaining to the holy priesthood." And the third discusses how the covenants of the endowment double as the primary covenants of temple marriage. All three insights center on Christ and covenants.

Chapter 2—Understanding the Keys of Temple Work

The 1836 restoration of priesthood keys in the Kirtland Temple by Moses, Elias, and Elijah make possible the work of salvation and exaltation. The keys of Moses provide for the gathering of Israel on both sides of the veil. Elias (whose identity is discussed) restored the keys of the Abrahamic covenant, which are transmitted to us through temple marriage. Elijah's keys seal all ordinances for the living and extend the same ordinances to the dead. The priesthood keys of the Restoration build on one another and extend the blessing of Christ's Atonement to all. Eternal, loving relationships are possible because of these keys of temple work.

Chapter 3—Eternal Families and Same-Sex Marriage

Our doctrine on the nature of eternal families is made clear through prophetic teachings on eternal seed, the nature of resurrected celestial bodies, the Abrahamic covenant, and the complementary natures of men and women. God's design for eternal families is incompatible with the concept of same-sex temple marriage. Historical policy changes regarding plural marriage and race restrictions show that those changes were rooted in preexisting scripture and doctrine, returning the Church to earlier norms, while no similar foundation exists for same-sex marriage. The doctrine presented in the family proclamation is eternal.

Chapter 4—Support for Sexual Minorities Through the Doctrine of Christ

We can support Latter-day Saints who experience same-sex attraction or related challenges by applying the doctrine of Christ, which is also called the law of the gospel of Jesus Christ. This doctrine has two dimensions: an upward relationship with Deity and outward relationships with others. The stories of people who are navigating same-sex attraction while remaining true to their covenants show success by focusing on Jesus Christ and engaging the support of friends. Opportunities for progress in the spirit world can give hope to those who live contrary to God's commandments in mortality, and Christ will judge who qualifies for those opportunities. We must teach both love and law.

Chapter 5—Sustaining the Lord's Imperfect Leaders

Instructions in the temple endowment and in the scriptures teach the importance of following living prophets and apostles despite their flaws. We can disagree without being disagreeable. Scriptures describe the purposes of prophets and apostles and tell how God guides them, including the trust He gives them through priesthood keys. God has directed some changes in the past; however, God's nature, purposes, and covenants will never change. A story about the author's grandmother recounts her choice to follow the living prophet when her own father chose to reject those teachings. Following Christ through the direction of His prophets and apostles is the safest path.

Chapter 6—Armed with Power: The Many Powers of Christ's Atonement

Jesus Christ is at the center of our temple worship, and our covenants give us access to the power of His Atonement. Four of the many powers of Christ's Atonement are taught or experienced through the temple: His redeeming, enabling, healing, and transforming powers. Personal stories from the author's family illustrate each of these. It is the Holy Ghost who transmits the powers of Christ's Atonement to us, and by keeping our covenants we have access to those powers.

Guidelines for Teaching About the Temple

We need to be cautious and respectful as we approach discussions about the temple ordinances. President Boyd K. Packer taught, "We do not discuss the temple ordinances outside the temples. . . . The ordinances and ceremonies of the temple . . . are sacred. They are kept confidential lest they be given to those who are unprepared."[5] While this remains true for some portions of the temple ceremonies, in more recent years our prophets and apostles have encouraged more openness and have shared publicly many aspects of these sacred temple ordinances, including the publication of many details about temple clothing, rituals, and covenants on the Church's website.[6]

In April 2019, Elder David A. Bednar spoke of ways in which "the programs and activities of the Church . . . are becoming more home centered and Church supported in this specific season of the dispensation

---

5. Boyd K. Packer, "The Holy Temple," *Ensign*, Oct. 2010, 29–30.
6. For example, see https://www.churchofjesuschrist.org/temples.

of the fulness of times."[7] He then encouraged more in-home temple preparation and quoted President Ezra Taft Benson, who said, "I believe *a proper understanding or background* will immeasurably help prepare our youth for the temple . . . [and] will foster within them a desire to seek their priesthood blessings just as Abraham sought his."[8]

Elder Bednar then instructed:

> Two basic guidelines can help us achieve the proper understanding emphasized by President Benson.
>
> Guideline #1. Because we love the Lord, we always should speak about His holy house with reverence. We should not disclose or describe the special symbols associated with the covenants we receive in sacred temple ceremonies. Neither should we discuss the holy information that we specifically promise in the temple not to reveal.
>
> Guideline #2. The temple is the house of the Lord. Everything in the temple points us to our Savior, Jesus Christ. We may discuss the basic purposes of and the doctrine and principles associated with temple ordinances and covenants.[9]

These two guidelines are rather generous, opening the door for more transparent discussions of many aspects of the temple ordinances and covenants than we might have felt comfortable with in the past. I believe that this flexibility and openness, encouraged by an Apostle of Jesus Christ "in this specific season of the dispensation of the fulness of times," is a sign that His Second Coming is near at hand.

Consistent with these guidelines, this book discusses some parts of our temple ceremonies more directly than might have been done prior to receiving Elder Bednar's counsel. Nevertheless, respect for the sacred nature of the temple is maintained. The injunction above the front door of every temple, "Holiness to the Lord," has been a guiding principle for this book.

---

7. David A. Bednar, "Prepared to Obtain Every Needful Thing," *Ensign* or *Liahona*, May 2019, 103.

8. Ezra Taft Benson, "What I Hope You Will Teach Your Children About the Temple," *Ensign*, Aug. 1985, 8; emphasis added.

9. David A. Bednar, "Prepared to Obtain Every Needful Thing," 103; emphasis in original.

The Temple Draws Us unto Christ

When Jesus visited the ancient Nephites at the temple in Bountiful, He taught, "My Father sent me that I might be lifted up upon the cross; and after that I had been lifted up upon the cross, that I might draw all men unto me" (3 Nephi 27:14). For those who have already entered into the covenant path, one of the most powerful tool sets that Christ uses to draw men and women unto Him is found in the doctrine, ordinances, and covenants of the temple.

Each of the essays in this book confirms that the temple principles presented can help draw us closer to Jesus Christ. He is the focus of our temple ceremonies and doctrine, as verified by the following statements, all made by President Russell M. Nelson:

- "The temple is the house of the Lord. The basis for every temple ordinance and covenant—the heart of the plan of salvation—is the Atonement of Jesus Christ."[10]
- "Because Jesus Christ is at the center of everything we do in the temple, as you think more about the temple you will be thinking more about Him."[11]
- "Each person who makes covenants in baptismal fonts and in temples—and keeps them—has increased access to the power of Jesus Christ. Please ponder that stunning truth! The reward for keeping covenants with God is heavenly power—power that strengthens us to withstand our trials, temptations, and heartaches better. This power eases our way."[12]
- "The temple is a place of revelation. There you are shown how to progress toward a celestial life. There you are drawn closer to the Savior and given greater access to His power. There you are guided in solving the problems in your life, even your most perplexing problems."[13]

---

10. Russell M. Nelson, "Personal Preparation for Temple Blessings," *Ensign*, May 2001, 32.
11. Russell M. Nelson, "Go Forward in Faith," *Ensign*, May 2020, 115.
12. Russell M. Nelson, "Overcome the World and Find Rest," *Liahona*, Nov. 2022, 96.
13. Russell M. Nelson, "Think Celestial!," *Liahona*, Nov. 2023, 119.

- "Nothing will help you more to hold fast to the iron rod than worshipping in the temple as regularly as your circumstances permit. Nothing will protect you more as you encounter the world's mists of darkness. Nothing will bolster your testimony of the Lord Jesus Christ and His Atonement or help you understand God's magnificent plan more. Nothing will soothe your spirit more during times of pain. Nothing will open the heavens more. Nothing!"[14]
- "In the house of the Lord, we focus on Jesus Christ. We learn of Him. We make covenants to follow Him. We come to know Him. As we keep our temple covenants, we gain greater access to the Lord's strengthening power. In the temple, we . . . experience the pure love of Jesus Christ and our Heavenly Father in great abundance! . . . Every sincere seeker of Jesus Christ will find Him in the temple. You will feel His mercy. You will find answers to your most vexing questions. You will better comprehend the joy of His gospel."[15]

The temples of God symbolize our highest aspirations as followers of Jesus Christ. These covenant cathedrals are all inscribed with the declaration "Holiness to the Lord," and they exist to provide opportunities for all of God's children to live eternally in His presence through His Son, Jesus Christ. As we embrace the doctrine and principles that underlie the temple ceremonies and abide by the covenants we make therein, we qualify to receive exaltation and eternal happiness.

May each of the following essays bless and strengthen all covenant-keeping Latter-day Saints as we journey together along the covenant path—"the Way of the New Covenant" that is through Jesus Christ. He is the heart of our covenants. May we all live true to the doctrines of His restored gospel as we strive to follow Him and receive all the blessings of His Atonement.

---

14. Russell M. Nelson, "Rejoice in the Gift of Priesthood Keys," *Liahona*, May 2024, 122.
15. Russell M. Nelson, "The Lord Jesus Christ Will Come Again," *Liahona*, Nov. 2024, 121–2.

1
Three Temple Insights

When I first went to the temple to receive my own endowment, I came away thinking that the purpose of the ceremony was to teach me about the Creation and the role of Adam and Eve. I thought it was mostly a review of the scriptures with a few additions or modifications that I would ponder on as if they were the most important insights I was to glean. Later, I began to see that Adam and Eve were not at the center of the endowment, but rather Jesus Christ and their relationship to Him and Heavenly Father were at the center.

The next stage of my growth was recognizing that my wife and I should see ourselves as Eve and Adam and that their journey symbolized our own journey through life. Their story teaches us that we should not be discouraged by our own fallen nature, but that we should look forward to "the joy of our redemption, and the eternal life which God giveth unto all the obedient" (Moses 5:11). I saw that God was offering us relational assistance, through covenants with Him, to help us stay on the path that leads back to His presence. I saw that God was also giving us special gifts to assist in our journey, including specific blessings for every part of our bodies and special clothing that would symbolize being wrapped in the power of Christ's Atonement.

Later, I realized that the temple marriage ceremony shows that our journey does not end with entrance into the presence of God but that my wife and I can become fully like our heavenly parents, blessed not only with immortality but also with eternal lives. By adding to my personal covenant relationship with God an additional three-way covenant with God and my wife, she and I can receive all that our heavenly parents have, including living together in a joyful familial relationship throughout eternity.

In recent years, I have learned about a narrative structure called "the hero's journey," and I recognized that the origin of this approach is the story of Adam and Eve. The hero's journey has been described as a class of stories that "involve a hero who goes on an adventure, is victorious in a decisive crisis, and comes home changed or transformed."[16] Modern stories such as *The Lord of the Rings*, *Star Wars*, and Disney's *The Lion King* are typical popular examples. This literary technique has been analyzed by different scholars and often includes stages such as:

- The call to adventure (often in a new world)
- Reluctance or refusal of the call
- Meeting a mentor
- The crossing of the first threshold
- Initiation (sometimes with the receipt of gifts or special clothing)
- The road of trials (and often overcoming them through an atonement)
- The road back
- The crossing of the return threshold
- Master of the two worlds[17]

I believe that hero's journey stories resonate so strongly with so many people because they are echoes of the story of Adam and Eve. They are the story of the plan of salvation and thus the storyline each one of us is destined to follow. The key to success in our own hero's journey is learning to access the divine powers of our Mentor, Jesus Christ, through the

---

16. Wikipedia, "Hero's journey," last modified Nov. 26, 2024, 17:27 (UTC), https://en.wikipedia.org/wiki/Hero%27s_journey.
17. Wikipedia, "Hero's journey."

greatest of all the gifts He has given us—the Holy Ghost. Along the way, we enter into covenants, which are anchoring guideposts to help us stay on the path back to God and acquire His attributes.

When we participate in the temple initiatory, endowment, and sealing ordinances, we are given a window into our own role in this eternal saga, as seen through the eyes of Adam and Eve. The temple initiatory ordinances prepare us with gifts and blessings to begin our journey, and the endowment teaches us about the struggles we will face and the covenants we will need to rely on in order to surmount those challenges. The endowment also teaches us what we need to know, do, and be so we can return to God's presence. Finally, the eternal marriage ceremony enables us to live the kind of life our heavenly parents live, in eternal joy and happiness. The initiatory ordinances reveal our potential, the endowment helps us acquire God's attributes through covenants, and the sealing ceremony enables us to live the kind of life He lives.

The following sections will discuss insights into three aspects of our temple ordinances—one associated with the initiatory ordinances, one related to the endowment, and one pertaining to marriage sealings. Understanding these will help us on our own hero's journey. The first section will review the purpose and blessings of wearing temple garments. The second will suggest how we can understand what President Brigham Young called "the signs and tokens, pertaining to the holy priesthood."[18] And the third will discuss the covenants of eternal marriage.

Clothed in Temple Garments

Our temple covenants are meant to guide us on the path back to God's presence and keep us safe from sin. This is symbolized in the temple garment. When we wear the garment, we carry sacred symbols of our temple covenants with us, and remembering this can strengthen and protect us. The Church's *General Handbook* says, "The garment is . . . a reminder of your temple covenants. . . . As you keep your covenants, including the sacred privilege to wear the garment as

---

18. Brigham Young, in *Journal of Discourses*, 2:31.

instructed in the initiatory ordinances, you will have greater access to the Savior's mercy, protection, strength, and power."[19]

Paul said, "I bear in my body the marks of the Lord Jesus" (Galatians 6:17). The same is true for us when we wear temple garments. In wearing them, we "bear the marks of the Lord Jesus," showing that we have taken upon us His name. The garment also resembles the veil of the temple, for they contain the same sacred symbols. So whenever we wear our temple garments, we carry symbols of both Christ and the temple with us.

Elder Allen D. Haynie spoke of the connection to Christ that comes through wearing the garment:

> The garment . . . helps us to honor the sacramental covenant to "always remember him and keep his commandments which he has given [us]; that [we] may always have his Spirit to be with [us]" (D&C 20:77).
>
> President Nelson recently taught something very profound about the temple garment that he gave me permission to share with you: "Your garment is symbolic of the veil [of the temple]; the veil is symbolic of the Lord Jesus Christ. So when you put on your garment, you may feel that you are truly putting upon yourself the very sacred symbol of the Lord Jesus Christ—His life, His ministry, and His mission, which was to atone for every daughter and son of God."
>
> We find Jesus in the temple, in every aspect of it, and we find Him in the symbolism of the garment. In wearing the garment, we declare to God that we rejoice in having Jesus's name placed upon us in His holy house (see D&C 109:26), and we remember Him always.[20]

The garment is a sacred covering for our bodies. In Hebrew, the word meaning to cover is *kaphar*, and this is the same root used to mean *atonement*. Thus, the garment is a constant reminder that we are covered by the Atonement of Jesus Christ. The first need for the power

---

19. *General Handbook: Serving in The Church of Jesus Christ of Latter-day Saints*, 38.5.5, Gospel Library.
20. Allen D. Haynie, "Meeting Jesus in the House of the Lord" (Brigham Young University devotional, Oct. 10, 2023), 6, speeches.byu.edu.

of this Atonement is recorded in Genesis 3, where it says that Adam and Eve partook of the fruit of the tree of knowledge of good and evil, after which they recognized their nakedness, covered themselves with aprons sewn from fig leaves, and then hid themselves from God. God called them out of hiding, gave them instructions, and then created covering garments for them made from animal skins—presumably from animals that had been sacrificed to God as a ceremonial atonement for their transgression. This biblical story provides a basis for wearing a holy garment as a covering and a symbol of Christ's Atonement.

President Russell M. Nelson expounded on how the Atonement covers and embraces us:

> Rich meaning is found in study of the word *atonement* in the Semitic languages of Old Testament times. In Hebrew, the basic word for atonement is *kaphar*, a verb that means "to cover" or "to forgive." Closely related is the Aramaic and Arabic word *kafat*, meaning "a close embrace"—no doubt related to the Egyptian ritual embrace. References to that embrace are evident in the Book of Mormon. One states that "the Lord hath redeemed my soul . . . ; I have beheld his glory, and I am encircled about eternally in the arms of his love" (2 Ne. 1:15). Another proffers the glorious hope of our being "clasped in the arms of Jesus" (Mormon 5:11).
>
> I weep for joy when I contemplate the significance of it all. To be redeemed is to be atoned—received in the close embrace of God with an expression not only of His forgiveness, but of our oneness of heart and mind. What a privilege![21]

Like the Atonement, our temple garments cover and embrace us. In the Book of Mormon, Amulek taught about the Atonement in ways that similarly remind us of the value of wearing our garments: "The intent of this last sacrifice [is] to bring about the bowels of mercy. . . . And thus mercy can satisfy the demands of justice, and *encircles them in the arms of safety*, while he that exercises no faith unto repentance *is exposed to the whole law* of the demands of justice; therefore only unto him that has faith unto repentance is brought about the great and eternal plan of redemption" (Alma 34:15–16; emphasis added). Wearing our garments shows our faith in that eternal plan of redemption and

---

21. Russell M. Nelson, "The Atonement," *Ensign*, Nov. 1996, 34.

encircles us in Christ's arms of safety so we are not exposed to sin and condemnation.

The scriptures often refer to the symbolism of marriage and the special clothing involved. The prophet Isaiah wrote, "I will greatly rejoice in the Lord, my soul shall be joyful in my God; for he hath clothed me with the garments of salvation, he hath covered me with the robe of righteousness, as a bridegroom decketh himself with ornaments, and as a bride adorneth herself with her jewels" (Isaiah 61:10). One interpretation of the temple endowment is that it is a marriage ceremony between Christ and us, as covenant members of His Church. As the bride of Christ, we need to be clothed in ceremonial wedding garments.

In the parable of the royal marriage feast, Jesus taught the importance of being clothed in proper garments for a royal wedding. The parable tells of a king who invited a group of strangers to a marriage feast for his son because the originally invited guests did not show up. The new guests had apparently all been given appropriate wedding clothing, yet one guest had not put on the garment provided. When the king saw this guest who was not properly attired, he inquired, "Friend, how camest thou in hither not having a wedding garment?" (Matthew 22:12). The careless guest was speechless, and the king cast him out, declaring, "For many are called, but few are chosen; *wherefore all do not have on the wedding garment*" (JST, Matthew 22:14 [in Matthew 22:14, footnote *b*]; emphasis added).

Elder David A. Bednar commented on this parable, saying, "An individual may . . . accept the invitation and sit down at the feast—yet not be chosen to partake because he or she does not have the appropriate wedding garment of converting faith in the Lord Jesus and His divine grace. . . . You and I ultimately can choose to be chosen through the righteous exercise of our moral agency."[22] Like the wedding garments in the parable, our temple garments are symbolic of our faith and our moral choices. By wearing our garments, we carry a constant reminder of our commitment to keep our temple covenants.

---

22. David A. Bednar, "Put On Thy Strength, O Zion," *Liahona*, Nov. 2022, 94.

Elder Lynn G. Robbins discussed this same parable and added, "The book of Revelation teaches us that the garment represents righteousness: 'The marriage of the Lamb is come, and his wife hath made herself ready . . . arrayed in fine linen, clean and white: for the fine linen is the *righteousness* of saints' (Revelation 19:7–8; emphasis added). In our day, the temple garment is clothing we always wear as a reminder of sacred temple covenants."[23]

One value of wearing this symbol of our covenants is that doing so can remind us that our outward behavior should be consistent with the godly nature of the spirit that resides within us. The *General Handbook* says, "When you put on your garment, you put on a sacred symbol of Jesus Christ. Wearing it is an outward expression of your inner commitment to follow Him."[24] This need for consistency between what is outward and what is inward can remind us of Christ's condemnation of hypocrisy:

> Woe unto you, scribes and Pharisees, hypocrites! for ye make clean the outside of the cup and of the platter, but within they are full of extortion and excess.
>
> Thou blind Pharisee, cleanse first that which is within the cup and platter, that the outside of them may be clean also.
>
> Woe unto you, scribes and Pharisees, hypocrites! for ye are like unto whited sepulchres, which indeed appear beautiful outward, but are within full of dead men's bones, and of all uncleanness.
>
> Even so ye also outwardly appear righteous unto men, but within ye are full of hypocrisy and iniquity. (Matthew 23:25–28)

Because our temple garments are worn beneath our outer clothing, they are a reminder of this same need to be pure and clean on the inside regardless of how we are dressed on the outside. They also provide a physical line of defense, or a shield, against breaking the law of chastity since it is hard to commit that sin without encountering the reminder of our temple covenants that our garments provide. Those who ignore this final barrier condemn themselves as they set aside their garments and their covenants to commit such a serious sin.

---

23. Lynn G. Robbins, "Oil in Our Lamps," *Ensign*, June 2007, 48.
24. *General Handbook*, 38.5.5.

Instead, we should try to be among the faithful Saints that John the Revelator described, "which have not defiled their garments; and they shall walk with me in white: for they are worthy. He that overcometh, the same shall be clothed in white raiment; and I will not blot out his name out of the book of life, but I will confess his name before my Father, and before his angels. He that hath an ear, let him hear" (Revelation 3:4–6).

John is describing the final Judgment Day when those who are righteous will stand with confidence before God in robes of righteousness. Wearing our garments in righteousness now foreshadows how we will be seen as we approach God for that Final Judgment: "Wherefore, we shall have a perfect knowledge of all our guilt, and our uncleanness, and our nakedness; and the righteous shall have a perfect knowledge of their enjoyment, and their righteousness, being clothed with purity, yea, even with the robe of righteousness. And . . . then cometh the judgment" (2 Nephi 9:14–15).

When we wear our garments in righteousness, they become spiritual armor for us. Elder Carlos E. Assay wrote:

> We must put on the armor of God spoken of by the Apostle Paul [see Ephesians 6:11–18] and reiterated in a modern revelation (see D&C 27:15–18). We must also "put on the armor of righteousness" (2 Nephi 1:23) symbolized by the temple garment. Otherwise, we may lose the war and perish.
>
> The heavy armor worn by soldiers of a former day, including helmets, shields, and breastplates, determined the outcome of some battles. However, the real battles of life in our modern day will be won by those who are clad in a spiritual armor—an armor consisting of faith in God, faith in self, faith in one's cause, and faith in one's leaders. The piece of armor called the temple garment not only provides the comfort and warmth of a cloth covering, it also strengthens the wearer to resist temptation, fend off evil influences, and stand firmly for the right.[25]

Moses was commanded to make holy garments for Aaron and his sons in preparation for officiating in their tabernacle temple: "And

---

25. Carlos E. Assay, "The Temple Garment: 'An Outward Expression of an Inward Commitment'," *Ensign*, Aug. 1997, 20–21.

take thou unto thee Aaron thy brother, and his sons with him, from among the children of Israel . . . And thou shalt make holy garments for Aaron thy brother for glory and for beauty . . . that he may minister unto me in the priest's office" (Exodus 28:1–3). God even specified this interesting detail: "And thou shalt make them linen breeches to cover their nakedness; from the loins even unto the thighs they shall reach" (Exodus 28:42). In similar fashion, we need to obtain the authorized style of temple garments from a Church Distribution Center before we participate in temple ordinances, and we should not modify their inspired design.

Later, when the tabernacle was ready, the Lord instructed Moses, "And thou shalt bring Aaron and his sons unto the door of the tabernacle of the congregation, and wash them with water. And thou shalt put upon Aaron the holy garments, and anoint him, and sanctify him" (Exodus 40:12–13). We also are formally authorized to wear our temple garments as part of the temple washing and anointing ordinances. The association emphasizes the importance of spiritual cleanliness and holiness in wearing our garments.

President James E. Faust has said:

> It is possible for us to be purged and purified and to have our sins washed away so that we may come before the Lord as clean, white, and spotless as the newly fallen snow.
>
> "Who shall ascend into the hill of the Lord?" We can see in vision the almost endless hosts of the elect, the devout, the believing who shall come to God's holy sanctuary to seek its blessings. As they enter those hallowed halls, Nephi would remind all that "the keeper of the gate is the Holy One of Israel; and he employeth no servant there; and there is none other way save it be by the gate; for he cannot be deceived, for the Lord God is his name" (2 Ne. 9:41).
>
> As the Saints come into the sacrosanct washing and anointing rooms and are washed, they will be spiritually cleansed. As they are anointed, they will be renewed and regenerated in soul and spirit.[26]

The washing and anointing ordinances, along with the wearing of our white temple garments, can remind us of the need to be purified

---

26. James E. Faust, "Who Shall Ascend into the Hill of the Lord?," *Ensign*, Aug. 2001, 4.

through Jesus Christ. The prophet Alma declared, "There can no man be saved except his garments are washed white; yea, his garments must be purified until they are cleansed from all stain, through the blood of him of whom it has been spoken by our fathers, who should come to redeem his people from their sins" (Alma 5:21).

President Jeffrey R. Holland taught that the formal name of the garment is "the garment of the holy priesthood." He explained, "This full name of the garment, like the full name of the Church, is instructive. The priesthood is the power of God, and wearing the garment is a reminder of godly power available to us when we make and keep covenants with God."[27]

The garment of the holy priesthood is both a vestment of godly power for this life and a mantle of godly potential for the life to come. BYU professor of ancient scripture, Daniel Belnap, has taught that temple garments include markings of a compass and a square, which are tools used by architects to build things, and that these symbols pertain to our potential to become like our Heavenly Father who designed and created the universe. Professor Belnap said:

> In the garment is this beautiful representation of the building tools that you will have: You can make perfect circles; you can make perfect squares. They represent the ability for you to become like a divine being who makes cosmos. And to have that right next to my skin underneath any other type of clothing—that I wear this beautiful piece of clothing that was given to me via an ordinance that represents the cosmic power to make cosmos like God Himself—I think that might change the way you act every day. What if every day we acted as if we were making a cosmos, having been given the tools and the identity to do so?[28]

Wearing our garments also sets an example for our children and shows them an outward, physical sign that our temple covenants are a priority to us. This became apparent to me when I watched a home

---

27. Jeffrey R. Holland, "The Garment of the Holy Priesthood," *Liahona*, Sept. 2024, footnote 6.
28. For All The Saints With Ben Hancock, "Astonishing Insights Into Sacred Rituals & Symbolic Clothing - Daniel Belnap," YouTube, Sept. 29, 2024, 1:16:10–1:17:51, https://www.youtube.com/watch?v=YhWvbKGMaBc.

video of my son, who was about four years old at the time. In the video, I asked him why he was wearing his summer pajamas in the middle of winter. The pajamas he had on were mostly white with short sleeves and short pant legs that reached a little above his knees. He looked down at them and declared, "I like 'em. They look like undies." It was apparent that he liked them because they made him feel like he was wearing garments like he had seen his dad wear, and he wanted to be like his dad. His positive attitude toward garments continued as he matured, and he was excited when he finally got to go to the temple and be clothed in the garment of the holy priesthood and be endowed with godly power in preparation for his mission. He is now setting a similar example of covenant living for his own sons.

In most wedding ceremonies, couples exchange rings, which they continue to wear as symbols of their unending love and commitment to one another. The temple garment is similarly given to us as part of a covenant ceremony and is to be continually worn thereafter to show our unending commitment to God and Jesus Christ. President Nelson emphasized the enduring value of the temple garment when he said, "Wearing the temple garment has deep symbolic significance. It represents a continuing commitment. Just as the Savior exemplified the need to endure to the end, we wear the garment faithfully as part of the enduring armor of God. Thus we demonstrate our faith in Him and in His eternal covenants with us."[29]

Wearing the temple garment is full of symbolism and meaning. When we understand the sanctity of the garment and its connection to our covenants and to the Atonement of Jesus Christ, we realize that it is not only a great privilege to wear the temple garment, but it is also a spiritual protection against the powers of Satan. We will then want to be wearing our temple garment in all circumstances where we can reasonably do so. Our faithfulness in wearing our temple garments will demonstrate to God our enduring faithfulness in keeping our covenants with Him, and He will bless us for our consecrated obedience.

---

29. Russell M. Nelson, "Personal Preparation for Temple Blessings," *Ensign*, May 2001, 33.

The Signs and Tokens Pertaining to the Holy Priesthood

Elder David A. Bednar has said, "From ancient times men and women have embraced sacred music, different forms of prayer, symbolic religious clothing, gestures, and rituals to express their innermost feelings of devotion to God."[30] Latter-day Saints who receive their endowments will find that they will experience "different forms of prayer, symbolic religious clothing, gestures, and rituals" than they are accustomed to experiencing during regular weekly church services. However, as they contemplate the spiritual significance of these religious symbols, they will come to find a richness and closeness to God that will settle any discomfort that comes with the newness of that experience.

President Brigham Young described the temple endowment as follows:

> Your endowment is, to receive all those ordinances in the House of the Lord, which are necessary for you, after you have departed this life, to enable you to walk back to the presence of the Father, passing the angels who stand as sentinels, being enabled to give them the key words, the signs and tokens, pertaining to the Holy Priesthood, and gain your eternal exaltation in spite of earth and hell.[31]

President Young's reference to the use of "signs and tokens" in the endowment is considered one of the more sacred aspects of temple ritual, and therefore it is not generally discussed outside of the temple. However, there are a few general things that may be said and analogies that may be made with some of the methods used historically in Scouting.[32]

First, what is a sign? It is a representation of something else. The first definition of *sign* in the *Merriam-Webster Dictionary* is "a motion

---

30. David A. Bednar, "Prepared to Obtain Every Needful Thing," *Ensign* or *Liahona*, May 2019, 104.
31. Brigham Young, in *Journal of Discourses*, 2:31.
32. Scouting has changed a lot over the years, and I am not endorsing its current trajectory; rather, I am pointing to some traditional practices by way of analogy.

or gesture by which a thought is expressed or a command or wish made known."[33]

The Boy Scout sign is an excellent example of this. *The Boy Scout Handbook* describes the Scout sign as follows:

> The Scout sign shows you are a Scout. Give it each time you recite the Scout Oath and Law. When a Scout or Scouter raises the Scout sign, all Scouts should make the sign, too, and come to silent attention.
>
> To give the Scout sign, cover the nail of your little finger of your right hand with your right thumb, then raise your right arm bent in a 90-degree angle, and hold the three middle fingers of your hand upward. Those fingers stand for the three parts of the Scout Oath. Your thumb and little finger touch to represent the bond that unites Scouts throughout the world.[34]

Notice that the Scout sign refers to something else—it refers to the Scout Oath and Law. The meaning of the Scout sign is found in the meaning of those commitments. Whenever a Scout makes the Scout sign, he is effectively saying that he will keep the promises contained in the Scout Oath and Law, even if he does not recite them. He is, in effect, affirming a covenant by making this sign.

Today, when we agree to a legal contract, we affirm this by affixing our "sign" to the document; that is, by *signing* our *signature*. In ancient times, when few people could read or write, a sign was not made by writing but rather with a gesture. This tradition continues in courts of law today where a witness is often asked to attest to the truth of his or her statement by raising the right arm to the square while affirming an oath.

Tokens are similar—they are used to represent something else of greater value. For example, a bus token is used to represent money for the fare. Such tokens are often carried in the hand, and thus the root

---

33. *Merriam-Webster.com Dictionary*, s.v. "sign," accessed Dec. 6, 2024, https://www.merriam-webster.com/dictionary/sign.
34. "Scout Sign," *Boy Scout Handbook, 11th Edition* (Boy Scouts of America, 1998), 7.

of the word *token* may be related to the word *touch*.[35] It is interesting to note that in Spanish, the word *tocan* is a verb meaning *they touch*, and it is pronounced the same as the English word *token*.

Most Latter-day Saints are familiar with the following use of the word *token* in the hymn "A Poor Wayfaring Man": "Then in a moment to my view / The stranger started from disguise. / The tokens in His hands I knew; / The Savior stood before my eyes."[36] In this case, the tokens in the Savior's hands are the scars He carries there as symbols of His atoning sacrifice and of His life given on the cross for us all.

One of the dictionary definitions of *token* is "something given or shown as a guarantee (as of authority, right, or identity)."[37] A handshake is such a token. In fact, the Boy Scout handshake has been described thusly: "The Scout handshake is made with the hand nearest the heart and is offered *as a token* of friendship. Extend your left hand to another Scout and firmly grasp his left hand."[38]

When I was a boy, the Scout handshake was a little more complex and included extending your three middle fingers in token of the three points of the Scout Oath as you grasped the left hand of the other Scout. Like the Scout sign, the Scout handshake was strongly linked to the Scout Oath. It was intended that any time the Scout sign or handshake was used, it would remind a Scout of his commitment to the ideals of scouting.

Sometimes signs and tokens can carry their own individual symbolic meanings in addition to alignment with an underlying oath. For example, notice that the above description of the Scout handshake says that it is made with the left hand, connecting it with the heart and thus with friendship. This is in addition to a connection to the Scout Oath and Law.

---

35. The etymology of *token* is traced to the Old English verb *tǽcan*, meaning to show, explain, or teach (see etymonline.com/word/token), and touching is one way to learn the nature of something.
36. "A Poor Wayfaring Man of Grief," *Hymns*, no. 29.
37. *Merriam-Webster.com Dictionary*, s.v. "token," accessed December 6, 2024, https://www.merriam-webster.com/dictionary/token.
38. "Scout Handshake," *Boy Scout Handbook*, 7; emphasis added.

Signs and tokens have no value or meaning in and of themselves. They only have meaning as symbols of commitment to the values or promises they represent. For me, the signs and tokens of the temple, referred to by Brigham Young, primarily represent the covenants of the temple. After we promise to keep each covenant, signs and tokens are presented, I believe, as further confirmation that we will keep those temple covenants. To me, they represent giving my signature and my handshake as a guarantee that I will abide by the temple covenants that accompany them. However, they are more than signatures and handshakes, for they have been received from God and are very holy.

Although Elder Bednar has described the covenants of the endowment as five separate laws,[39] President Ezra Taft Benson combined the first two, resulting in only four: "the law of obedience and sacrifice, the law of the gospel, the law of chastity, and the law of consecration."[40] As President Russell M. Nelson has taught, "The laws of obedience and sacrifice are indelibly intertwined."[41] Because of this, only four sets of signs and tokens are needed to confirm all of the covenants of the endowment.[42] (Incidentally, the four marks on the garment can also be aligned with these four covenants.)

Besides signs and tokens, President Young referred to "key words." With the combination of these, the temple engages our eyes, our arms and hands, our ears, and our voice. Ancient temples also included incense and shewbread, adding nose and mouth to complete the involvement of our entire body and all its senses in the temple experience. God does not want a partial commitment; He wants to engage

---

39. See David A. Bednar, "Prepared to Obtain Every Needful Thing."
40. Ezra Taft Benson, "A Vision and a Hope for the Youth of Zion" (Brigham Young University devotional, Apr. 12, 1977), 1, speeches.byu.edu.
41. Russell M. Nelson, "Lessons from Eve," *Ensign*, Nov. 1987, 88.
42. Obedience and sacrifice are often linked in the scriptures: (1) Adam was commanded to offer animal sacrifices, and he obeyed without knowing why (see Moses 5:7–8). (2) King Saul failed to obey God's command to destroy a wicked people including their animals, claiming he kept them for sacrifices, so the prophet Samuel reprimanded Saul, saying, "To obey is better than sacrifice" (1 Samuel 15:22). (3) Jesus said, "As the Father gave me commandment, even so I do" (John 14:31), and then He obediently and willingly sacrificed His life for us, declaring, "Not my will, but thine, be done" (Luke 22:42).

every part of us—our seeing, feeling, hearing, speaking, smelling, and tasting. He wants our heart, might, mind, and strength. He wants our whole souls in consecrated covenant commitment to Him.

President Nelson said, "Temple patterns are as old as human life on earth. Actually, the plan for temples was established even before the foundation of the world."[43] These ancient temple patterns would need to accommodate the faithful Saints of all ages, whether they were schooled or unschooled, literate or illiterate. It would make sense that God would include in these ancient temple patterns methods of giving and receiving covenants that would not require modern-day written documents and signatures.

Our covenants also come with promises to keep them private. When we covenant to never disclose the signs and tokens we receive, our integrity is tested. Just as fully as we promise to guard them as sacred and private, we should also keep our temple covenants sacred and personal. They are between us and God, and He knows, better than anyone else, whether we are keeping them or not. As cited earlier, Brigham Young explained that in order to receive exaltation in God's presence, we are going to have to give signs and tokens to angels who stand as sentinels guarding the entrance to the celestial kingdom. I believe that these signs and tokens stand as symbols of our covenants, and only those who have kept their covenants will remember their signs and tokens when they face those sentinel angels, regardless of how many times they may have gone through an endowment session on earth to learn them.

I wrote elsewhere about an experience I had in the temple when I tried to correct a small verbal mistake a temple worker made as he was representing the Lord.[44] As soon as I attempted to do so, my mind went completely blank. It was as if a white sheet had suddenly been pulled over my brain. I had to pause and humble myself, collect my thoughts, and start again. I learned that the Lord will likewise have influence over my memory when I approach Him or one of His

---

43. Russell M. Nelson, "Temples and Temple Work," *Teachings of Russell M. Nelson* (Deseret Book, 2018), 365.
44. See Valiant K. Jones, *The Covenant Path: Finding the Temple in the Book of Mormon* (Cedar Fort, 2020), 94.

servants at the entrance to His kingdom. By keeping my covenants I will have access to that memory when I need it.

President Boyd K. Packer said, "Life is a homeward journey for all of us, back to the presence of God in His celestial kingdom. Ordinances and covenants become our credentials for admission into His presence."[45] I consider the signs and tokens of the priesthood to be affirmations of those credentials. When I give signs and tokens in the temple, I like to think of the temple covenants that correspond to them. When we are true and faithful to these covenants, we ensure the protection and blessings of God. President Joseph Fielding Smith said:

> If we go into the temple, we raise our hands and covenant that we will serve the Lord and observe his commandments and keep ourselves unspotted from the world. If we realize what we are doing, then the endowment will be a protection to us all our lives—a protection which a man who does not go to the temple does not have.
>
> I have heard my father say that in the hour of trial, in the hour of temptation, he would think of the promises, the covenants that he made in the House of the Lord, and they were a protection to him. . . . This protection is what these ceremonies are for, in part. They save us now and they exalt us hereafter if we will honor them. I know that this protection is given, for I too have realized it, as have thousands of others who have remembered their obligations.[46]

I have also had times when, faced with temptations, I have thought upon my temple covenants, and this has brought me strength to withstand those temptations. I feel grateful every time I participate in the rituals and ordinances of the temple. They remind me of my covenants with God, and they bring me closer to my Savior, Jesus Christ. I love my Savior and the rites and ordinances of His holy house. They are symbolically beautiful and deeply meaningful to me.

---

45. Boyd K. Packer, "Covenants," *Ensign*, May 1987, 24.
46. *Teachings of Presidents of the Church: Joseph Fielding Smith* (2013), 235–6; punctuation updated.

The Covenants of Eternal Marriage

In the Church publication *Preparing to Enter the Holy Temple*, President Boyd K. Packer taught that the endowment and the marriage sealing are connected. He said that in preparation for the sealing ceremony, a temple officiator might say to a bride and groom, "Each of you has received your endowment. In that endowment you received an investment of eternal potential. But all of these things, in one sense, *were preliminary and preparatory to your coming to the altar to be sealed* as husband and wife for time and for all eternity."[47] Later he added, "When sealed at the altar a person is the recipient of glorious blessings, powers, and honors *as part of his or her endowment.*"[48]

We should not think of the endowment ceremony and the marriage sealing ceremony as two distinct and unrelated ordinances. They are connected. The endowment can be seen as the first part of a ritually elaborate wedding ceremony where the bride and groom each make covenants with God in preparation for being sealed together eternally. Indeed, the covenants of the endowment can be seen as the primary covenants of an eternal marriage.

Eternal marriage is a three-way covenant between a man, a woman, and God. One Latter-day Saint institute manual presents the marriage covenant with a triangle diagram like the following:[49]

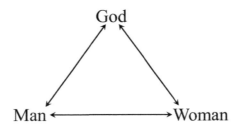

This triangle model can be carried a little further: The two sides of the triangle, which form covenant links to God, are established when

---

47. Boyd K. Packer, *Preparing to Enter the Holy Temple* (2012), 15; emphasis added.
48. Boyd K. Packer, *Preparing to Enter the Holy Temple*, 31; emphasis added.
49. "Keeping the Sacred Covenant of Marriage," *Building an Eternal Marriage Teacher Manual* (2003), 14.

a man and a woman, individually, receive their endowments. And the base of the triangle, connecting the man and the woman together, is formed during the marriage sealing ceremony. So the triangle becomes this:

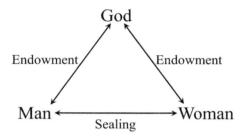

With this perspective, the endowment is seen as the first half of the marriage ceremony. Many aspects of the endowment point toward this conclusion: the seating of men and women on separate sides of the room before they pass through the veil; the covenants themselves, each of which helps ensure a successful marriage; the manner of progression through the veil for couples who are about to be sealed; and the fact that in older temples, the sealing rooms lie beyond the celestial room, sometimes at a higher level, implying that eternal marriage is the next step in progression toward exaltation.

President James A. Faust affirmed a connection between the endowment and eternal marriage, saying, "The crowning blessings of life come through obedience to the covenants and honoring of the ordinances received in the holy temples, including the new and everlasting covenant of *marriage, which is the capstone of the holy endowment.*"[50] If eternal marriage is the capstone of the endowment, then we should not think of the two as independent ordinances but as progressive ordinances, with marriage built upon the foundation of the endowment.

Those who have been present at a temple marriage ceremony know that there is no exchange of vows in the traditional language often used by other churches. For example, the bride and groom do not promise to take one another "for better, for worse, for richer, for

---

50. James E. Faust, "Keeping Covenants and Honoring the Priesthood," *Ensign*, Nov. 1993, 39.

poorer, in sickness and in health, to love and to cherish."[51] In fact, historically, the eternal marriage ceremony has included very little language describing the marriage vows.

In spite of the lack of traditional vows, Elder Orson Pratt explained that the eternal marriage ceremony includes "a covenant and promise . . . [to] fulfill all the laws, rites, and ordinances, pertaining to this holy matrimony."[52] His spelling of *rites* is not r-i-g-h-t-s, as in entitlements or privileges, but rather r-i-t-e-s, as in rituals. Also, Elder Pratt did not specify what these "laws, rites, and ordinances" are. As I contemplated what they might refer to, the first thought that came to my mind was that they would have to be "laws, rites, and ordinances" administered by the priesthood. Then I realized that they are perfectly encompassed in the covenants of the endowment.

The endowment covenants are presented as laws, they are administered in temple rites, and they are part of a priesthood ordinance. I believe they are the laws, rites, and ordinances we promise to abide by when we are married in the temple. Thus, the covenants of the endowment double as the primary covenants of eternal marriage.

When we see the covenants of the endowment in this light, we recognize that everyone who has received his or her endowment has received the foundational covenants upon which eternal marriage is built. Even if an endowed person is not sealed to a spouse during mortal life, the covenant bond to God has been formed with nothing held back in that leg of the three-way relationship of marriage. Only the final sealing to a spouse, with its majestic, crowning promises, has yet to occur. This is a beautiful concept that affirms the love and mercy of God for all of His children, married or single. God's covenant ways are marvelous. They include blessings and promises that are certain for all who desire to follow His covenant path, regardless of their marital status.

Many priesthood ordinances have two parts. Baptism is not complete without confirmation, and when the sick are anointed with consecrated oil, a separate ordinance seals that anointing. The same is true

---

51. Wikipedia, "Wedding Vows," last modified Nov. 6, 2024, 15:10 (UTC), https://en.wikipedia.org/wiki/Marriage_vows.
52. Orson Pratt, "Celestial Marriage," *The Seer* 1, no. 2 (Feb. 1853): 31.

for temple washings and anointings—each is followed by a separate sealing or confirmation. These paired ordinances have one part that includes a physical action and another part that focuses more on the spiritual. They can remind us that Christ's Atonement was also completed in two parts: in Gethsemane and on Golgotha. This two-part pattern shows us that whenever we see a priesthood ordinance called a sealing or a confirmation, there is a preceding ordinance associated with it. So what is the antecedent, companion ordinance for the sealing we call an eternal marriage? It is the endowment. The two go together. The first prepares for the second. The covenants of the endowment are the covenants of an eternal marriage. The sealing that occurs with an eternal marriage not only seals the couple together, but it also seals the ordinance of the endowment for each participant, confirming one of the primary purposes for which they were endowed: to form an eternal family.

When we see the endowment as the first half of the marriage ceremony, new insights can come. As we review the Creation story in this context, we can remember that the whole purpose of the earth is to provide a place where families can be established for growth and learning. As we view the story of Adam and Eve played out, we can see that first marriage as a model for us, teaching the purpose of opposition and the temptations that will come to every marriage and family. And when we see the Apostles Peter, James, and John come on the scene, we can recognize the importance of following the counsel of modern-day prophets and apostles in our families.

Those who have been married in the temple will remember that before going into the sealing room, they were taken to an endowment room to participate in a special veil ceremony as a couple. This alone should be sufficient witness that the endowment and eternal marriage are linked. I once taught a Sunday School lesson on eternal marriage as part of a class for new members. The class included a newly baptized couple who were looking forward to their temple sealing. When they learned that they would first need to receive their endowments, the wife asked, "What is the endowment?" I replied, "I like to think of the endowment as the first half of the wedding ceremony—the part where we make covenants with God before we are sealed together as a couple." The sister responded with a simple and contented "Oh!" and a look of satisfaction on her face. The explanation fit her understanding of the whole reason she wanted to go to the temple—to be sealed to her husband forever. The endowment truly does prepare us for our marriage sealing. The covenants of the endowment are antecedent covenants that we must agree to as part of the new and everlasting covenant of marriage.

In the Church's *General Handbook*, the instructions for performing a civil marriage ceremony state, "Before performing a civil marriage, a Church officer may counsel the couple on the sacred nature of the marriage vows. He may add other counsel as the Spirit directs."[53] I expect that similar instructions are given to those who perform temple marriages. At the temple marriage of one of my children, I was thrilled when the temple sealer reviewed the covenants of the endowment as part of his counsel to the bride and groom.

During the height of the COVID-19 pandemic, about a year after Elder David A. Bednar empowered us to "discuss the basic purposes of and the doctrine and principles associated with temple ordinances and covenants,"[54] I had occasion to perform two civil marriages for members of the Church. The following reflects the marriage counsel I gave, putting Elder Bednar's guidance into practice:

> Today you will be married in a union that will last for the remainder of your mortal lives together. This ceremony is a foreshadowing of an even higher ceremony which we hope you will choose to receive at a future time: marriage for time and all eternity in a holy temple of God. A temple marriage makes it possible for you to live eternally as husband and wife—not only in this life but also in the next. I encourage you two to set eternal marriage as a goal and work toward it.
>
> Those who enter into eternal marriage must first make covenant promises to follow five specific laws of God. These promises are made individually by the man and the woman to secure their relationship with God, but they also form the foundation of a

---

53. *General Handbook*, 38.3.6.
54. David A. Bednar, "Prepared to Obtain Every Needful Thing," 103.

strong and happy marriage. These covenantal laws, along with my commentary, are as follows:

1. The Law of Obedience: God's commandments are not meant to be restrictions to control us but rather guideposts to keep us on the path of happiness. If you will always keep God's commandments, your marriage will be on a sure foundation, and you will avoid a lot of pain and sadness.

2. The Law of Sacrifice: If you will always remember the sacrifice of our Lord, Jesus Christ, and then sacrifice for one another and for the future children the Lord might send you, then you will find a level of joy that is not available to those who are self-centered and only seek after their own comforts.

3. The Law of the Gospel of Jesus Christ: If you will come unto Christ and always remember Him, repenting when needed as you strive to be a better person, then you will have the guidance of the Holy Ghost in your marriage. That guidance is critical.

4. The Law of Chastity: Physical desires for one another are God-given, for they have the potential to bring you children and draw you closer as a couple. However, their use outside of marriage, either through real or virtual means, can destroy a marriage. Make sure you always remain faithful to one another in your marriage.

5. The Law of Consecration: If you will consecrate your lives to God and serve others, your family will grow in an atmosphere of benevolence and love. Remember that "whosoever will lose his life for [Christ's] sake shall find it" (Matthew 16:25).

Following this five-step covenant path will put Christ at the center of your marriage and give you a strong foundation for a happy family life.[55]

In the world today, many people enter into prenuptial agreements before marriage. These are legal covenants between the two betrothed parties. Engaged Latter-day Saint couples also enter into prenuptial covenants—these are called the covenants of the endowment. However, there are significant differences between the world's ways and God's ways. The prenuptial covenants of the world are entered into to assure the rights of the individuals and to establish the ownership of assets in case the marriage fails. The prenuptial covenants of

---

55. Valiant K. Jones, "Wedding Ceremony," personal notes, Aug. 2020.

God, received through the endowment, are entered into to ensure that the marriage will last for eternity.

Oh, what beauty, glory, and magnificence we see in the ordinances established by our loving Father in Heaven! The blessings He provides through the endowment and sealing ordinances in His holy temples are powerful and eternal. No wonder He declared, "And this greater [Melchizedek] priesthood administereth the gospel and holdeth the key of the mysteries of the kingdom, even the key of the knowledge of God. Therefore, in the ordinances thereof, the power of godliness is manifest" (D&C 84:19–20). As President Russell M. Nelson declared, "The supreme benefits of membership in the Church can only be realized only through the exalting ordinances of the temple. These blessings qualify us for 'thrones, kingdoms, principalities, and powers' in the celestial kingdom."[56]

The Temple Centers on Covenants and Jesus Christ

A common element in each of the topics discussed in this chapter is our temple covenants. Whenever we clothe ourselves in our temple garments, we are reminded that we are covered by the Atonement of Jesus Christ as we keep our covenants. When we participate in the signs and tokens of the temple, we can use them to remember our commitments to keep our temple covenants. And in order to receive the blessings promised in a temple marriage ceremony, we must first commit to following the covenants of the endowment. All things in the temple revolve around our covenants.

All things in the temple also revolve around Jesus Christ. President Nelson said, "Because Jesus Christ is at the center of everything we do in the temple, as you think more about the temple you will be thinking more about Him. Study and pray to learn more about the power and knowledge with which you have been endowed—or with which you will yet be endowed."[57] That power comes by keeping our temple covenants.

---

56. Russell M. Nelson, "Endure and Be Lifted Up," *Ensign*, May 1997, 72.
57. Russell M. Nelson, "Go Forward in Faith," *Ensign* or *Liahona*, May 2020, 115.

The more we learn about our temple covenants, the more we learn the ways of Jesus Christ. It was Jesus who modeled perfect obedience, declaring, "I came down from heaven, not to do mine own will, but the will of him that sent me" (John 6:38). It was Jesus who gave the greatest example of sacrifice the world has ever known by what He experienced in Gethsemane and on Golgotha: "He . . . put away sin by the sacrifice of himself" (Hebrews 9:26). It was Jesus who taught the law of His gospel—that salvation comes through Him by faith, repentance, baptism, and following the guidance of the Holy Ghost as we endure to the end (see 3 Nephi 27:13–21). It was Jesus who expounded on the importance of the law of chastity, declaring "that whosoever looketh on a woman to lust after her hath committed adultery with her already in his heart" (Matthew 5:28). And it was Jesus who, in the premortal realms, consecrated to the Father all He was and all He would become when He committed, "Here am I, send me" (Moses 4:1).

If we will follow Jesus by keeping our covenants, we will receive the power of Christ's Atonement in our lives in greater measure. President Nelson made the following promise regarding our covenants:

> Entering into a covenant relationship with God binds us to Him in a way that makes everything about life easier. Please do not misunderstand me: I did not say that making covenants makes life easy. In fact, expect opposition, because the adversary does not want you to discover the power of Jesus Christ. But yoking yourself with the Savior means you have access to His strength and redeeming power. . . .
>
> Spend more time in the temple, and seek to understand how the temple teaches you to rise above this fallen world. . . . Cherish and honor your covenants above all other commitments. . . . Because Jesus Christ overcame this world, you can too.[58]

We can all gain greater insights into the temple ceremonies and our temple covenants as we consistently and prayerfully attend the house of the Lord to engage in the work of salvation for ourselves and

---

58. Russell M. Nelson, "Overcome the World and Find Rest," *Liahona*, Nov. 2022, 97–98.

for our kindred dead. We can be strengthened by those covenants and by the power of the Atonement of Jesus Christ inherent in them as we exit the temple doors to face the challenges of this world in our real-life hero's journey. We will then find that we do not face those challenges alone, but rather we go forth clothed with power and authority from God so that we can become like our heavenly parents and like our Savior, Jesus Christ.

2
Understanding the Keys of Temple Work

While serving as a branch president, I was asked to perform a civil marriage for a young couple. Before I could do so, I needed to make sure I had the proper authorization from both the Church and the government. I learned that I had received the authority from the Church to perform a civil wedding when I was set apart in my calling as branch president, with two limitations: I could only marry couples where at least one was a member of my congregation, and I had to be legally authorized in the jurisdiction where the marriage would be performed.

The first requirement was not an issue, but I wondered if I needed to register my church calling with a government agency in order to be legally authorized. I learned that my state only required that I be ordained or otherwise authorized by a church and that I would need to list my church affiliation on the marriage certificate, a copy of which would be filed with the county clerk.

I performed the marriage and completed the paperwork, which the couple filed as required. It was a beautiful ceremony that started the couple on a lifelong journey of love and commitment. I was grateful to have learned the procedures I needed to follow to make sure the civil marriage ceremony I performed was considered legal and binding for both the government and the Church. I had to make sure I was doing things correctly in the eyes of higher authorities because they held the keys of that ceremony. I was merely the officiator.

Keys are important. As one Church magazine article explained, "With a set of keys, you can do a lot of things that you wouldn't otherwise be able to do—enter buildings, drive cars, and open trunks, among other things. Keys, basically, mean authority and access. The same is true of priesthood keys. They control access to the blessings and ordinances of the priesthood."[59] President Russell M. Nelson taught that priesthood keys "refer to the right to preside over priesthood authority in the name of the Lord Jesus Christ."[60]

Just as I needed to receive authorization from those who held the keys of civil marriage, those who perform any priesthood ordinance must do so under the direction of those who hold proper priesthood keys. This chapter will review the restoration of the keys of temple work.

The Restoration of Priesthood Keys

When Jesus Christ visited the Nephites after His Resurrection, He recited the words that had been given to the prophet Malachi in the old world. These included a prophecy of the future return of Elijah: "Behold, I will send you Elijah the prophet before the coming of the great and dreadful day of the Lord; And he shall turn the heart of the fathers to the children, and the heart of the children to their fathers, lest I come and smite the earth with a curse" (3 Nephi 25:5–6; see also Malachi 4:5–6). Moroni repeated this prophecy, with some modifications, when he appeared to Joseph Smith (see D&C 2 and JS—H 1:36–38).

This prophecy was fulfilled when Joseph Smith and Oliver Cowdery received a remarkable series of visions in the Kirtland Temple on April 3, 1836. The first was an appearance of Jehovah—Jesus Christ

---

59. "Priesthood Keys," *New Era*, May 2012, 38.
60. Russell M. Nelson, "Keys of the Priesthood," *Ensign*, Oct. 2005, 40.

Himself—who accepted the newly completed and dedicated Kirtland Temple. Following this, visions of three special messengers appeared, in sequence, which Joseph described as follows:

> The heavens were again opened unto us; and Moses appeared before us, and committed unto us the keys of the gathering of Israel from the four parts of the earth, and the leading of the ten tribes from the land of the north.
>
> After this, Elias appeared, and committed the dispensation of the gospel of Abraham, saying that in us and our seed all generations after us should be blessed.
>
> After this vision had closed, another great and glorious vision burst upon us; for Elijah the prophet, who was taken to heaven without tasting death, stood before us, and said:
>
> Behold, the time has fully come, which was spoken of by the mouth of Malachi—testifying that he [Elijah] should be sent, before the great and dreadful day of the Lord come—
>
> To turn the hearts of the fathers to the children, and the children to the fathers, lest the whole earth be smitten with a curse—
>
> Therefore, the keys of this dispensation are committed into your hands; and by this ye may know that the great and dreadful day of the Lord is near, even at the doors. (D&C 110:11–16)

These three heavenly messengers bestowed upon Joseph Smith and Oliver Cowdery important priesthood keys, including the keys of missionary work and the keys of temple ordinances for the living and for the dead.

Moses was a fitting custodian of the keys of the gathering of Israel because it was he who led the children of Israel from Egypt as one body before they were dispersed. That dispersion was first into separate lands of inheritance in Canaan and later among all the nations of the earth. The keys that Moses bestowed on Joseph and Oliver authorized global missionary work, imparting priesthood power to those who would spread the gospel under the direction of all the modern prophets who have carried those keys since 1836. Every missionary of this dispensation has preached gospel truths with power and authority because of the restoration of these priesthood keys.

However, the keys restored by Moses were not given solely for the gathering of people into the gospel net of salvation. They were also given for the gathering of people to temples so that all souls born in all time periods could have the opportunity to receive the blessing of exaltation and eternal families. The keys that Moses restored prepare receptive children of God to receive the blessings of the keys of Elias and Elijah that followed. The keys of Moses needed to be imparted before temple work could begin because, as President Nelson has pointed out, the gathering of Israel occurs "on both sides of the veil."[61] When we search out the names of our ancestors, we are functioning within the spirit of the keys of Moses as much as within the spirit of the keys of Elijah. The restored keys of the gathering of Israel function both on the earth and in the spirit world.

The final visitor was the prophet Elijah. Much has been written about this ancient seer and the restoration of the sealing keys he carried. The Bible Dictionary says of him:

> Elijah held the sealing power of the Melchizedek Priesthood. He appeared on the Mount of Transfiguration in company with Moses (also translated) and conferred the keys of the priesthood on Peter, James, and John (Matt 17:3). He appeared again, in company with Moses and others, on April 3, 1836, in the Kirtland (Ohio) Temple and conferred the same keys upon Joseph Smith and Oliver Cowdery. All of this was in preparation for the coming of the Lord, as spoken of in Mal. 4:5–6 (D&C 110:13–16). As demonstrated by his miraculous deeds, the power of Elijah is the sealing power of the priesthood by which things bound or loosed on earth are bound or loosed in heaven. Thus the keys of this power are once again operative on the earth and are used in performing all the ordinances of the gospel for the living and the dead.[62]

The keys Elijah restored are clear and beautiful—they make sense. However, our understanding of his predecessor, Elias, and the keys he restored is less clear. Frankly, Elias has long been a bit of an enigma for many members of the Church. Part of this is because even his historical identity is unclear. In addition, there is the issue of Elias

---

61. Russell M. Nelson, "Hope of Israel" (worldwide youth devotional, June 3, 2018), Gospel Library; see also Russell M. Nelson, "The Gathering of Scattered Israel," *Ensign* or *Liahona*, Nov. 2006.

62. Bible Dictionary, "Elijah"

being both a person and a title. And what is the relationship between the keys of Elias and those of Elijah? Also, at first glance, the keys restored by Elias are not aligned in an obvious way with any particular ordinance. It is all rather confusing. The following discussion will be an attempt to shed some light on all of this.

Who Was Elias?

It is important to recognize that Elijah and Elias are the same name coming to us in English from two other languages. They are like Pedro and Pierre or Carlos and Charles. Elijah is a transliteration into English from the Hebrew form of the name, and Elias is a transliteration from the Greek form of the same name.

Hebrew, Greek, and English are all written in different alphabets or scripts, so when proper names are translated, the best available equivalent letters are typically chosen. However, sometimes adjustments are made because there is no equivalent letter or in order to make the name appear more reasonable in the new language. Thus, when doing a translation directly from Hebrew, early writers chose *Elijah* in English, but when early translators started with the Greek transliteration of the same name and then anglicized that, they chose *Elias*. Other equivalent names in the King James Version (KJV) Old Testament and New Testament include Elisha/Eliseus (see Luke 4:27), Isaiah/Esaias (see John 12:38), Joshua/Jesus (see Acts 7:45), Judah/Judas (see Matthew 1:2–3), and Noah/Noe (see Matthew 24:38). Additional equivalent names include Miriam/Mary, Hannah/Anna, and Jacob/James.[63]

When Jesus said, as written in the King James Bible, "But I tell you of a truth, many widows were in Israel in the days of Elias, when the heaven was shut up three years and six months, when great famine was throughout all the land" (Luke 4:25), He was clearly referring to the Old Testament prophet we know of as Elijah the Tishbite. Likewise, when John the Baptist told the priests and Levites that he was not the Christ or Messiah, and they asked, "What then? Art thou

---

63. Even though Jacob and James are equivalent names, both are used in the KJV New Testament. For an interesting discussion of these names, see https://www.gotquestions.org/James-vs-Jacob.html.

Elias?" (John 1:21), they were asking if he was the Old Testament prophet Elijah—for they knew of the prophecy that Elijah would appear before the coming of the Messiah (see Malachi 4:5–6). It would not be wrong for us to substitute *Elijah* in place of *Elias* in our minds wherever the latter is encountered in the KJV New Testament. In fact, most of the other English translations of the Bible use Elijah in all passages in the New Testament where the KJV uses Elias. So first and foremost, Elias refers to Elijah the Tishbite.

In addition, Jesus referred to John the Baptist as Elias, meaning Elijah (see Matthew 11:13–14). When the angel Gabriel appeared to Zacharias and prophesied that his wife, Elizabeth, would bear a son who should be named John, the angel said of him, "And many of the children of Israel shall he turn to the Lord their God. And he shall go before him in the spirit and power of Elias [i.e., Elijah], to turn the hearts of the fathers to the children, and the disobedient to the wisdom of the just; to make ready a people prepared for the Lord" (Luke 1:16–17). Thus, John the Baptist was to be a forerunner of the first coming of Christ "in the spirit and power of Elias [i.e., Elijah]" just as Elijah himself was to be a forerunner of the Second Coming of Christ. Both would prepare people's hearts to receive Jesus Christ before He arrived. This provides the basis for the use of *Elias* as a title, meaning forerunner.

The Prophet Joseph Smith expounded on this second use of *Elias*. He taught, "The spirit of Elias is to prepare the way for a greater revelation of God. . . . And when God sends a man into the world to prepare for a greater work, holding the keys of the power of Elias, it was called the doctrine of Elias, even from the early ages of the world."[64]

Joseph Smith used Elias in other ways as well. The Bible Dictionary summarizes all these ways and then states, "Thus the word *Elias* has many applications and has been placed upon many persons as a title pertaining to both preparatory and restorative functions."[65] Apparently, the duplication of this name in two forms in the King James Bible—Elijah and Elias—provided an impetus for the Lord to

---

64. *Teachings of the Prophet Joseph Smith*, sel. Joseph Fielding Smith (1976), 335–6.
65. Bible Dictionary, "Elias."

inspire Joseph Smith in many ways regarding Elias and the doctrine of Elias.

For Latter-day Saints, the most important event that occurred under the name of Elias took place when the Lord sent a heavenly messenger under that appellation to Joseph Smith and Oliver Cowdery in the Kirtland Temple on April 3, 1836. The Bible Dictionary says of this messenger, "A man called Elias apparently lived in mortality in the days of Abraham, who committed the dispensation of the gospel of Abraham to Joseph Smith and Oliver Cowdery. . . . We have no specific information as to the details of his mortal life or ministry."[66]

The lack of specific information regarding this restorer of priesthood keys has led some to conjecture that this angel may have been a prophet known in the Old Testament by some other name. President Joseph Fielding Smith, as an Apostle, stated that Elias and Noah are the same person.[67] President Smith also stated that "some think him to be Melchizedek."[68] Elder Bruce R. McConkie confirmed the uncertainty of the identity of the Elias who appeared in the Kirtland Temple, writing, "Whether he was Abraham or Melchizedek or some other prophet, we do not know."[69] Elder McConkie later conjectured, "Apparently this Elias lived in the day of Abraham, and may even have been Abraham himself."[70] It is also possible that the Elias who

---

66. Bible Dictionary, "Elias."

67. Joseph Fielding Smith, in Conference Report, Apr. 1960, 72; see also Joseph Fielding Smith, *Answers to Gospel Questions* (Deseret Book, 1960), 3:139–141. This conclusion is based on D&C 27:6–7, which says that Elias announced to Zacharias the birth of his future son, John the Baptist. In Luke 1:19, this birth announcement is attributed to the angel Gabriel, whom Joseph Smith declared to be Noah (see *Teachings of the Prophet Joseph Smith*, 157). The conclusion of all of this is that Elias is Noah. However, when we remember that Elias is sometimes used as a title meaning forerunner, we realize that the scripture in D&C 27 is probably saying that the angel Gabriel was a forerunner. He was a forerunner to John the Baptist who was a forerunner to Christ. Both Gabriel and John the Baptist were each an Elias.

68. Joseph Fielding Smith, *Doctrines of Salvation*, comp. Bruce R. McConkie (1955), 1:107.

69. Bruce R. McConkie, "Elias," *Mormon Doctrine*, 2nd ed. (1966), 220.

70. Bruce R. McConkie, "This Final Glorious Gospel Dispensation," *Ensign*, Apr. 1980, 22.

appeared in the Kirtland Temple was none of these but was a separate prophet who lived in ancient times and whose earthly name was the Hebrew equivalent of *Elijah* and *Elias*. The statement on Elias from the Bible Dictionary, cited earlier, seems to agree with this possibility.[71]

In addition to all these possibilities regarding the identity of Elias, I offer another proposal. It is possible that the two separate visions in the Kirtland Temple, wherein a single messenger appeared each time—the first in the name of Elias and the second in the name of Elijah—were both carried out by the same ancient prophet: Elijah the Tishbite. Perhaps he was directed by God to appear twice under his two separate but related names in order to restore two separate but related priesthood keys, both of which he held.

It is interesting to note that in the New Testament record of a similar occasion—when keys were given to Peter, James, and John on the Mount of Transfiguration—Moses and Elijah appeared together at the same time (see Matthew 17:3; Mark 9:4). Yet in the Kirtland Temple, the three messengers appeared sequentially—an arrangement that would have accommodated a repeat appearance by Elijah. Also, this theory creates a stronger parallel with the New Testament record, which speaks of a visit by only those two messengers (see Matthew 17:1–13; Mark 9:2–13; Luke 9:28–26). Perhaps Joseph and Oliver also received only two messengers, with one of them appearing twice in subsequent visions. Perhaps these modern seers were so taken by the glory of their visions and so focused on the messengers' words that they did not recognize the equality of the angels' features in the two appearances.

---

71. The Bible Dictionary statement that "a man called Elias apparently lived in mortality in the days of Abraham" raises some questions. To suggest that this unknown man carried a name that was distinct from the name Elijah ignores the etymology of the name Elias. Remember that Elias is derived from the same Hebrew name as Elijah after passing through Greek, so it is highly unlikely that an ancient prophet would have carried the Greco-Hebrew name Elias. However, it is possible there were two separate ancient prophets with the same Hebrew name and that the Lord has chosen to distinguish them in our day by calling one Elijah and the other Elias. The Old Testament has no record of a second prophet named Elijah, but it is not unreasonable to consider that there could have been multiple men with that name. I assume that this is what the Bible Dictionary statement is suggesting as a possibility.

God often works within the paradigms we hold ourselves to, and if Joseph Smith believed that the references to Elias and Elijah in his KJV Bible were references to two separate prophets (and some of the ways Joseph used *Elias* suggest that he did), then it is possible that God chose to use that paradigm to emphasize the restoration of two separate but related priesthood keys. God rarely clarifies our misunderstandings unless we ask, and it is possible that Joseph never even considered that Elias and Elijah could have been the same person.

Of course, this proposal is only a conjecture; however, there is nothing in Doctrine and Covenants 110 that is inconsistent with this theory. Joseph's many and varied references to Elias confirm he was not settled on who Elias was. However, this does not affect his stature as a prophet; it simply makes him human. The Lord stated that the revelations in the Doctrine and Covenants "were given unto my servants in their weakness, after the manner of their language, that they might come to understanding" (D&C 1:24; see also 2 Nephi 31:3). In other words, the revelations were given in the imperfect language paradigms that Joseph comprehended so that the principles God deemed most important could be revealed.

Remember also that Jesus Himself contributed to the complexity of this issue when he referred to John the Baptist as Elias/Elijah (see Matthew 11:7–14). Regardless of all this, if we were to take the second key-bearer at his word when he said he was Elias and then invoke the simplest interpretation of his name, we would conclude that this messenger was Elijah the Tishbite.

Regarding the identity of Elias, Elder John A. Widtsoe wrote, "When Elias, the man, lived, and what he did in his life, must for the present remain in the field of conjecture."[72] Both the Bible and the Book of Mormon refer to many unnamed prophets, confirming that ancient prophets were not always identified.[73] The messenger who came as Elias to the Kirtland Temple was undoubtedly a great prophet when he lived on earth, but when he appeared to Joseph and Oliver, his

---

72. John A. Widtsoe, *Evidences and Reconciliations: Aids to Faith in a Modern Day* (Bookcraft, 1943), 243–4.
73. See Hosea 12:13; 1 Samuel 2:27; 1 Kings 13:1–3, 11; 1 Kings 20:13, 22; 1 Kings 28; 2 Kings 23:18; Zechariah 7:3; 1 Nephi 1:4.

mortal life and mission were secondary in importance to the keys that he was restoring. Maybe this is why the Lord provided this messenger with some anonymity by having him introduce himself as Elias.

All this aside, we must not be so concerned about the identity of Elias that we overlook his purpose. This is an issue faced by people who become attached to a particular missionary who has been teaching them the gospel. If that missionary gets transferred before their baptism, they must decide if it is the missionary or the underlying priesthood authority that matters for their baptism. As a young missionary in Argentina many years ago, I saw this principle at work when I got transferred from Córdoba to Mendoza. I arrived in my new area on a Monday, and the following Saturday we had a baptism scheduled for a kind widow who had been receiving the discussions before I arrived. She had known the departing missionary well, and I'm sure she was disappointed to see him leave just before her baptism. Nevertheless, she had greater faith in the gospel message and in the power of the priesthood than in the person of the missionary who had departed, so she moved forward with her baptism and even asked me to perform it.

So it is with Elias. His specific identity and background were not as important as his priesthood authority. Regardless of who this Elias was in mortal life, the most important thing we need to know about him is that he restored important priesthood keys to Joseph Smith and Oliver Cowdery in the Kirtland Temple in 1836. That much is certain, and that part is what matters most.

Elias and the Dispensation of the Gospel of Abraham

Regarding the purpose of the heavenly messenger who came in the name of Elias, Joseph and Oliver wrote that he "committed the dispensation of the gospel of Abraham" (D&C 110:12). To understand this declaration, it is helpful to recognize that the word *gospel* can sometimes be used as a synonym for the word *covenant*[74] and to

---

74. In D&C 39:11 and 66:2, the Lord refers to the gospel as a covenant. These verses likely refer to the covenant called *the law of the gospel*; however, they also suggest that *gospel* and *covenant* can be synonyms.

understand the word *dispensation* in the sense of dispensing or bestowing rather than as an epoch of time on the earth. With these clarifications, this passage can be interpreted as saying that Elias "committed the *bestowing* of the *covenant* of Abraham." Consistent with this interpretation, the 2025 *Doctrine and Covenants Seminary Teacher Manual* explains, "Elias committed the dispensation of the gospel of Abraham. This includes the restoration of the Abrahamic covenant."[75] The fulness of this covenant, which includes the promises of endless posterity, priesthood power, and an eternal promised land inheritance in God's presence,[76] is bestowed through the ordinance of temple marriage. Thus, the keys restored by Elias are the keys of eternal marriage.

This link to eternal marriage becomes clearer when we consider the promise given by Elias "that in us and our seed all generations after us should be blessed" (D&C 110:12). This statement echoes the promise Abraham received that "in thy seed after thee . . . shall all the families of the earth be blessed" (Abraham 2:11). This promise could only be fulfilled through the union of Abraham with Sarah. Likewise, these same blessings are bestowed on couples married in the temple, where they are sealed together eternally and bestowed the blessings of Abraham, Isaac, and Jacob.

President Nelson confirmed this understanding of the keys of Elias, teaching:

> In 1836, keys of "the gospel of Abraham" were conferred (D&C 110:12). In 1843 the Lord declared to the Prophet Joseph Smith that "Abraham received promises concerning his seed, and of the fruit of his loins—from whose loins ye are. . . . This promise is yours also, because ye are of Abraham" (D&C 132:30–31). . . .
>
> The ultimate blessings of the Abrahamic covenant are conferred in holy temples. These blessings allow us to come forth in the First Resurrection and inherit thrones, kingdoms, powers, principalities,

---

75. "Lesson 124—D&C 110, Part 2: The Restoration of Priesthood Keys," *Doctrine and Covenants Seminary Teacher Manual* (2025).

76. See Kent P. Jackson, "The Abrahamic Covenant: A Blessing for All People," *Ensign*, Feb. 1990, 50–53; see also "The Abrahamic Covenant," *Liahona*, Feb. 2022.

and dominions, to our "exaltation and glory in all things" (D&C 132:19).[77]

Of course, these blessings described by President Nelson are the blessings pronounced upon every couple sealed in eternal marriage.

To paraphrase a little differently the Doctrine and Covenants 110 declaration of the keys restored by Elias, we could say that he bestowed upon Joseph and Oliver a dispensing of the same good news that many generations earlier had been given to Abraham. And what was this particular good news or gospel? It was that Joseph and Oliver now had the power to administer a binding, covenant-marriage link for men and women on earth so that all generations that would come after them would be blessed. Elder Bruce R. McConkie taught, "Elias restored the great commission, given of God to Abraham our father, whereby the seed of Abraham has power to gain eternal blessings forever through eternal marriage; that is, Elias restored the marriage discipline that had eternal efficacy, virtue, and force in the days of Abraham, Isaac, and Jacob."[78]

The authority to bind couples in eternal marriage has existed since Adam, but it was strongly associated with Abraham, who was promised that his seed would be as vast as the sands of the sea (see Genesis 22:17; 32:12), so this authority was also called the good news of Abraham or the gospel of Abraham (see Abraham 2:9–11). This approach of naming a divine power after a remarkable prophet is similar to what occurred with the Melchizedek Priesthood, which also existed on the earth since Adam but was renamed "because Melchizedek was such a great high priest" (D&C 107:2). Similarly, the Lord said to Abraham, "For as many as receive this Gospel shall be called after thy name, and shall be accounted thy seed, and shall rise up and bless thee, as their father" (Abraham 2:10). So the new and everlasting covenant

---

77. Russell M. Nelson, "Special Witnesses of Christ," *Ensign*, Apr. 2001, 8; see also Russell M. Nelson, "The Everlasting Covenant," *Liahona*, Oct. 2022.

78. Bruce R. McConkie, *A New Witness for the Articles of Faith* (Deseret Book, 1985), 508; quoted by Robert L. Millet, "The Ancient Covenant Restored," *Ensign*, Mar. 1998, 43. See also Bruce R. McConkie, "The Keys of the Kingdom," *Ensign*, May 1983, 21–23.

of marriage is also called the gospel of Abraham or the Abrahamic covenant, and Elias restored the keys of this covenant.

Elder McConkie elaborated further on this role of Elias:

> This Elias . . . "committed the dispensation of the gospel of Abraham" (D&C 110:12) . . . meaning the great commission which God gave Abraham in his day. That commission dealt with families, those of Abraham and his seed, who were and are promised continuance "in the world and out of the world . . . as innumerable as the stars; or, if ye were to count the sand upon the seashore ye could not number them" (D&C 132:30).
>
> As Joseph Smith records it, what Elias actually said to him and Oliver Cowdery was that "in us and our seed all generations after us should be blessed" (D&C 110:12). And so, the Lord be praised, the marriage discipline of Abraham was restored; it is the system that enables a family unit to continue in eternity; it is the system out of which eternal life grows.[79]

The heavenly messenger who declared himself to be Elias restored the keys of eternal marriage. I believe these keys encompass not only the temple marriage ceremony but also the temple endowment ceremony, since the endowment prepares us for eternal marriage.[80]

Elias and the Restoration of All Things

Another interesting insight showing a link between Elias and eternal marriage can be found in considering the role of Elias as a restorer. A search of the scriptures for the phrase "restore all things" or its variant, "restoration of all things," yields seven occurrences of these phrases. Four of them clearly specify Elias as the restorer of all things (see D&C 27:6; D&C 77:9; JST, Matthew 17:10; JST, John 1:26), and two other occurrences are related to eternal marriage (see D&C 132:40, 45). There is a connection between these two approaches.

In Doctrine and Covenants 132, the Lord taught about the importance of the eternal marriage covenant and then said, "I am the Lord

---

79. Bruce R. McConkie, "This Final Glorious Gospel Dispensation," 22.
80. For a discussion of how the endowment can be seen as the first part of the eternal marriage ceremony, see the section "The Covenants of Eternal Marriage" in chapter 1 of this book.

thy God, and I gave unto thee, my servant Joseph, an appointment, *and restore all things*" (D&C 132:40; emphasis added). A few verses later, the Lord added, "For I have conferred upon you the keys and power of the priesthood, wherein *I restore all things*, and make known unto you all things in due time" (D&C 132:45; emphasis added). In both verses, the Lord used *restore* in the present tense, suggesting that by revealing this doctrine on eternal marriage, the restoration of all things was now complete.[81]

It appears that the restoration of the keys of the Abrahamic covenant of eternal marriage was such a significant crowning event that once the Lord revealed a full understanding of that covenant by revealing Doctrine and Covenants 132, He considered the restoration of all the core doctrines and keys of the gospel to be complete. This does not mean that further light and understanding would not later occur in the ongoing Restoration, for the Lord added that He will "make known unto you all things in due time" (D&C 132:45). For example, a knowledge of our Heavenly Mother was also a part of this restoration of all things because Her existence is inherent in the doctrine of the eternal family, even though Joseph only later taught explicitly of Her existence to some early Church members.[82] Nevertheless, it appears that the revelation on eternal marriage was the capstone for the restoration of the keys of temple work, making it clear why Elias would be associated with the restoration of all things.

In Doctrine and Covenants 27, the Lord revealed, "The hour cometh that I will drink of the fruit of the vine with you on the earth, . . . and also with Elias, to whom I have committed the keys of

---

81. In the Joseph Smith Translation of John 1:26–28, Joseph Smith associated the title of Elias with Jesus Christ, making that reference to Elias unique; however, this does not change the fact that Joseph repeatedly associated the prophet Elias with the restoration of all things. When we realize that Christ accomplishes things through His prophets, then it is not unreasonable for Christ to be called an Elias based on the actions of the prophet Elias who acted in Christ's name. In addition, the Lord Himself took an active part in this restoration of all things by giving to Joseph Smith the revelation on eternal marriage, wherein He said, "I restore all things" (D&C 132:45). So both the prophet Elias and Jesus Christ actively participated in the restoration of all things.
82. See Gospel Topics Essays, "Mother in Heaven," Gospel Library.

bringing to pass the restoration of all things spoken by the mouth of all the holy prophets since the world began, concerning the last days" (D&C 27:5–6). The restoration of the doctrine of eternal marriage is the glorious doctrine that was spoken of by all the holy prophets since the world began and restored by Elias in the climactic event of the restoration of all things. Personally, I can think of no other doctrine of the Restoration that is more expansive and ennobling, revealing the divine potential of all covenant men and women to become like our Heavenly Father and Heavenly Mother as joint heirs with Jesus Christ and promising continued family relationships eternally. It makes me want to exclaim, as did Joseph Smith, "Now, what do we hear in the gospel which we have received? A voice of gladness! . . . A voice of gladness for the living and the dead; glad tidings of great joy" (D&C 128:19)!

Six of the seven scriptural references to the restoration of all things have been discussed. In the seventh occurrence, the Lord told Joseph Smith in 1832, "Therefore your life and the priesthood have remained, and must needs remain through you and your lineage until the restoration of all things spoken by the mouths of all the holy prophets since the world began" (D&C 86:10). In fulfillment of this, not only did Joseph live to receive the restoration of the keys of temple work and the revelation on eternal marriage, but he continued to live until a temple was designed and under construction and all of the keys of the kingdom had been transmitted to the members of the Quorum of the Twelve Apostles, presided over by Brigham Young.[83] So even this seventh reference to the restoration of all things points to eternal marriage.

As we have seen, Joseph Smith's revelations regarding the restoration of all things provide additional evidence that the keys restored by Elias are the keys of eternal marriage. However, on their own, these keys are limited to ceremonies performed for the living. When Elias bestowed his priesthood keys, he said, "All generations *after us* should be blessed" (D&C 110:12; emphasis added). The keys of Elias provide blessing to posterity who come after us, but they do nothing for

---

83. This event will be discussed later in this chapter.

ancestors who came before us. In order to bring the same blessings to them, additional priesthood keys were needed. The subsequent visit by Elijah restored the keys that extended those sealing ordinances to the dead—to those progenitors in the spirit world who had not entered into gospel covenants with God while they were living on the earth.

Work for the Dead Commenced After Christ's Death

Work for the dead was not performed on the earth until after Christ initiated the preaching of the gospel to the spirits in prison at the time of His death. No proxy work for the dead could occur until after Christ opened the door for this by doing the greatest proxy work of all—atoning for our sins. Peter wrote:

> For Christ also hath once suffered for sins, the just for the unjust, that he might bring us to God, being put to death in the flesh, but quickened by the Spirit:
> By which also he went and preached unto the spirits in prison;
> Which sometime were disobedient, when once the longsuffering of God waited in the days of Noah, while the ark was a preparing, wherein few, that is, eight souls were saved by water. . . .
> For for this cause was the gospel preached also to them that are dead, that they might be judged according to men in the flesh, but live according to God in the spirit. (1 Peter 3:18–20; 4:6)

President Joseph F. Smith's vision of the spirit world makes it clear that, when Christ died, the dead "were assembled awaiting the advent of the Son of God into the spirit world" (D&C 138:16), apparently with no change in the status of each since their deaths. Christ arrived and organized the faithful to be teachers to those who were in darkness. President Smith described how the Lord initiated this work of redemption of the dead:

> I perceived that the Lord went not in person among the wicked and the disobedient who had rejected the truth, to teach them;
> But behold, from among the righteous, he organized his forces and appointed messengers, clothed with power and authority, and commissioned them to go forth and carry the light of the gospel to

them that were in darkness, even to all the spirits of men; and thus was the gospel preached to the dead. . . .

Thus was it made known that our Redeemer spent his time during his sojourn in the world of spirits, instructing and preparing the faithful spirits of the prophets who had testified of him in the flesh;

That they might carry the message of redemption unto all the dead. (D&C 138:29–30, 36–37)

Christ's ministry in the spirit world had to occur before authorized proxy ordinances for the dead could be performed on earth. The Bible Dictionary entry for "Temple" confirms this, declaring, "From Adam to the time of Jesus, ordinances were performed in temples for the living only. After Jesus opened the way for the gospel to be preached in the world of spirits, ceremonial work for the dead, as well as for the living, has been done in temples on the earth by faithful members of the Church."[84]

Confirming this, President Nelson taught, "From the days of Adam to the meridian of time, temple ordinances were performed for the living only. Ordinances for the dead had to await the Atonement and postmortal ministry of the Savior."[85] This same principle also was taught by President Brigham Young[86] and President Joseph Fielding Smith.[87] Understanding that temple ordinances were performed only for the living until after Christ's Resurrection will help us understand the keys of Elijah.

Elijah's Keys Seal All Ordinances for the Living

We often say that Elijah brought the sealing keys of temple work for the dead, and this is true; however, since proxy temple work for the dead did not occur until after the Resurrection of Jesus, what purpose did these keys fulfill in Old Testament times? The answer lies in the dual nature of these keys: They apply to ordinances performed both

---

84. Bible Dictionary, "Temple"
85. Russell M. Nelson, "The Spirit of Elijah," *Ensign*, Nov. 1994, 85.
86. See Brigham Young, in *Journal of Discourses*, 4:285.
87. See Joseph Fielding Smith, *Doctrines of Salvation*, 2:320–1.

for the living and for the dead. Elijah's keys seal in heaven all priesthood ordinances performed on earth, regardless of which side of the veil the souls reside on when they are named in the ordinances.

The way in which the sealing keys of Elijah were used in his day was to make sure all ordinances done for the living applied eternally. For priesthood ordinances to apply eternally, they must be performed under the direction of a prophet or apostle who holds the sealing keys of Elijah. Regarding these keys, the Prophet Joseph Smith declared, "It may seem to some to be a very bold doctrine that we talk of—a power which records or binds on earth and binds in heaven. Nevertheless, in all ages of the world, whenever the Lord has given a dispensation of the priesthood to any man by actual revelation, or any set of men, this power has always been given" (D&C 128:9).

One of the defining characteristics of the Great Apostasy was the loss of these sealing keys. The Catholic Church claims an unbroken line of authority from their popes back to Peter. However, even if the earliest popes, who were serving as bishops in Rome, could trace their priesthood ordinations to Peter, this would not be enough. All priesthood ordinances must be performed under the direction of a prophet or apostle who holds proper priesthood keys. The eventual lack of oversight by an authorized apostle on the earth who possessed the keys of Elijah means that any ordinances performed during that absence would not be recognized by God and would not be sealed in heaven. This is why Elijah had to return from heaven to restore those sealing keys to Joseph Smith.

President Boyd K. Packer described the keys of Elijah: "The sealing power . . . gives substance and eternal permanence to all ordinances performed with proper authority for both the living and the dead."[88] This was first taught by Joseph Smith, who said, "Why send Elijah? Because he holds the keys of the authority to administer in *all the ordinances of the priesthood*; and without the authority is given, the ordinances could not be administered in righteousness."[89] As BYU professor Mark Mathews explained, "Sealing power is the authority to

---

88. Boyd K. Packer, "Ordinances" (Brigham Young University devotional, Feb. 3, 1980), 6, speeches.byu.edu.
89. *Teachings of the Prophet Joseph Smith*, 172; emphasis added.

preside over and seal all ordinances of the temple and all ordinances for the living and the dead."[90]

President Joseph Fielding Smith elaborated on this doctrine as follows:

> Elijah restored to this Church . . . the keys of the sealing power; and that sealing power puts the stamp of approval upon every ordinance that is done in this Church and more particularly those that are performed in the temples of the Lord. . . . Some members of the Church have been confused in thinking that Elijah came with the keys of baptism for the dead or of salvation for the dead. Elijah's keys were greater than that. They were the keys of sealing, and those keys of sealing pertain to the living and embrace the dead who are willing to repent.[91]

> This priesthood holds the keys of binding and sealing on earth and in heaven of all the ordinances and principles pertaining to the salvation of man, that they may thus become valid in the celestial kingdom of God.[92]

In summary, the way the sealing power of Elijah functions for the living is to assure that ordinances performed under proper priesthood authority on earth are recognized by God in heaven, giving them eternal permanence. For this reason, under "Elijah" in the Bible Dictionary, we read, "The power of Elijah is the sealing power of the priesthood by which things bound or loosed on earth are bound or loosed in heaven. Thus the keys of this power are once again operative on the earth and are used in performing all the ordinances of the gospel for the living and the dead."[93] The way in which Elijah's keys apply to ordinances for the dead will be discussed next.

---

90. Mark Mathews, "Understanding Priesthood Keys in Leadership | An Interview with Mark Mathews," *Leading Saints* (podcast), Sept. 23, 2018, 33:44, https://leadingsaints.org/understanding-priesthood-keys-in-leadership/.
91. Joseph Fielding Smith, *Doctrines of Salvation*, 3:129–130; see also Joseph Fielding Smith, "Chapter 17: Sealing Power and Temple Blessings," *Teachings of Presidents of the Church: Joseph Fielding Smith* (2013).
92. Joseph Fielding Smith, *Doctrines of Salvation*, 2:117.
93. Bible Dictionary, "Elijah."

Elijah's Keys Extend Exalting Ordinances to the Dead

After Christ broke open the doors of spirit prison, an additional purpose for those keys became viable: The sealing keys of Elijah could then also be used to validate in heaven saving ordinances performed by proxies on earth for those who had already died without those ordinances but later repented and accepted Christ in the spirit world. During His ministry, Jesus Christ explained to Peter that he would receive the priesthood keys of the sealing power for his dispensation, saying, "And I will give unto thee the keys of the kingdom of heaven: and whatsoever thou shalt bind on earth shall be bound in heaven: and whatsoever thou shalt loose on earth shall be loosed in heaven" (Matthew 16:19). Christ later reiterated this, saying, "Verily I say unto you, Whatsoever ye shall bind on earth shall be bound in heaven: and whatsoever ye shall loose on earth shall be loosed in heaven" (Matthew 18:18).

Notice that the Lord told Peter, "I *will* give thee." Christ fulfilled this promise when he took Peter, James, and John to the Mount of Transfiguration and presided over the transfer of priesthood keys from Moses and Elijah to these three leading Apostles (see Matthew 17; Mark 9; Luke 9). Also notice the use of the term *whatsoever*. Under the keys of Elijah, *all* saving ordinances performed on earth are sealed as permanent, eternal, and binding in heaven, as previously explained.

In addition, Peter learned that in his dispensation, a particular new use for the keys of Elijah would be initiated: After the Resurrection of Jesus Christ, Peter and his fellow Apostles would be able to employ Elijah's sealing keys in proxy ordinance work for the dead. It should not surprise us to find that it is an epistle from Peter that explains the preaching of the gospel in the spirit prison (see 1 Peter 3:18–20; 4:6). The foundation for Peter's understanding of the doctrine of work for the dead undoubtedly came from his experience on the Mount of Transfiguration.

Joseph Smith likewise received a foundation for his understanding of the doctrine of work for the dead when he received from Elijah those same keys for his dispensation in the Kirtland Temple. Joseph continued to learn through revelation more about work for the dead until it became a primary focus of his life during his final years in Nauvoo. The Prophet taught how members of the Church in this last dispensation are to participate in fulfilling the mission of Elijah through the keys that the ancient Tishbite restored:

> How are [the Saints] to become saviors on Mount Zion? By building their temples, erecting their baptismal fonts, and going forth and receiving all the ordinances, baptisms, confirmations, washings, anointings, ordinations and sealing powers upon their heads, in behalf of all their progenitors who are dead, and redeem them that they may come forth in the first resurrection and be exalted to thrones of glory with them; and herein is the chain that binds the hearts of the fathers to the children, and the children to the fathers, which fulfills the mission of Elijah.[94]

Joseph Smith also taught, "The doctrine or sealing power of Elijah is as follows: If you have power to seal on earth and in heaven, then we should be wise. The first thing you do, go and seal on earth your sons and daughters unto yourself, and yourself unto your fathers in eternal glory."[95] Notice that the Prophet spoke of two separate sealing experiences—one to your children and another to your fathers or ancestors. The way to "seal on earth your sons and daughters unto yourself" is by being married in the temple so that your children are born in the covenant, or, if they are already born, by having them sealed to you after you are sealed to your spouse in a temple marriage. Such marriages and sealings for the living are performed under the keys of Elias. And the way to seal "yourself unto your fathers" is by performing proxy marriages and sealings for your deceased ancestors. Such ordinances for the dead are possible because of the additional keys of Elijah.

What glorious, good news we find in the combination of this gospel of Abraham and this doctrine of Elijah! A temple marriage for

---

94. *Teachings of the Prophet Joseph Smith*, 330; see also "Chapter 41: Becoming Saviors on Mount Zion," *Teachings of Presidents of the Church: Joseph Smith* (2011).

95. *Teachings of the Prophet Joseph Smith*, 340; see also "Chapter 26: Elijah and the Restoration of the Sealing Keys," *Teachings of Presidents of the Church: Joseph Smith*.

the living will bind a couple's children to them eternally, for they are born in the covenant. However, there is little value in being sealed to those who come in the future if we are not also sealed to those in the past through the keys of Elijah. Without this ability to form sealing links backward, the purposes of the earth would be wasted at the Lord's Second Coming (see D&C 2:1–3). Joseph Smith wrote, "These are principles in relation to the dead and the living that cannot be lightly passed over, as pertaining to our salvation. For their salvation is necessary and essential to our salvation, as Paul says concerning the fathers—that they without us cannot be made perfect—neither can we without our dead be made perfect" (D&C 128:15).

Joseph exulted in the restoration of these priesthood keys in his dispensation, writing, "Let your hearts rejoice, and be exceedingly glad. Let the earth break forth into singing. Let the dead speak forth anthems of eternal praise to the King Immanuel, who hath ordained, before the world was, that which would enable us to redeem them out of their prison; for the prisoners shall go free" (D&C 128:22).

Sometimes when we want something to be held very securely, we give keys to two different individuals and require that both come and bring their separate keys to unlock a treasure. This is true of Elias and Elijah. If the keys of Elias enabled eternal marriage for the living, this unlocked only part of the treasure of eternal families. Elijah had to follow and bring his keys to not only validate ordinances for the living but also to make proxy priesthood ordinances effective for the dead so that the living and the dead could be connected in eternal family bonds.

No wonder the building of temples and the work of salvation and exaltation for the dead is moving forward in our day at such a fantastic pace. These efforts are part of President Nelson's invitation to "help gather Israel on both sides of the veil."[96] He has said, "That gathering is the most important thing taking place on earth today. Nothing else compares in magnitude, nothing else compares in importance, nothing else compares in majesty. And if you choose to, if you want

---

96. Russell M. Nelson, "Sisters' Participation in the Gathering of Israel," *Ensign* or *Liahona*, Nov. 2018, 69.

to, you can be a big part of it. You can be a big part of something big, something grand, something majestic!"[97]

A Culmination of the Restoration

This chapter has expounded on the remarkable series of visions that occurred in the Kirtland Temple on April 3, 1836. The reception of priesthood keys on this occasion was a culmination of a series of restoration experiences. The following table summarizes the most significant of the priesthood restoration events of this dispensation.

Priesthood Restoration Events for Joseph Smith and Oliver Cowdery

Restorer	When	Where	Purpose and Keys Restored
John the Baptist	May 15, 1829	On the banks of the Susquehanna River, near Harmony, Pennsylvania	Aaronic Priesthood: The keys of the ministering of angels and of repentance and baptism (see D&C 13)
Peter, James, and John	Most likely in late May 1829[98]	In the wilderness between Harmony and Colesville, Pennsylvania (see D&C 128:20)	Melchizedek Priesthood: The keys of spiritual blessings, including the Holy Ghost, and the keys of Church administration (see D&C 27, 84, 107)
Moses	April 3, 1836	The Kirtland Temple	The keys of the gathering of Israel (see D&C 110)
Elias	April 3, 1836	The Kirtland Temple	The keys of the Abrahamic covenant, including eternal marriage (see D&C 110)
Elijah	April 3, 1836	The Kirtland Temple	The keys of sealing for all ordinances for the living and the dead (see D&C 110)

Let us review the succession of the receipt of these priesthood keys and see how they build on one another. John the Baptist first appeared to Joseph Smith and Oliver Cowdery to "confer the Priesthood of Aaron, which holds the keys of the ministering of angels, and of the gospel of repentance, and of baptism by immersion for the remission

---

97. Russell M. Nelson, "Hope of Israel."

98. Larry C. Porter, "The Restoration of the Aaronic and Melchizedek Priesthoods," *Ensign*, Dec. 1996, 30–47. In June 1829 Joseph Smith received D&C 18, which stated that Oliver Cowdery and David Whitmer were to be called as Apostles (see verse 9) and were to select additional members of that Quorum. This implies that the Melchizedek Priesthood had already been restored by that time.

of sins" (D&C 13:1). Next, Peter, James, and John restored the Priesthood of Melchizedek, which holds the "keys of all the spiritual blessings of the church" (D&C 107:18), including the gift of the Holy Ghost. They also "committed the keys of the kingdom, and a dispensation of the gospel for the last times" (D&C 27:13). Furthermore, "this greater priesthood administereth the gospel and holdeth the key of the mysteries of the kingdom, even the key of the knowledge of God" (D&C 84:19).

At this point, Joseph and Oliver possessed the keys and authority to perform all the ordinances of salvation, but they lacked the authority to spread this work of salvation globally. Moses came and filled this gap, providing "the keys of the gathering of Israel from the four parts of the earth" (D&C 110:11). Joseph and Oliver also lacked the keys and authority necessary to perform the exaltation ordinances of the endowment and eternal marriage. This was remedied with the bestowal of the keys of the Abrahamic covenant by Elias who "committed the dispensation of the gospel of Abraham" (D&C 110:12).

The keys and authority necessary to perform all ordinances had now been restored; however, this was still not enough. Up to this point, any ordinances were provisional and could only be performed for the living. Additional keys were needed to be able to seal the eternal validity of these ordinances in heaven and to make it possible to perform the same ordinances for the dead. These keys were restored by Elijah, who restored keys "to turn the hearts of the fathers to the children, and the children to the fathers, lest the whole earth be smitten with a curse" (D&C 110:15).

We might ask why Jesus could not have conferred all these priesthood keys Himself. Certainly He held all priesthood keys, so surely He could have. However, Christ respects and honors those He calls into stewardship under Him, and He provides opportunities for participation and personal growth as broadly as He can.

Similar to Joseph and Oliver, Christ's Apostles Peter, James, and John received priesthood keys from Moses and Elijah on the Mount of Transfiguration (see Mathew 17; Mark 9; Luke 9). These two Old Testament prophets had gone to heaven without tasting death, allowing them to be able to return and corporally lay their hands on the heads of Peter, James, and John for the transmission of priesthood keys before Christ broke the bands of death and made resurrection possible. In addition, Joseph Smith has implied that John the Baptist was present.[99] However, the Baptist could only have been there in spirit since he had recently died (see Matthew 14:1–12). Therefore, his presence could not have been for the transfer of his keys. That transfer of Aaronic Priesthood keys, although not recorded in the New Testament, had undoubtedly occurred while John the Baptist was living. Perhaps the Baptist came in spirit to the Mount of Transfiguration in order to be instructed by Jesus on the future transfer of the priesthood keys that everyone present would participate in 1,800 years later: Jesus, John the Baptist, Peter, James, John, Moses, and Elijah.

We might wonder why the keys of Moses, Elias, and Elijah needed to be restored to Joseph Smith, since the work of the priesthood was already underway by the time they came. Their visits occurred in April of 1836, yet the Church had been organized in April of 1830. During the intervening six years, many members had been baptized and received the gift of the Holy Ghost, and many brethren had been ordained to the priesthood. Were these ordinances performed on earth without being sealed in heaven? Also, Samuel Smith had already been set apart in June of 1830 as the first official missionary of the Church, and he had already been sharing copies of the Book of Mormon throughout New England.[100] Was this not the start of the gathering of Israel? Furthermore, Joseph Smith had received some degree of revelation regarding eternal marriage as early as 1831,[101] and

---

99. The Joseph Smith Translation of Mark 9:3 says, "And there appeared unto them Elias with Moses, or in other words, John the Baptist and Moses," and under "Elias" in the Bible Dictionary, it says, "The curious wording of JST Mark 9:3 does not imply that the Elias at the Transfiguration was John the Baptist, but that in addition to Elijah the prophet, John the Baptist was present."

100. See Ryan Carr, "The First Latter-day Missionary," *New Era*, Sept. 2004.

101. The heading to D&C 132 says, "Evidence indicates that some of the principles involved in this revelation [on eternal marriage] were known by the Prophet as early as 1831."

he performed anointings in the upper rooms of the incomplete temple in January of 1836.[102]

Clearly, the spirit of the restoration of the priesthood keys was already at work on the earth before Moses, Elias, and Elijah appeared. However, all of those early events were very limited in scope. Until the final restoration of the priesthood keys in the Kirtland Temple, those actions and ordinances were only provisional. The Lord was laying the foundation of the Restoration line upon line and precept upon precept. The work of gathering Israel and the work of forming eternal families could not expand beyond their early limited scopes until all priesthood keys were restored. In addition, the work of salvation for the dead could not and did not occur until after Elijah's visit.

It appears that Joseph Smith was able to take those initial steps to begin the work of salvation under the authority of the Melchizedek priesthood and the mantle of his prophetic calling. This preliminary authority may have been what Joseph and Oliver received as a pronouncement from God when "the voice of God in the chamber of old Father Whitmer, in Fayette, Seneca county" (D&C 128:21) instructed them on steps to take to establish the Church. In his 1838 history, Joseph Smith placed this sacred, authorizing event shortly after the visit of John the Baptist.[103] BYU professor Michael Hubbard MacKay has researched this event and suggested that it brought priesthood authority to Joseph before the bestowal of the keys of the Melchizedek Priesthood by Peter, James, and John.[104]

Clearly, the scope of Joseph's early priesthood efforts was limited until he received the fulness of priesthood keys in the Kirtland Temple. It is interesting to note that the Quorum of the Twelve Apostles had only been established less than a year prior to the restoration of these priesthood keys, and their missionary endeavors had not yet extended

---

102. See Richard O. Cowan, "The Unfolding Restoration of Temple Work," *Ensign*, Dec. 2001, 34–39.

103. Joseph Smith, in History, 1838–1856, volume A-1 [23 December 1805–30 August 1834], 27, josephsmithpapers.org.

104. See Michael Hubbard MacKay, "Event or Process?: How 'the Chamber of Old Father Whitmer' Helps Us Understand Priesthood Restoration," *BYU Studies Quarterly* 60, no. 1 (2021): 73.

beyond short regional missions in North America. The foundation was being laid so that Joseph could share these keys with the new Apostles. After these keys were restored, Joseph started sending missionaries to distant nations across the oceans.[105] All the priesthood keys necessary to direct the work of salvation for the living and the dead were once again upon the earth.

President Packer taught, "Elijah came . . . and bestowed the keys of the sealing power. Thereafter ordinances were not tentative, but permanent. The sealing power was with us. No authorization transcends it in value. That power gives substance and eternal permanence to all ordinances performed with proper authority for both the living and the dead."[106]

Restored Keys Extend Christ's Atonement to All

Because of the events at the Kirtland Temple on April 3, 1836, the restored keys of Moses, Elias, and Elijah are now carried out as a unified system of priesthood ordinances in hundreds of temples scattered throughout the world. The purpose of these keys is to expand the reach of the Atonement of Jesus Christ to everyone who has ever lived upon the earth. The Prophet Joseph Smith explained why this work is so important:

> The greatest responsibility in this world that God has laid upon us is to seek after our dead. The apostle says, "They without us cannot be made perfect" (Hebrews 11:40) for it is necessary that the sealing power should be in our hands to seal our children and our dead for the fulness of the dispensation of times—a dispensation to meet the promises made by Jesus Christ before the foundation of the world for the salvation of man. . . .
>
> It is necessary that those who are going before and those who come after us should have salvation in common with us; and thus hath God made it obligatory upon man. Hence, God said, "I will send you Elijah the prophet before the coming of the great and dreadful day of the Lord: he shall turn the heart of the fathers to

---

105. See "Chapter 24 Truth Shall Prevail," *Saints: The Story of the Church of Jesus Christ in the Latter Days*, vol. 1, *The Standard of Truth, 1815–1846* (2018).
106. Boyd K. Packer, "Ordinances," 6.

the children, and the heart of the children to their fathers, lest I come and smite the earth with a curse." (Malachi 4:5.)[107]

Without the keys restored by Moses, Elias, and Elijah, "the whole earth would be utterly wasted at [Christ's] coming" (D&C 2:3). But now, through the great work of gathering Israel on both sides of the veil, and through temple work performed under the keys of Elias and Elijah for the living and the dead, the purpose of the Creation of the earth is being fulfilled, and Christ will not need to smite it with a curse when He comes. Instead, He will be joyful knowing that the earth's purpose has been fulfilled, facilitated by the restoration of priesthood keys.

Whenever we perform any ordinances under the power and authority of these restored priesthood keys, we draw ourselves and others nearer to Jesus Christ. We expand the influence of Christ's Atonement by participating in the work of salvation and thus become "saviors on Mount Zion" ourselves. Joseph Smith taught, "How are [the Saints] to become saviors on Mount Zion? By building their temples, erecting their baptismal fonts, and going forth and receiving all the ordinances, baptisms, confirmations, washings, anointings, ordinations and sealing powers upon their heads, in behalf of all their progenitors who are dead, and redeem them that they may come forth in the first resurrection and be exalted to thrones of glory with them."[108]

The keys of the priesthood under which these ordinances are performed continue with us today. At the time of the death of Joseph Smith, most of the Twelve Apostles were away on missions. Apostles Wilford Woodruff and Brigham Young were in New England, and they met together in Boston shortly after learning of the martyrdom. Later, when President Woodruff was prophet himself, he recounted the following memory of that occasion:

> We were overwhelmed with grief and our faces were soon bathed in a flood of tears. . . . After we had done weeping we began to converse together concerning the death of the prophets [Joseph and

---

107. *Teachings of the Prophet Joseph Smith*, 356; see also *Teachings of Presidents of the Church: Joseph Smith*, 475.
108. *Teachings of Presidents of the Church: Joseph Smith*, 473.

Hyrum Smith]. In the course of the conversation, [Brigham] smote his hand upon his thigh and said, "Thank God, the keys of the kingdom are here." . . .

President Young . . . referred to the last instructions at the last meeting we had with the Prophet Joseph before starting on our mission. . . . The Prophet Joseph, I am now satisfied, had a thorough presentiment that that was the last meeting we would hold together here in the flesh. We had had our endowments; we had had all the blessings sealed upon our heads that were ever given to the apostles or prophets on the face of the earth. On that occasion the Prophet Joseph rose up and said to us: "Brethren, I have desired to live to see this temple built. I shall never live to see it, but you will. I have sealed upon your heads all the keys of the kingdom of God. I have sealed upon you every key, power, principle that the God of heaven has revealed to me. Now, no matter where I may go or what I may do, the kingdom rests upon you." . . .

The keys of the kingdom of God are here, and they are going to stay here, too, until the coming of the Son of Man. Let all Israel understand that. They may not rest upon my head but a short time, but they will then rest on the head of another Apostle, and another after him, and so continue until the coming of the Lord Jesus Christ in the clouds of heaven.[109]

Research has determined that this transfer of priesthood keys from Joseph Smith to the Twelve Apostles most likely occurred on March 26, 1844.[110] We are blessed to have these keys with us today, held active and viable by a living prophet who is a modern Apostle of Jesus Christ. It is under the direction of these keys that sacred priesthood ordinances are now performed in temples throughout the earth. President Nelson said:

---

109. Wilford Woodruff, "The Keys of the Kingdom," *Ensign*, Apr. 2004, 30–31.
110. See Jeffrey M. Bradshaw, "'There's the Boy I Can Trust': Dennison Lott Harris' First-Person Account of the Conspiracy of Nauvoo and Events Surrounding Joseph Smith's 'Last Charge' to the Twelve Apostles," *Interpreter: A Journal of Mormon Scripture* 21 (2016): 23–117, https://journal.interpreterfoundation.org/theres-the-boy-i-can-trust-dennison-lott-harris-first-person-account-of-the-conspiracy-of-nauvoo-and-events-surrounding-joseph-smiths-last-charge/.

> Consider how *your* life would be different if priesthood keys had not been restored to the earth. Without priesthood keys, you could not be endowed with the power of God. Without priesthood keys, the Church could serve only as a significant teaching and humanitarian organization but not much more. Without priesthood keys, none of us would have access to essential ordinances and covenants that bind us to our loved ones eternally and allow us eventually to live with God.
>
> Priesthood keys distinguish The Church of Jesus Christ of Latter-day Saints from any other organization on earth. Many other organizations *can* and *do* make your life better here in mortality. But no other organization *can* and *will* influence your life after death.
>
> Priesthood keys give us the authority to extend all of the blessings promised to Abraham to every covenant-keeping man and woman. Temple work makes these exquisite blessings available to *all* of God's children, regardless of *where* or *when* they lived or now live. Let us rejoice that priesthood keys are once again on the earth![111]

We do rejoice! We are blessed to live in a time when these priesthood keys are active on the earth, allowing us to participate in the work of salvation and exaltation on both sides of the veil. Besides maintaining our own personal righteousness, there is no better way to show our love for Jesus Christ and to prepare for His Second Coming than to gather the children of Israel under the direction of these priesthood keys so that all have the opportunity to progress along the covenant path toward exaltation.

I Shall Love Thee Better After Death

Many poets have written about a romantic love that will last forever. Eternal love has been a topic of sonnets, songs, and poems throughout all literature. Such longings speak to one of the deepest and most profound emotions men and women experience. However, simply declaring one's love for another person will not create a bond

---

111. Russell M. Nelson, "Rejoice in the Gift of Priesthood Keys," *Liahona*, May 2024, 121.

that will last throughout eternity. Only sealing ordinances administered through priesthood keys will do that.

In her sonnet "How Do I Love Thee," Elizabeth Barrett Browning wrote:

> How do I love thee? Let me count the ways.
> I love thee to the depth and breadth and height
> My soul can reach, when feeling out of sight
> For the ends of being and ideal grace.
> . . .
> I love thee with the breath,
> Smiles, tears, of all my life; and, if God choose,
> I shall but love thee better after death.[112]

Desires expressed in poems and songs cannot create bonds that will be sanctioned by God throughout eternity. A person may claim, "I shall but love thee better after death," but this is only possible if two conditions are met. First, a couple must have an eternal marriage that is solemnized by an authorized temple sealer who has been set apart under the delegated authority of the living prophet of God. And second, that couple must embrace their temple covenants in such a way that those covenants start to change their natures. Only through living our temple covenants can we become sanctified in Christ and have our marriage "sealed by the holy spirit of promise" (D&C 132:7). That process may not be completed in this life, but if we will stay on the path—the covenant path—it will eventually be achieved with the help and grace of Jesus Christ.

This is why the keys of temple work matter. They create the foundation of sanctioned authority upon which eternal marriages can be established as well as the covenant environment in which eternal family relationships can flourish. In his own poetic prose, Elder Parley P. Pratt described the feelings he experienced when he first learned the doctrine of eternal families and the joy that came to him from knowing these eternal truths:

---

112. Elizabeth Barrett Browning, "How Do I Love Thee? (Sonnet 43)," Academy of American Poets, accessed Oct. 20, 2024, https://poets.org/poem/how-do-i-love-thee-sonnet-43.

> It was at this time [during the winter of 1839–40] that I received from [Joseph Smith] the first idea of eternal family organization, and the eternal union of the sexes in those inexpressibly endearing relationships which none but the highly intellectual, the refined and pure in heart, know how to prize, and which are at the very foundation of everything worthy to be called happiness.
>
> Till then I had learned to esteem kindred affections and sympathies as appertaining solely to this transitory state, as something from which the heart must be entirely weaned, in order to be fitted for its heavenly state. It was Joseph Smith who taught me how to prize the endearing relationships of father and mother, husband and wife; of brother and sister, son and daughter.
>
> It was from him that I learned that the wife of my bosom might be secured to me for time and all eternity; and that the refined sympathies and affections which endeared us to each other emanated from the fountain of divine eternal love. It was from him that I learned that we might cultivate these affections and grow and increase in the same to all eternity. . . .
>
> I had loved before, but I knew not why. But now I loved—with a pureness—an intensity of elevated, exalted feeling, which would lift my soul from the transitory things of this groveling sphere and expand it as the ocean. I felt that God was my heavenly Father indeed; that Jesus was my brother, and that the wife of my bosom was an immortal, eternal companion. . . . I could now love with the spirit and with the understanding also.[113]

This eternal love, so beautifully described by Elder Pratt, is possible because of the sacred temple keys that were restored in the Kirtland Temple on April 3, 1836. What a blessing to have these keys effective today under the direction of a living prophet of God in hundreds of temples throughout the world. Like Elder Pratt, I too am grateful to be sealed to the wife and children of my bosom for eternity. Only in The Church of Jesus Christ of Latter-day Saints are these eternal blessings available because of the restoration of the sacred priesthood keys of temple work. This is the foundation for a love that truly will be "better after death."

---

113. Parley P. Pratt, "He Taught Me the Heavenly Order of Eternity," *Ensign*, Aug. 2015, 80; punctuation modified.

3

Eternal Families and Same-Sex Marriage

For many decades, our Church's doctrine on eternal marriage and the family had been a point of righteous pride within the Church and a reason for admiration from without. In the 1980s, Krister Stendahl, the Lutheran Bishop of Stockholm, declared that he felt "holy envy" for our Church's doctrine related to temple work for our deceased ancestors.[114] Others have shown similar respect for Latter-day Saint teachings and lifestyle in past years.

More recently, however, the Church's doctrine on eternal families has been criticized from both within and without. This criticism has coincided with a deterioration of the institution of the family and a growth in political and social support for alternative lifestyles. Some people have been especially critical of the Church's policies regarding same-sex marriage. They call Church leaders old-fashioned and advocate for change, saying that the Church should allow same-sex temple marriage.

---

114. See Wikipedia, "Krister Stendahl," last modified Sept. 12, 2024, 18:05 (UTC), https://en.wikipedia.org/wiki/Krister_Stendahl.

Can the doctrine of the Church accommodate such a change? Could the Church open the door to same-sex eternal marriage without altering many of the foundational doctrines that make our Church unique from all other Christian denominations? This chapter will examine pertinent scriptures and statements from prophets and apostles that underscore the doctrine of the Church regarding eternal families and eternal seed. It will also discuss whether our doctrine can accommodate the calls for change surrounding this complex issue.

Be Fruitful and Multiply

The first commandment God gave Adam and Eve, recorded in the first chapter of Genesis, was to "be fruitful, and multiply, and replenish the earth" (Genesis 1:28). In the second chapter, we learn that Adam and Eve "shall be one flesh. And they were both naked, the man and his wife, and were not ashamed" (Genesis 2:24–25). After their Fall and expulsion from the garden, we read that "Adam knew Eve his wife; and she conceived, and bare [a son]" (Genesis 4:1). The opening chapters of God's holy word clearly emphasize the propriety of sexual union between a husband and a wife.

As Latter-day Saints, we believe that sexual intimacy in marriage is good. God has not placed barriers around sex because it is a bad thing but rather because it is such a supremely good thing. The *General Handbook* of the Church states, "Physical intimacy between husband and wife is intended to be beautiful and sacred. It is ordained of God for the creation of children and for the expression of love between husband and wife."[115] An article in the *Encyclopedia of Mormonism* on procreation states:

> Latter-day Saints have an exceptionally positive view of procreation. After God commanded Adam and Eve to "multiply and replenish the earth" (Gen. 1:28), he pronounced all of his creation, including the power of procreation, "very good" (Gen. 1:31). President Joseph F. Smith noted, "The lawful association of the sexes is ordained of God, not only as the sole means of race perpetuation, but for the development of the higher faculties and nobler traits of human

---

115. *General Handbook: Serving in The Church of Jesus Christ of Latter-day Saints*, 2.1.2, Gospel Library.

nature, which the love-inspired companionship of man and woman alone can insure" (*Improvement Era* 20:739). . . .

To beget and bear children is central to God's plan for the development of his children on earth. The powers of procreation therefore are of divine origin. An early LDS apostle, Parley P. Pratt, noted that the desires and feelings associated with procreation are not evil, but are ordained of God for sacred purposes: "The fact is, God made man, male and female; he planted in their bosoms those affections which are calculated to promote their happiness and union. That by that union they might fulfill the first and great commandment, 'To multiply and replenish the earth, and subdue it.' From this union of affection, springs all the other relationships, social joys and affections diffused through every branch of human existence. And were it not for this, earth would be a desert wild, an uncultivated wilderness" (Pratt, Parley P., *The Writings of Parley P. Pratt*, ed. Parker Robison. Salt Lake City, 1952, 52–54). . . .

Using the power of procreation does not alienate one from God. Rather, properly used, it enables mortals to become cocreators with him in the divine Plan of Salvation.[116]

Marriage between a man and a woman, including procreation, is tied to the purpose of the earth. The Lord revealed, "And again, verily I say unto you, that whoso forbiddeth to marry is not ordained of God, for marriage is ordained of God unto man. Wherefore, it is lawful that he should have one wife, and *they twain shall be one flesh, and all this that the earth might answer the end of its creation*; And that it might be filled with the measure of man, according to his creation before the world was made" (D&C 49:15–17; emphasis added).

Literal Children of Heavenly Parents

During a cholera epidemic in Nauvoo in 1839, eighteen-year-old Zina Diantha Huntington and her mother contracted the disease, and the mother passed away. Zina recovered after being cared for in the home of Joseph and Emma Smith.[117] In her later years, Zina recount-

---

116. Brent A. Barlow, "Procreation," *Encyclopedia of Mormonism* (Macmillan, 1992), 1157, https://eom.byu.edu/index.php/Procreation.
117. See Wikipedia, "Zina D. H. Young," last modified Nov. 21, 2024, 12:20 (UTC), https://en.wikipedia.org/wiki/Zina_D._H._Young.

ed a dialogue that occurred one day while talking with the Prophet about her grief over the loss of her mother. Zina asked the Prophet, "Will I know my mother as my mother when I get over on the Other Side?" "Certainly you will," he quickly replied. "More than that, you will meet and become acquainted with your eternal Mother, the wife of your Father in Heaven." Zina then exclaimed in astonishment, "And have I then a Mother in Heaven?" To which Joseph affirmed, "You assuredly have. How could a Father claim His title unless there were also a Mother to share that parenthood?"[118]

President Dallin H. Oaks taught, "Our theology begins with heavenly parents. Our highest aspiration is to be like them. . . . As earthly parents we participate in the gospel plan by providing mortal bodies for the spirit children of God. The fulness of eternal salvation is a family matter."[119] The Church's Gospel Topics essay on Mother in Heaven states, "The Church of Jesus Christ of Latter-day Saints teaches that all human beings, male and female, are beloved spirit children of heavenly parents, a Heavenly Father and a Heavenly Mother."[120] The *Encyclopedia of Mormonism* adds this:

> The Church of Jesus Christ of Latter-day Saints rejects the idea found in some religions that the spirits or souls of individual human beings are created ex nihilo. Rather it accepts literally the vital scriptural teaching as worded by Paul: "The Spirit itself beareth witness with our spirit, that we are the children of God." This and other scriptures underscore not only spiritual sibling relationships but heirship with God, and a destiny of joint heirship with Christ (Rom. 8:16–18; cf. Mal. 2:10).
>
> Latter-day Saints believe that all the people of earth who lived or will live are actual spiritual offspring of God the Eternal Father (Num. 16:22; Heb. 12:9). In this perspective, *parenthood requires*

---

118. Susa Young Gates, *History of the Ladies' Mutual Improvement Association of the Church of Jesus Christ of L.D.S., from Nov. 1869 to June 1910*, 16, https://contentdm.lib.byu.edu/digital/collection/NCMP1820-1846/id/26618.

119. Dallin H. Oaks, "Apostasy and Restoration," *Ensign*, May 1995, 87.

120. Gospel Topics Essays, "Mother in Heaven," Gospel Library.

both father and mother, whether for the creation of spirits in the premortal life or of physical tabernacles on earth.[121]

In the Doctrine and Covenants, we read that "the inhabitants [of the world] are begotten sons and daughters unto God" (D&C 76:24). To beget means to produce offspring. The belief that our spirits are literal offspring of our heavenly parents is a fundamental building block of our doctrine that has been affirmed by a myriad of Church leaders in statements such as the following:

- President John Taylor: "[Man] is a son of God, and being his son, he is, of course, his offspring, an emanation from God, in whose likeness, we are told, he is made. He did not originate from a chaotic mass of matter, moving or inert, but came forth possessing, in an embryonic state, all the faculties and powers of a God."[122]
- The First Presidency (1909): "The Father of Jesus is our Father also. Jesus . . . is our elder brother, and we, like him, are in the image of God. All men and women are in the similitude of the universal Father and Mother and are literally the sons and daughters of Deity."[123]
- Sister Bonnie H. Cordon: "You are literally the spirit daughters of heavenly parents, and nothing can separate you from Their love and the love of your Savior."[124]
- President Dieter F. Uchtdorf: "We are the literal spirit children of divine, immortal, and omnipotent heavenly parents!"[125]
- Sister Julie B. Beck: "You have light because you are literally spirit daughters of Deity, 'offspring of exalted parents' with a

---

121. Elaine Anderson Cannon, "Mother in Heaven," *Encyclopedia of Mormonism*, 961, https://eom.byu.edu/index.php/Mother_in_Heaven; emphasis added.
122. *Teachings of Presidents of the Church: John Taylor* (2011), 3.
123. The First Presidency of the Church, "The Origin of Man," *Improvement Era* 13, no. 1 (Nov. 1909), 78; reprinted in *Ensign*, Feb. 2002, 26–30.
124. Bonnie H. Cordon, "Beloved Daughters," *Ensign* or *Liahona*, Nov. 2019, 67.
125. Dieter F. Uchtdorf, "O How Great the Plan of Our God!" *Ensign* or *Liahona*, Nov. 2016, 21.

divine nature and an eternal destiny. You received your first lessons in the world of spirits from your heavenly parents."[126]
- Elder James E. Talmage: "We, the human family, literally the sons and daughters of Divine Parents, the spiritual progeny of God our Eternal Father, and of our God Mother, are away from home for a season, studying and working as pupils."[127]

What does it mean to say that we are the *literal* offspring of heavenly parents? If you google the word *literal*, you will get this definition: "taking words in their usual or most basic sense without metaphor or allegory."[128] So our status as children of God is not metaphorical—it is literal. This is our doctrine.

To say that we are literal and not metaphorical offspring of both our Heavenly Father and our Heavenly Mother implies that our spirit bodies formed as a result of some sort of union between them. Elder Franklin D. Richards quoted Moses 6:8–9: "In the day that God created man, in the likeness of God made he him; in the image of his own body, male and female, created he them, and blessed them, and called their name Adam." He then explained, "Here we are informed that it required the male and female, united to make one image of [God's] own body."[129]

This concept may make some people uncomfortable, but it should not. As discussed earlier, we believe that sexual intimacy in marriage is good, not bad. Consider this statement by President Brigham Young: "God has made His children like Himself . . . and has endowed them with intelligence and power and dominion over all His works, and given them the same attributes which He himself possesses. *He created man, as we create our children*; for there is no other process of creation

---

126. Julie B. Beck, "You Have a Noble Birthright," *Ensign* or *Liahona*, May 2006, 106.

127. James E. Talmage, "The Philosophical Basis of Mormonism," *Improvement Era* 18, no. 11 (Sept. 1915): 950, catalog.churchofjesuschrist.org/assets/ccee17ce-7dcb-40e1-afaa-7b23a50d1670/0/0.

128. *Google Dictionary*, s.v. "literal," accessed December 10, 2024, https://www.google.com/search?q=literal.

129. Franklin D. Richards, *A Compendium of the Doctrines of the Gospel* (Harvard College, 1894), 120.

in heaven, on the earth, in the earth, or under the earth, or in all the eternities, that is, that were, or that ever will be."[130]

The Prophet Joseph Smith taught, "When the Savior shall appear we shall see him as he is. We shall see that he is a man like ourselves" (D&C 130:1). Gospel writers Scot and Maurine Proctor have added, "In other words, we are not of a different species than God. We are not His creatures, nor His subjects, nor His possessions, but His children at a different stage of progression."[131] As such, it makes sense to suggest that the process of creating spiritual offspring in the eternal worlds would be similar to the process we experience in the mortal world.

This idea may be a challenge to grasp. As President Brigham Young said, "The whole subject of the marriage relation is not in my reach, nor in any other man's reach on this earth. It is without beginning of days or end of years; it is a hard matter to reach. We can tell some things with regard to it; it lays the foundation for worlds, for angels, and for the Gods; for intelligent beings to be crowned with glory, immortality, and eternal lives. In fact, it is the thread which runs from the beginning to the end of the holy Gospel of Salvation—of the Gospel of the Son of God; it is from eternity to eternity."[132]

There Are Also Celestial Bodies

As Latter-day Saints, we believe in a physical resurrection of our bodies. I have attended several funerals in other Christian denominations, and in every case, the priest or pastor spoke of resurrection and eternal life as if they were only spiritual experiences. There was talk of the soul or spirit living on but not of the physical body coming to life again. In contrast, the doctrine of The Church of Jesus Christ of

---

130. Brigham Young, in *Journal of Discourses*, 11:122; emphasis added.
131. Scot and Maurine Proctor, "Come Follow Me Podcast #46: 'When We Obtain Any Blessing it is from God', D&C 129–132," *Meridian Magazine Podcast* (podcast), Nov. 7, 2021, https://latterdaysaintmag.com/come-follow-me-podcast-46-when-we-obtain-any-blessing-it-is-from-god-doctrine-and-covenants-129-132/.
132. Brigham Young, in *Journal of Discourses*, 2:90.

Latter-day Saints teaches that our physical bodies will rise again in a literal, corporeal resurrection.

On occasion, I have reviewed with my Christian friends the story of the resurrected Christ suddenly appearing in a closed room where His disciples were meeting together. They supposed they were only seeing a spirit, but Jesus said to them, "Behold my hands and my feet, that it is I myself: handle me, and see; for a spirit hath not flesh and bones, as ye see me have" (Luke 24:39). He then ate some broiled fish and honeycomb as further proof that His resurrected body was physical. I then ask my Christian friends, "What do you think Jesus did with His resurrected body before He returned to heaven? Did He hang it in a closet, and He only embodies it when He's on earth? No. His Apostles saw him ascend into heaven in His resurrected body (see Acts 1:9–11), and He will retain it for eternity. It is true that His resurrected body has immortal, spiritual abilities; after all, He had suddenly appeared to His disciples behind closed doors before He declared, 'Handle me, and see.' So His resurrected body has spiritual powers, but it is nonetheless composed of flesh and bones. And we will have the same type of body when we are resurrected."

Speaking of the Resurrection of all mankind, the great Book of Mormon missionary and theologian Amulek taught:

> The spirit and the body shall be reunited again in its perfect form; both limb and joint shall be restored to its proper frame, even as we now are at this time. . . .
>
> Now, this restoration shall come to all, both old and young, both bond and free, both male and female, both the wicked and the righteous; and even there shall not so much as a hair of their heads be lost. (Alma 11:43–44)

The Apostle Paul also taught that we will all be resurrected, but he added that there will be differences in the nature of our resurrected bodies depending on the kingdom we have been resurrected to abide in:

> For since by man came death, by man came also the resurrection of the dead.
>
> For as in Adam all die, even so in Christ shall all be made alive.

> But every man in his own order: . . .
> *All flesh is not the same flesh.* . . .
> *There are also celestial bodies, and bodies terrestrial*: but the glory of the celestial is one, and the glory of the terrestrial is another.
> There is one glory of the sun, and another glory of the moon, and another glory of the stars: for one star differeth from another star in glory.
> *So also is the resurrection of the dead.* (1 Corinthians 15:21–23, 39–42; emphasis added)

Paul's message lays a foundation for the following instruction by President Joseph Fielding Smith, which teaches that the ability to procreate eternally will be restricted only to those who inherit the celestial kingdom:

> Some will gain celestial bodies with all the powers of exaltation and eternal increase. . . . Those who receive the exaltation in the celestial kingdom will have the "continuation of the seeds forever" (D&C 132:19). They will live in the family relationship. In the terrestrial and in the telestial kingdoms there will be no marriage. Those who enter there will remain "separately and singly" forever (D&C 132:15–32). Some of the functions in the celestial body will not appear in the terrestrial body, neither in the telestial body,[133] and the power of procreation will be removed.[134]

These teachings are consistent with the following revelations received by the Prophet Joseph Smith and recorded in our scriptural canon:

> In the celestial glory there are three heavens or degrees;
> And in order to obtain the highest, a man must enter into this order of the priesthood [meaning the new and everlasting covenant of marriage];
> And if he does not, he cannot obtain it.
> He may enter into the other, but that is the end of his kingdom; *he cannot have an increase.* (D&C 131:1–4; emphasis added)

---

133. Note that President Smith stated that some functions will not appear, not that some organs will not appear.

134. Joseph Fielding Smith, *Doctrines of Salvation*, comp. Bruce R. McConkie (1955), 2:396–7; formatting modified.

And again, verily I say unto you, if a man marry a wife by my word, which is my law, and by the new and everlasting covenant, . . . and if [they] abide in my covenant, . . . they shall pass by the angels, and the gods . . . to their exaltation and glory in all things, . . . which glory shall be a fulness and *a continuation of the seeds forever and ever.*

Then shall they be gods, because they have no end; therefore shall they be from everlasting to everlasting, because they continue; . . . because they have all power, . . . *and continuation of the lives.* (D&C 132:19–22; emphasis added)

Clearly, God has designed eternal marriage so that His covenant children can enjoy the blessings of eternal increase themselves. President James E. Faust described the sacred temple marriage ceremony in these words:

> We can see in vision the countless couples in their youth and beauty coming to be married. We see clearly the unspeakable joy on their countenances as they are sealed together and as there is sealed upon them, through their faithfulness, the blessing of the holy Resurrection, with power to come forth in the morning of the First Resurrection clothed with glory, immortality, and eternal lives.[135]

President Faust makes it clear that those being married in the temple are given "the blessing of the holy Resurrection, with power to come forth in the morning of the First Resurrection." I used to wonder why this would be pronounced as a blessing of temple marriage since we know that everyone will be resurrected and that all the righteous will come forth on the morning of the First Resurrection, whether they receive a temple marriage or not. Then I realized that this promise comes with a critical modifying phrase: "clothed with glory, immortality, and eternal lives." This is the crowning blessing of eternal marriage: Couples sealed together will come forth on the morning of the First Resurrection clothed in glorious, immortal bodies that will have the capability of bringing forth additional eternal lives.

---

135. James E. Faust, "Who Shall Ascend into the Hill of the Lord?," *Ensign*, Aug. 2001, 4.

This glorious promise is given only to those who are married in the temple for eternity and is contingent upon staying true to holy covenants. As President Joseph Fielding Smith taught, "Those who are married in the temple for all time and eternity obtain the blessing of eternal lives. I put stress on eternal lives. Eternal life is God's life, that is, to be like Him. Eternal lives means eternal increase—the continuation, as the revelation says, of the seeds forever."[136]

We should not think of this doctrine of eternal seed as obscure. It is one of the most fundamental truths of the restored gospel of Jesus Christ, and it is the culminating objective of our temple ordinances. The following quotes reiterate this truth:

- Joseph Smith: "Except a man and his wife enter into an everlasting covenant and be married for eternity, while in this probation, by the power and authority of the Holy Priesthood, they will cease to increase when they die; that is, they will not have any children after the resurrection. But those who are married by the power and authority of the priesthood in this life, and continue without committing the sin against the Holy Ghost, will *continue to increase and have children in the celestial glory*."[137]
- Joseph Fielding Smith: "The Father has promised us that through our faithfulness . . . we will have the privilege of becoming like him. To become like him we must have all the powers of godhood; *thus a man and his wife when glorified will have spirit children* who eventually will go on an earth like this one we are on and pass through the same kind of experiences, being subject to mortal conditions, and if faithful, then they also will receive the fulness of exaltation and partake of the same blessings. There is no end to this development; it will go on forever. We will become gods and have jurisdiction over

---

136. Joseph Fielding Smith, *Answers to Gospel Questions*, comp. Joseph Fielding Smith Jr. (1966), 4:197.
137. *Teachings of the Prophet Joseph Smith*, sel. Joseph Fielding Smith (1976), 300–301; emphasis added.

worlds, and *these worlds will be peopled by our own offspring.* We will have an endless eternity for this."[138]

- Melvin J. Ballard: "What do we mean by endless or eternal increase? We mean that through the righteousness and faithfulness of men and women who keep the commandments of God they will come forth with celestial bodies, fitted and prepared to enter into their great, high and eternal glory in the celestial kingdom of God; and unto them, through their preparation, there will come children, who will be spirit children. I don't think that is very difficult to comprehend and understand."[139]

Why is this doctrine of eternal increase so important? Because it points to the fact that eternal seed can only be propagated between a man and a woman who have been sealed together in eternal marriage and have then been resurrected with celestial bodies.

Families in Heaven

As members of The Church of Jesus Christ of Latter-day Saints, we often talk about the blessing of living together as families in the celestial kingdom. But how will each family unit be composed? Will families be groupings of a husband and wife living in a heavenly household with their children who are sealed to them? If so, will I live eternally as a single young man in a household led by my parents, or will my wife and I be adult parents with our children existing as youths in that eternal world? I can't be both a single youth and a married adult at the same time. How will eternal families be organized?

Before answering this, let us look at Church teachings regarding those who die as children. The restored gospel teaches that children who die before the age of accountability will be saved through the Atonement of Jesus Christ (see D&C 29:46–47; Moroni 8). In addition, Joseph Smith taught that these children will rise in the Resurrection to be raised by their faithful parents in a family setting.

---

138. Joseph Fielding Smith, *Doctrines of Salvation*, 2:429; emphasis added.
139. Melvin J. Ballard, *Three Degrees of Glory* (Zion's Printing and Publishing Co., 1922), 10.

Sister M. Isabella Horne told of the following experience that she witnessed while with the Prophet as he ministered to the wife of John Taylor:

> In conversation with the Prophet Joseph Smith once in Nauvoo, the subject of children in the resurrection was broached. I believe it was in Sister Leonora Cannon Taylor's house. She had just lost one of her children, and I had also lost one previously. The Prophet wanted to comfort us, and he told us that we should receive those children in the morning of the resurrection just as we laid them down, in purity and innocence, and we should nourish and care for them as their mothers. He said that children would be raised in the resurrection just as they were laid down, and that they would obtain all the intelligence necessary to occupy thrones, principalities and powers. The idea that I got from what he said was that the children would grow and develop *in the Millennium*, and that the mothers would have the pleasure of training and caring for them, which they had been deprived of in this life.[140]

We presume that deceased children of parents who do not qualify to come forth in the morning of the First Resurrection to raise their children will be raised by suitable, worthy surrogate parents. Regardless, after these children have grown to maturity, they will be given all the opportunities of the faithful who lived longer lives on earth. President Lorenzo Snow taught:

> There is no Latter-day Saint who dies after having lived a faithful life who will lose anything because of having failed to do certain things when opportunities were not furnished him or her. In other words, if a young man or a young woman has no opportunity of getting married, and they live faithful lives up to the time of their death, they will have all the blessings, exaltation and glory that any man or woman will have who had this opportunity and improved it. That is sure and positive.[141]

---

140. *History of the Church*, 4:556, footnote 7; emphasis added.
141. *Teachings of Presidents of the Church: Lorenzo Snow* (2012), 130.

This truth applies equally to those who die in their infancy as well as to those who die after the age of accountability. President Joseph F. Smith said:

> Our beloved friends who are now deprived of their little one, have great cause for joy and rejoicing, even in the midst of the deep sorrow that they feel at the loss of their little one for a time. . . . Such children are in the bosom of the Father. They will inherit their glory and their exaltation, and they will not be deprived of the blessings that belong to them; for, . . . all that could have been obtained and enjoyed by them if they had been permitted to live in the flesh will be provided for them hereafter. They will lose nothing by being taken away from us in this way.[142]

So those who die young will be resurrected during the Millennium at the same age at which they died, and they will be raised in a family setting by resurrected parents. After they mature, such children will have the opportunity to find a companion and receive eternal marriage and all the blessings of exaltation.

Those who die when they are older will be transformed into perfect bodies when they are resurrected. Amulek described the ultimate state of our resurrected bodies, saying that in the Resurrection, "the spirit and the body shall be reunited again in its perfect form; . . . every thing shall be restored to its perfect frame" (Alma 11:43–44). Alma similarly taught that in the Resurrection, "all things shall be restored to their proper and perfect frame" (Alma 40:23). President Dallin H. Oaks described this ultimate resurrected state as being "in the prime of life."[143] So in the end, everyone, whether they died as children or as aged adults, will have eternal bodies that appear to be about the same age.

Now let us return to the question of what will constitute a nuclear family unit for eternity in the celestial kingdom, after the Millennium has passed. Such families will necessarily be comprised of only a husband and wife plus any of their children sealed to them but who, for whatever reason, are not themselves sealed to an eternal companion.

---

142. *Teachings of Presidents of the Church: Joseph F. Smith* (2011), 129.
143. Dallin H. Oaks, "Resurrection," *Ensign*, May 2000, 15.

Likely these single children who are heirs to celestial glory will be relatively few in number, given the statements above assuring that no righteous person will be denied any desired blessing, and they will serve their families as ministering angels (see D&C 132:16). Other worthy earthly offspring of each couple who are themselves sealed eternally to a spouse will form their own separate family unit. Each couple is linked to other couples through sealing bonds, but at the nucleus of most eternal family units in the celestial kingdom, there will be only a husband and a wife. This nucleus will be added to as the couple perpetuates eternal offspring, but it will begin with only a husband and a wife.

Until a few years ago, my aged parents were both alive, and they lived independently as a couple. My siblings and I had also reached the age where most of us were "empty nesters." Although our children were just beginning to raise their own offspring, the older two generations were comfortable living only as couples. When children leave the nest, each couple remains an independent family unit even though they are linked to their parents and to their children and grandchildren. In modern times, technology makes it possible for us to maintain loving communication and have influence with all the other families we are connected to. This is similar to how families will be constituted in the celestial kingdom. We will initially be mostly couples linked to other couples. Add to this the additional blessing and complexity that each covenant husband and wife comes from a separate family, each with its own network of sealing bonds, and we see that the eternal family network is bounteous and strong, with connecting links in many directions.

Imagine a three-dimensional net.[144] Each knot in the net is a married couple, and they are linked in multiple directions to many other knots: to the husband's parents, to the wife's parents, and to each of their own children who themselves have spouses. Each of these pairs is likewise connected to similar knots formed by eternal sealings in other directions. The sealing ordinances also connect each person to our heavenly parents and to Jesus Christ. This is why we should not

---

144. Think of several nets layered on top of one another, with connections in both vertical and horizontal directions.

be worried about eternal family bonds if our parents get divorced and are later sealed to someone new—it just means we have more couples we are connected to. Likewise, we should not worry if parents or other ancestors have not lived true to their covenants and therefore are not included in the net. No faithful person is left dangling. All who keep their covenants are bound by so many ligatures in so many directions that their covenant belonging is secure. We who are sealed by covenant ceremonies in holy temples of God on earth will be bound by a network of eternal covenant connections in heaven.

Again, the knots at each locus in this celestial family network will be formed by couples, sealed together for eternity in the new and everlasting covenant of marriage, and the connections between them will be formed by sealings between parents and children. The promised innumerable seed that will come to these eternal family couples will be spirit offspring that will emanate from them after these couples progress further and have established their own eternal kingdoms.

This family network organization will be led by our first parents, Adam and Eve. And prominent in leadership among all the couples will be Abraham, Isaac, and Jacob along with their wives. These ancient patriarchs and matriarchs form the model for fulfillment of the promises given to all couples who are sealed for eternity in the holy temples of God.

The Abrahamic Blessing of Posterity or Seed

The scriptures are replete with promises of fruit and seed both in this life and in the next. God promised Abraham, "I will multiply thy seed as the stars of the heaven, and as the sand which is upon the sea shore" (Genesis 22:17). The blessings of Abraham, Isaac, and Jacob are likewise promised to us when we are sealed as husband and wife in the temple.

Fruit and seed are instructive euphemisms. In the plant world, fruit and seed cannot form if the plant's flowers are not pollinated by another plant or another part of the plant. I remember learning in my high school biology class that these different plant parts are designated male or female. Consider the following scholastic description:

Flowers are how plants produce seeds to reproduce. In many cases, the flower contains male and female parts, roughly equivalent to the male and female sexes of animals. The male parts of the flower are called the stamens and are made up of the anther at the top and the stalk or filament that supports the anther. The female elements are collectively called the pistil. The top of the pistil is called the stigma, which is a sticky surface receptive to pollen. The bottom of the pistil contains the ovary and the narrowed region in between is called the style. The male contribution or pollen is produced in the anther, and seeds develop in the ovary. Many of the fruits we eat are the thickened ovary walls surrounding the seeds.[145]

So the use of *fruit* and *seed* in the scriptures to imply the offspring of sexual fertilization has a basis in biology. Elder Milton R. Hunter taught:

> The Prophet Joseph Smith explained that this continuation of "the seeds" forever and ever, meant the power of procreation; in other words, the power to beget spirit children on the same principle as we were born to our heavenly parents, God the Eternal Father and our Eternal Mother. Therefore, a man cannot receive the highest exaltation without a woman, his wife, nor can a woman be exalted without her husband (1 Corinthians 11:11). That is the fulness of the gospel of Jesus Christ, the plan of salvation.[146]

The Bible is anchored in stories about families, each formed by the marriage of a man and a woman. It begins with the story of the formation of the first family through Adam and Eve. We also learn of Noah and his wife and family that repeopled the earth after the flood. We are then introduced to Abraham, the father of many nations, and his wife Sarah. The covenant promises to Abraham could only be fulfilled with Sarah. Likewise, there could be no greatness in Isaac without Rebekah and no fulfillment of covenant blessings for Jacob without his wives.

---

145. "Africanized Honey Bees on the Move Lesson Plans | Information Sheet: 9 Parts of Flowers," The University of Arizona, accessed July 11, 2022, https://cales.arizona.edu/pubs/insects/ahb/inf9.html.
146. Milton R. Hunter, in Conference Report, Apr. 1949, 71.

Elder Bruce R. McConkie wrote, "Every person married in the temple for time and for all eternity has sealed upon him, conditioned upon his faithfulness, all of the blessings of the ancient patriarchs."[147] These are the blessings of Abraham, Isaac, and Jacob. These are the blessings of being heirs of the Abrahamic covenant. This covenant includes promises of posterity, priesthood, and a promised land along with the blessings of prosperity and exaltation in the presence of God eternally. However, it is important to recognize that these promises will be fulfilled in their fulness only after the Resurrection and only for those who qualify for the highest level of the celestial kingdom. There, each couple will be blessed with posterity as numerous as the sands of the seas or the stars of the heavens. There, each couple will enjoy the blessings of priesthood power together. There, each couple will inherit their own prosperous eternal promised land and kingdom. There, each couple will experience the joy of exaltation under the tutelage of our heavenly parents as we emulate their godly ways.

Brigham Young taught, "The Lord has blessed us with the ability to enjoy an eternal life with the Gods, and this is pronounced the greatest gift of God. The . . . Lord has bestowed on us the privilege of becoming fathers [and mothers] of lives. What is a father of lives as mentioned in the Scriptures? A man who has a posterity to an eternal continuance. That is the blessing Abraham received, and it perfectly satisfied his soul. He obtained the promise that he should be the father of lives."[148] Likewise, Sarah became the mother of lives.

Taken together, the ordinances that we receive in the temple point us toward eternal marriage and the fulfillment of the blessings of the ancient patriarchs. The temple ordinances are a continuum that prepares us for exaltation as gods and goddesses, as described in an earlier chapter. In the initiatory ordinances, we are washed and anointed and given promises that point toward eternal marriage. In the endowment, we enter into holy covenants whose purposes are to perfect us and make us godly. These covenants also become the core of our marriage covenants. And in the marriage sealing ceremony itself, we are

---

147. Bruce R. McConkie, *The Millennial Messiah: The Second Coming of the Son of Man* (Deseret Book, 1982), 264.

148. *Teachings of Presidents of the Church: Brigham Young* (1997), 89.

bestowed the blessings of Abraham, Isaac, and Jacob. Joseph Smith revealed the desired outcome of these ordinances: "And they shall pass by the angels, and the gods, which are set there, to their exaltation and glory in all things, as hath been sealed upon their heads, which glory shall be a fulness and a continuation of the seeds forever and ever. Then shall they be gods, because they have no end; therefore shall they be from everlasting to everlasting, because they continue" (D&C 132:19–20).

We should remember the purpose of the blessings promised in the temple. President John Taylor said, "Have you forgotten who you are, and what your object is? Have you forgotten that you profess to be Saints of the Most High God, clothed upon with the holy priesthood? Have you forgotten that you are aiming to become kings and priests to the Lord, and queens and priestesses to him?"[149]

President Joseph Fielding Smith added:

> The main purpose for our mortal existence is that we might obtain tabernacles of flesh and bones for our spirits that we might advance after the resurrection to the fulness of the blessings which the Lord has promised to those who are faithful. They have been promised that they shall become sons and daughters of God, joint heirs with Jesus Christ, and if they have been true to the commandments and covenants the Lord has given us, to be kings and priests and queens and priestesses, possessing the fulness of the blessings of the celestial kingdom.[150]

The stories of Abraham, Isaac, and Jacob and their wives demonstrate that women matter and therefore gender matters. The promises to the ancient prophets could not be fulfilled without their covenant wives. It is the same for us. In the highest level of the celestial kingdom, there will be no king without his queen, no priest without his priestess, no god without his goddess. If the Church were to eliminate the need for gender distinctions, this would diminish the eternal role of women. This will never happen. As President Russell M. Nelson

---

149. John Taylor, *The Gospel Kingdom: Selections from the Writings and Discourses of John Taylor, Third President of the Church of Jesus Christ of Latter-Day Saints*, ed. G. Homer Durham (Deseret Book, 2002), 229–230.

150. Joseph Fielding Smith, *Answers to Gospel Questions*, 4:61

has said, "The kingdom of God is not and cannot be complete without women who make sacred covenants and then keep them."[151]

Complementary Natures

Besides the biological necessity of joining male and female for procreation, the combination of the two sexes in marriage joins two different but complementary natures that can only become whole and complete when sealed together as one in eternal union. Elder Bruce D. Porter said, "The differences between men and women are not simply biological. They are woven into the fabric of the universe, a vital, foundational element of eternal life and divine nature."[152] Both are needed. President Henry B. Eyring demonstrated this when he said, referring to the complementary relationship he had with his wife, Kathleen, "Our differences combined as if they were designed to create a better whole."[153]

Elder David A. Bednar elaborated on this topic:

> The natures of male and female spirits complete and perfect each other, and therefore men and women are intended to progress together toward exaltation. . . . For divine purposes, male and female spirits are different, distinctive, and complementary.
>
> After the earth was created, Adam was placed in the Garden of Eden. Importantly, however, God said it was "not good that the man should be alone" (Genesis 2:18; Moses 3:18), and Eve became Adam's companion and helpmeet. The unique combination of spiritual, physical, mental, and emotional capacities of both males and females were needed to implement the plan of happiness. Alone, neither the man nor the woman could fulfill the purposes of his or her creation.
>
> By divine design, men and women are intended to progress together toward perfection and a fulness of glory. Because of their distinctive temperaments and capacities, males and females each

---

151. Russell M. Nelson, "A Plea to My Sisters," *Ensign* or *Liahona*, Nov. 2015, 96.
152. Bruce D. Porter, "Defending the Family in a Troubled World," *Ensign*, June 2011, 13.
153. Henry B. Eyring, "Transcript: President Eyring Addresses the Vatican Summit on Marriage" (given Nov. 18, 2014), newsroom.ChurchofJesusChrist.org.

bring to a marriage relationship unique perspectives and experiences. The man and the woman contribute differently but equally to a oneness and a unity that can be achieved in no other way. The man completes and perfects the woman, and the woman completes and perfects the man as they learn from and mutually strengthen and bless each other.[154]

The divine feminine can be found in ancient scripture, often associated with such characteristics as wisdom, spirit, mercy, compassion, and love,[155] whereas the divine masculine is sometimes associated with companion attributes such as knowledge, strength, justice, vengeance, and law. These are balancing characteristics. Both natures are needed to complete the whole. Elder D. Todd Christofferson taught, "It is [God] who in the beginning created Adam and Eve in His image, male and female, and joined them as husband and wife to become 'one flesh' and to multiply and replenish the earth. Each individual carries the divine image, but it is in the matrimonial union of male and female as one that we attain perhaps the most complete meaning of our having been made in the image of God—male and female."[156]

We have both a Heavenly Mother and a Heavenly Father who are cocreators of our spirits. This is likely the reason we read in the Creation story, "And God said, Let *us* make man in *our* image, after *our* likeness" (Genesis 1:26; emphasis added). In ancient Semitic languages, *El* refers to God, and its plural form in the Hebrew language is *Elohim*. When we hear this plural name, we may wonder if our Father in Heaven is subtly trying to tell us that He is not alone. Perhaps *Elohim* is a name that signifies the Entity that is our Heavenly Father united with our Heavenly Mother. Only together are they a

---

154. David A. Bednar, "Marriage Is Essential to His Eternal Plan," *Ensign*, June 2006, 83–85.

155. See FAIR - Faithful Answers, "The Mother in Heaven and Her Children - Margaret Barker - 2015 Fair Mormon Conference," YouTube, Sept. 3, 2017, https://www.youtube.com/watch?v=ilF9NXEl6Xs&t=2860s; The Stick of Joseph, "Margaret Barker | Solomon's Temple, Isaiah, and The Divine Feminine," YouTube, Aug. 18, 2024, https://www.youtube.com/watch?v=44ruz-_KjAM&t=3434s.

156. D. Todd Christofferson, "Why Marriage, Why Family," *Ensign* or *Liahona*, May 2015, 52.

complete God—male and female—and it will be the same in eternity for all who attain exaltation.

Elder Erastus Snow elaborated on the necessity of both male and female in Deity:

> If I believe anything that God has ever said about himself, and anything pertaining to the creation and organization of man upon the earth, I must believe that Deity consists of man and woman....
>
> I sometimes illustrate this matter by taking up a pair of shears, if I have one, but then you all know they are composed of two halves, but they are necessarily parts, one of another, and to perform their work for each other, as designed, they belong together, and neither one of them is fitted for the accomplishment of their works alone. And for this reason says St. Paul, "the man is not without the woman, nor the woman without the man in the Lord." In other words, there can be no God except he is composed of the man and woman united, and there is not in all the eternities that exist, nor ever will be, a God in any other way. I have another description: There never was a God, and there never will be in all eternities, except they are made of these two component parts; a man and a woman; the male and the female.[157]

Paul's seminal statement on marriage, "Neither is the man without the woman, neither the woman without the man, in the Lord" (1 Corinthians 11:11), is true both in earth life and in exaltation. Only in the union of the two sexes can be found the best family environment on earth and the only exalted family arrangement in heaven. President Nelson said, "No man in this Church can obtain the highest degree of celestial glory without a worthy woman who is sealed to him. This temple ordinance enables eventual exaltation for both of them.... In God's eternal plan, salvation is an individual matter; exaltation is a family matter."[158]

The divine role of women alongside men is critical in our beliefs. Our doctrine takes the sectarian view of Mother Eve and flips it on its head. Other traditions denigrate all women because Eve was the first

---

157. Erastus Snow, in *Journal of Discourses*, 19:269–70.
158. Russell M. Nelson, "Salvation and Exaltation," *Ensign* or *Liahona*, May 2008, 9–10.

to transgress a commandment from God, but we see her differently. Although we acknowledge that Eve was beguiled and thus needed a Savior, we also see her as a wise woman who came to recognize a greater purpose in her choice to partake of the fruit of the tree of knowledge of good and evil. She realized that this was the only way to learn the attributes of godhood and to fulfill the first commandment of God to multiply and replenish the earth (see Moses 5:11). We honor her for her choice, which opened the door for the rest of us to come to earth, making her the mother of all living. She was a full partner with Adam, combining her unique characteristics with his, strengthening them together as one united whole. It will be the same for all exalted couples in the celestial kingdom where male and female couples will live forever, united as one.

Implications of Our Doctrine

The previous sections have approached the doctrine of eternal families from several different angles, and they all converge in a consistent message: Eternal marriage can only be between a man and a woman because their natural differences make it possible for the union to be elevated to a godly level and because the biological nature of eternal procreation, like mortal procreation, requires it. These are not things that God or His Church can change. The many prophetic quotes that have been presented all support the same conclusion, providing a consistent and clear doctrine regarding eternal marriage. President Dallin H. Oaks reiterated this doctrine when he stated, "Exaltation or eternal life . . . is possible only through marriage for eternity. Eternal life includes the creative powers inherent in the combination of male and female—what modern revelation describes as the 'continuation of the seeds forever and ever.'"[159]

God is not like Pinocchio's father, Geppetto, creating children from wood or clay. It is true that our mortal bodies are composed of elements from the earth and thus are said to come from dust, but that is not where we had our beginnings. As the poet William Wordsworth

---

159. Dallin H. Oaks, *"Two* Great Commandments," *Ensign* or *Liahona*, Nov. 2019, 74.

penned, "The Soul that rises with us, our life's Star, / Hath had elsewhere its setting and cometh from afar."[160] His insight is consistent with the teachings of President Lorenzo Snow, who said, "We were born in the image of God our Father; he begat us like unto himself. There is the nature of deity in the composition of our spiritual organization; in our spiritual birth our Father transmitted to us the capabilities, powers and faculties which he himself possessed."[161] Our spirit bodies come from our heavenly parents, just as an acorn comes from an oak tree and has the potential to grow into a mighty oak itself. Likewise, our own eternal progeny will spring from the seed of our exalted bodies.

A false doctrine that arose out of the Great Apostasy is that the original sin of Adam and Eve was sexual intercourse and that all sexual behavior is bad and is only tolerated by God because it is necessary for procreation in our fallen world. As a result, much of the sectarian world has traditionally seen sexual intimacy as inherently evil[162] and the main reason children are born with original sin.[163] With this view deeply embedded in the religious traditions around us, if we Latter-day Saints emphasize that procreation will continue in the eternities, we are seen as carnal and sex-focused. To avoid such accusations, our rhetoric has instead focused on the more agreeable "families can be forever" dialogue. However, the full implications are more personal.

---

160. William Wordsworth, "Ode on Intimations of Immortality from Recollections of Early Childhood," Academy of American Poets, accessed Oct. 20, 2024, https://poets.org/poem/ode-intimations-immortality-recollections-early-childhood.

161. *Teachings of Presidents of the Church: Lorenzo Snow*, 84.

162. See, for example, Arthur Frederick Ide, "Woman as Priest, Bishop and Laity in the Early Church to 440 A.D." (1984), published in "Women and Sex in Early Christianity," Wijngaards Institute for Catholic Research, accessed Dec. 10, 2024, https://womenpriests.org/articles-books/ide-07-women-and-sex-in-early-christianity/.

163. For one interesting review of these traditions, see Daniel Kohanski, "Why the Catholic Church Is So Conflicted About Sex," TheHumanist.com, Dec. 27, 2018, https://thehumanist.com/magazine/january-february-2019/features/why-the-catholic-church-is-so-conflicted-about-sex/.

It is important to understand that even though we believe that procreation is good, both on earth and in the eternities, we also believe that it should be kept private and sacred, as an intimate sacrament between a husband and a wife. Anyone who gets to know us as a people will observe that our Church culture strongly encourages modesty in dress, dialogue, and behavior. Chastity and virtue are standards we embrace alongside our belief in the rightness of procreation within the bonds of marriage.

Independent of religious dogma, the concept of sexual relations in the eternities can still be distasteful to some people, both within the Church and without, even though others may find the concept pleasing. It is important to acknowledge that we really do not know much about eternal procreation other than that it takes both a man and a woman to create eternal offspring. No Latter-day Saint sister needs to be worried that her eternal life will consist of endless pregnancies. As Elder Henry B. Eyring said, quoting an unnamed prophet of God, "You are worrying about the wrong problem. You just live worthy of the celestial kingdom, and the family arrangements will be more wonderful than you can imagine."[164]

In spite of discomfort surrounding the topic and in light of modern efforts to normalize same-sex relations, we may now find it prudent to emphasize our belief in the goodness of the intimate marital relationship between a husband and a wife and the role it will play in our eternal lives as resurrected beings. We may now be at a crossroads where the rise of same-sex marriage requires us to be bolder in the declaration of our doctrine regarding eternal marriage. We cannot be shy in explaining that we believe in eternal increase and that this requires a man and a woman as a simple, biological fact. We must become more open in explaining why our doctrine of the eternal family is physically incompatible with progressive LGBT+ philosophies.

The Church's *General Handbook* says that the law of chastity "means abstaining from sexual relations outside of a legal marriage

---

164. Henry B. Eyring, "The Hope of Eternal Family Love," *Ensign* or *Liahona*, Aug. 2018, 5; see also "A Home Where the Spirit of the Lord Dwells," *Ensign* or *Liahona*, May 2019, 22–25.

between a man and a woman, which is according to God's law."[165] It also describes that law, stating, "God has commanded that sexual intimacy is to be reserved for marriage between a man and a woman."[166] In spite of this, some people may suggest that the law of chastity should not be considered violated if a same-sex couple is married and both partners remain monogamous. They may say that same-sex couples should be allowed to be married for eternity in the temple, but to what end? Certainly, they could provide eternal companionship for one another, but they could never produce eternal seed between themselves, and that is clearly one of the primary objectives of eternal marriage.

Can you imagine a temple sealer giving a newly married same-sex couple the same directive that was told to Adam and Eve: "Be fruitful, and multiply, and replenish the earth" (Genesis 1:28)? That just won't work. The laws of nature require the union of male and female for the creation of new lives. As Elder Joseph W. Sitati has said, "Marriage between a man and a woman is the institution that God ordained for the fulfillment of the charge to multiply. A same-gender relationship does not multiply."[167]

On earth, a same-sex couple can adopt a child, or one partner can provide half of the "seed" for a child, but in the end, biology dictates that a female's egg be fertilized by a male's sperm in order for offspring to develop. In the celestial world, a man and a woman, married for eternity, will have only themselves with whom they can create eternal offspring. Same-sex eternal marriage simply will not work. It is against the eternal laws of nature—laws that even God must follow.

Even though modern legislation allows same-sex couples to join in civil marriage, these unions cannot produce offspring by themselves. Medical operations and hormone therapies can be administered to change some of a person's physical characteristics so that they mimic a person of the opposite gender, but no amount of medical intervention will enable someone born as a woman to produce sperm or someone

---

165. *General Handbook*, 7.2.
166. *General Handbook*, 2.1.2.
167. Joseph W. Sitati, "Be Fruitful, Multiply, and Subdue the Earth," *Ensign* or *Liahona*, May 2015, 127.

born as a man to ovulate and gestate a child. There are some natural laws that cannot be circumvented no matter how much people try. Even if a proposed uterine transplant becomes viable in the future, this would only be putting part of a donor female body into a male body.

We cannot get around the fact that the foundational doctrine of our Church regarding eternal families is in direct conflict with the concept of same-sex marriage. Some people may continue to advocate for a change in Church policy to allow temple marriage for same-sex couples; however, this would not only require a change in policy, but it would also require that we throw out our entire doctrine on eternal families, and "the whole earth would be utterly wasted at [Christ's] coming" (D&C 2:3). That will not happen. God will not allow it. A change in policy would have no effect on the nature of the eternal world God has created.

In the celestial kingdom of God, eternal, natural laws will control the propagation of seed just as they do on earth. We cannot change these laws; we can only accept them and prepare to live within their boundaries. This preparation includes marriages on earth in relationships that most closely resemble the marriages that will exist in the eternities—marriages modeled after the relationship our heavenly parents share. "For strait is the gate, and narrow the way that leadeth unto the exaltation and continuation of the lives, and few there be that find it" (D&C 132:22).

The Church of Jesus Christ of Latter-day Saints is not a democracy. Elder David B. Haight has said, "Conferences of this Church are far more than a convention where views are expressed or policies adopted by vote, but they are assemblies where the mind and the will of the Lord is manifest by His servants. The Church is not a democracy—it is a kingdom."[168] It is the kingdom of God on earth, and Christ is the King. God sets the laws under which we fall subject, and these laws are based on eternal principles. We may not fully understand how the life experiences of those who experience same-sex attraction fit within these laws; however, we should remember that God has a history of giving requirements to His children without explanations

---

168. David B. Haight, "Successful Living of Gospel Principles," *Ensign*, Nov. 1992, 74.

(see Moses 5:5–6). Nevertheless, it is not humankind's prerogative to change things to suit their limited understanding. As the prophet Isaiah wrote, "For my thoughts are not your thoughts, neither are your ways my ways, saith the Lord" (Isaiah 55:8).

Our Doctrine on Gender and Sexuality

The Church has clarified our doctrine on gender in "The Family: A Proclamation to the World." It is based on the principles explained above. This inspired document contains the following pertinent statements:

- "We . . . proclaim that marriage between a man and a woman is ordained of God and that the family is central to the Creator's plan for the eternal destiny of His children."
- "Gender is an essential characteristic of individual premortal, mortal, and eternal identity and purpose."
- "The first commandment that God gave to Adam and Eve pertained to their potential for parenthood as husband and wife."
- "God has commanded that the sacred powers of procreation are to be employed only between man and woman, lawfully wedded as husband and wife."
- "We declare the means by which mortal life is created to be divinely appointed."
- "The family is ordained of God. Marriage between man and woman is essential to His eternal plan."
- "Children are entitled to birth within the bonds of matrimony, and to be reared by a father and a mother who honor marital vows with complete fidelity."[169]

In addition, President Dallin H. Oaks has clarified, "The intended meaning of gender in the family proclamation and as used in Church statements and publications since that time is biological sex at birth."[170]

---

169. "The Family: A Proclamation to the World," Gospel Library.
170. "General Conference Leadership Meetings Begin," Oct. 2, 2019, newsroom. ChurchofJesusChrist.org; see also "How Does the Church Define Gender?," Life Help | Transgender, Gospel Library.

The family proclamation was published in 1995, and some have suggested that it was merely a reaction to shifting social trends in the 1990s. However, the family proclamation is not the first time Church leaders taught about the eternal nature of gender. Similar statements were made in the early 1900s; however, in those earlier statements, the word *sex* was used to mean *gender at birth*. This was simply a matter of English usage, which has changed over time. In the 1913 edition of *Webster's Dictionary*, the word *sex* has three definitions, all of which refer to the distinctive differences of male and female in animals or plants, with no reference to sexual acts.[171] A modern secular article states, "'Sex' . . . begins to appear in text in sexual terms in 1948, shortly after the Kinsey Institute released its initial reports on human sexuality."[172] Before that, it had the meaning we now attribute to the phrase *gender at birth*.

Elder James E. Talmage was one who taught about the eternal nature of what we now call gender at birth. In 1922 he wrote:

> We affirm as reasonable, scriptural, and true, the eternity of sex [i.e., gender at birth] among the children of God. The distinction between male and female is no condition peculiar to the relatively brief period of mortal life. It was an essential characteristic of our pre-existent condition, even as it shall continue after death, in both disembodied and resurrected states. . . . [The] scriptures attest a state of existence preceding mortality, in which the spirit children of God lived, doubtless with distinguishing characteristics, including the distinction of sex [i.e., gender], "before they were [created] naturally upon the face of the earth" (Moses 3:5).[173]

Elder John A. Widtsoe likewise authored the following in a 1915 Melchizedek Priesthood manual:

---

171. *Websters 1913 Dictionary*, s.v. "sex," accessed December 10, 2024, https://www.websters1913.com/words/Sex.

172. Jillian Kramer, "A Brief History of the Word Sex Over the Past Two Centuries," *Glamour Newsletter*, July 21, 2015, https://www.glamour.com/story/history-of-the-word-sex.

173. James E. Talmage, "The Eternity of Sex," *Millennial Star*, Aug. 24, 1922, 539, https://catalog.churchofjesuschrist.org/assets/bc02d406-b283-411c-926e-3f0f9d55ba09/0/0.

Sex [i.e., Gender at birth], which is indispensable on this earth for the perpetuation of the human race, is an eternal quality [i.e., characteristic] which has its equivalent everywhere. It is indestructible. The relationship between men and women is eternal and must continue eternally. In accordance with Gospel philosophy there are males and females in heaven. Since we have a Father, who is our God, we must also have a mother, who possesses the attributes of Godhood. This simply carries onward the logic of things earthly, and conforms with the doctrine that whatever is on this earth is simply a representation of spiritual conditions of deeper meaning than we can here fathom.[174]

The doctrinal teaching that gender is eternal is not new. The truth is that for most of the history of mankind, the immutability of gender was considered self-evident. When the family proclamation was first published in 1995, nothing in it was considered new doctrine; the proclamation merely consolidated our family doctrine into one clear and concise document. President Dallin H. Oaks said, "Those who do not believe in or aspire to exaltation and are most persuaded by the ways of the world consider this family proclamation as just a statement of policy that should be changed. In contrast, Latter-day Saints affirm that the family proclamation defines the kind of family relationships where the most important part of our eternal development can occur."[175]

The Church's policy on sexuality is described in the *General Handbook*. The section titled "Same-Sex Attraction and Same-Sex Behavior" begins by stating, "The Church encourages families and members to reach out with sensitivity, love, and respect to persons who are attracted to others of the same sex." It distinguishes between same-sex attraction and same-sex behavior, affirming that, "Feeling same-sex attraction is not a sin," while also declaring "God's commandments forbid all unchaste behavior, either heterosexual or

---

174. John A. Widtsoe, *Rational Theology: As Taught by The Church of Jesus Christ of Latter-day Saints, Published for the Use of the Melchizedek Priesthood by the General Priesthood Committee* (1915), 64–65, https://gutenberg.org/cache/epub/35562/pg35562-images.html.

175. Dallin H. Oaks, "The Plan and the Proclamation," *Ensign* or *Liahona*, Nov. 2017, 29.

same-sex."[176] The *Handbook* specifically condemns same-sex marriage, stating:

> As a doctrinal principle, based on the scriptures, the Church affirms that marriage between a man and a woman is essential to the Creator's plan for the eternal destiny of His children. The Church also affirms that God's law defines marriage as the legal and lawful union between a man and a woman.
>
> Only a man and a woman who are legally and lawfully wedded as husband and wife should have sexual relations. Any other sexual relations, including those between persons of the same sex, are sinful and undermine the divinely created institution of the family.[177]

The Church does acknowledge that "in extremely rare circumstances, a baby is born with genitals that are not clearly male or female," and it makes accommodations for these situations.[178] However, they are not placed in the same category as people who experience same-sex attraction or identify as transgender.

Scripturally, critics of the Church would be hard-pressed to find anything that would condone same-gender sexual relations or same-sex marriage. Indeed, there are many verses that condemn such things.[179] However, there is one Old Testament story that has been interpreted by some people as supporting same-sex love: the story of Jonathan and David. The prophet Samuel recorded, "The soul of Jonathan was knit with the soul of David, and Jonathan loved him as his own soul" (1 Samuel 18:1). Samuel also described an emotional departure where the two close friends "kissed one another, and wept one with another" (1 Samuel 20:41).

Some people have interpreted this as evidence that Jonathan and David had been engaging in a same-sex relationship. However, as scriptural scholar Jared Halverson has said, "There is nothing in the text that requires that kind of interpretation, and, in fact, there is

---

176. *General Handbook*, 38.6.15.
177. *General Handbook*, 38.6.16.
178. *General Handbook*, 38.7.7.
179. See Leviticus 18:22; Leviticus 20:13; Romans 1:27; 1 Corinthians 6:9.

so much in the text that would cast doubt on that interpretation."[180] This includes David marrying many wives (see 2 Samuel 3:2–5; 5:13) and lusting after Bathsheba (see 2 Samuel 11:2–4) as well as the fact that Jonathan fathered at least one son (see 2 Samuel 4:4). While it is possible that either man was bisexual and got married only out of social expectations, their behaviors with women do raise some doubts about claims of same-sex attraction, especially for David. However, even if one or both young men did experience such feelings, there is nothing in their story to suggest that God condones same-sex physical intimacy. In fact, if anything, it shows that a person can have strong feelings of love toward another of the same gender and not act on them sexually, for there is nothing in the biblical story saying that these two men did so.

Nothing in our scriptural canon supports same-gender sexual behavior. On the other hand, there are many scriptures that promote a heteronormative view of sexuality. For example, Jesus taught, "From the beginning of the creation God made them male and female. For this cause shall a man leave his father and mother, and cleave to his wife; And they twain shall be one flesh: so then they are no more twain, but one flesh. What therefore God hath joined together, let not man put asunder" (Mark 10:6–9; see also Matthew 19:4–6). And Paul declared, "Neither is the man without the woman, neither the woman without the man, in the Lord" (1 Corinthians 11:11).

A Look at Two Historical Changes

Many advocates of same-sex temple marriage point to historical changes in the Church regarding plural marriage and race restrictions and suggest that these provide a basis for a policy change that would allow same-sex marriage. However, as we shall see, both of these historical changes moved us toward practices that are rooted in scripture and doctrine, returning us to earlier norms.

It is true that during the nearly forty-year period in which plural marriage was publicly endorsed in this dispensation, it was promoted

---

180. Unshaken, "Come Follow Me—1 Samuel 8–31, Part 2 (chapters 18–31): Bound in the Bundle of Life," YouTube, June 8, 2022, 32:39, https://www.youtube.com/watch?v=rNGwfMVQ7nM.

by many Church leaders as an eternal principle, and many members were encouraged to practice it. However, after the practice ended, clear statements in scripture and by Joseph Smith were amplified to show that plural marriage is not required for exaltation and that "monogamy is God's standard for marriage unless He declares otherwise" (Official Declaration 1, heading).

In the Book of Mormon, we read that the prophet Jacob told his people, "Wherefore, my brethren, hear me, and hearken to the word of the Lord: For there shall not any man among you have save it be one wife; and concubines he shall have none. . . . For if I will, saith the Lord of Hosts, raise up seed unto me, I will command my people; otherwise they shall hearken unto these things" (Jacob 2:27, 30). Furthermore, Joseph Smith said, "I have constantly said no man shall have but one wife at a time, unless the Lord directs otherwise."[181] Polygamy scholars Brian and Laura Hales have documented statements from several contemporaries of Joseph Smith who confirmed that he taught that exaltation does not require polygamy.[182]

Even though the Church changed its policy from encouraging plural marriage to disallowing it, it is clear that the doctrinal foundation for monogamy had already existed. In fact, the halting of plural marriage was not a change in doctrine at all but rather a return to the norm of monogamy. Nevertheless, this change only occurred after the living prophet, who held the keys of eternal marriage, received a revelation that the change should occur.

The other significant shift in Church policy that some people point to when advocating for same-sex marriage is the change that occurred in 1978 when race restrictions for priesthood and temple participation were lifted. However, those restrictions were found to have a shaky foundation. Historical research pointed to early statements and actions by the Prophet Joseph Smith that confirmed that he had ordained a few Black men of African descent to the priesthood. The Church essay "Race and Priesthood" explains, "During the first

---

181. *Teachings of the Prophet Joseph Smith*, 324.
182. See "Does Exaltation Require Polygamy?," Joseph Smith's Polygamy, accessed July 1, 2022, https://josephsmithspolygamy.org/common-questions/polygamy-exaltation/.

two decades of the Church's existence, a few black men were ordained to the priesthood. One of these men, Elijah Abel, also participated in temple ceremonies in Kirtland, Ohio, and was later baptized as proxy for deceased relatives in Nauvoo, Illinois. There is no reliable evidence that any black men were denied the priesthood during Joseph Smith's lifetime."[183]

In addition, the Book of Mormon decries discrimination, stating, "And he [the Lord] inviteth them all to come unto him and partake of his goodness; and he denieth none that come unto him, black and white, bond and free, male and female; and he remembereth the heathen; and all are alike unto God, both Jew and Gentile" (2 Nephi 26:33).

For many years, Church leaders sought revelation to confirm that the priesthood and temple restrictions should be lifted. This revelation was finally received, and it was announced on June 8, 1978. Official Declaration 2 confirms that the lifting of the priesthood restriction was not a doctrinal change but an arrival to a previously prophesied state:

> Aware of the *promises made by the prophets and presidents of the Church who have preceded us* that at some time, in God's eternal plan, all of our brethren who are worthy may receive the priesthood, and witnessing the faithfulness of those from whom the priesthood has been withheld, we have pleaded long and earnestly in behalf of these, our faithful brethren, spending many hours in the Upper Room of the Temple supplicating the Lord for divine guidance.
>
> He has heard our prayers, and by revelation has confirmed *that the long-promised day has come* when every faithful, worthy man in the Church may receive the holy priesthood, with power to exercise its divine authority, and enjoy with his loved ones every blessing that flows therefrom, including the blessings of the temple. (Official Declaration 2; emphasis added)

Similar to the issue of polygamy, there was a preexisting doctrinal basis for the change whereby priesthood and temple restrictions on race were lifted. With both issues, the changes had a doctrinal

---

183. Gospel Topics Essays, "Race and the Priesthood," Gospel Library.

foundation in scripture and in the teachings and practices of our founding prophet, Joseph Smith.

If we were to predict future changes in doctrine or policy toward same-sex-attracted Saints based on these two past changes, then the new changes would have to have a similar preexisting foundation. However, as seen in the earlier sections of this chapter, our doctrine has no such foundation—not in scripture nor in the teachings of any Church leaders—that would justify a change in policy to allow same-sex marriage. In fact, to the contrary, we have seen clear and consistent teachings that in the celestial kingdom, families will consist of a husband and wife along with their eternal offspring who will come forth in a natural way as seed from their own resurrected, celestial bodies. Their eternal children will come as spirit offspring in the same way we are spirit offspring of our heavenly parents. Such children can only come from the union of a male and a female in the eternal realms, just like on earth.

Irrevocable Doctrine

President Dallin H. Oaks referred to the Church's 1995 family proclamation and declared, "Those who do not fully understand the Father's loving plan for His children may consider this family proclamation no more than a changeable statement of policy. In contrast, we affirm that the family proclamation, *founded on irrevocable doctrine*, defines the kind of family relationships where the most important part of our eternal development can occur."[184]

Similarly, President Nelson has said, "Marriage between a man and a woman is God's pattern for a fulness of life *on earth and in heaven*. . . . The doctrine of the Lord regarding marriage and morality *cannot be changed*. . . . While we are to emulate our Savior's kindness and compassion, while we are to value the rights and feelings of all

---

184. Dallin H. Oaks, "Divine Love in the Father's Plan," *Liahona*, May 2022, 103, emphasis added; see also Dallin H. Oaks, "Kingdoms of Glory," *Liahona*, Nov. 2023, 27.

of God's children, we cannot change His doctrine. It is not ours to change. His doctrine is ours to study, understand, and uphold."[185]

The symphony of prophetic statements that has been presented in this chapter bears witness that this doctrine is true. However, we must also recognize that this doctrine can be difficult to accept for Saints who experience same-sex attraction or related challenges. They may question whether there is a place in the Church for people whose life experiences do not seem to align with these doctrines. For this reason, we must embrace these brothers and sisters in Christ with empathy, love, and understanding.

Eternal truth cannot be changed. Truths revealed through prophets must be acknowledged, and then we can grapple with how to make sense of life experiences that do not fit the ideal template that these truths present. Elder Joseph W. Sitati said, "[The] timeless constancy of the onset of day and night is one daily reminder of realities that govern our lives that we cannot change. When we respect and align what we do with these eternal realities, we experience internal peace and harmony. When we don't, we are unsettled, and things do not work as we expect."[186] So it is with all truth.

The doctrine proclaimed in the family proclamation is with us for eternity. It is a doctrine that will bring eternal fulfillment and happiness to all who abide by its principles. However, we must remember that this eternal family doctrine is made possible because of Jesus Christ, for, as President Nelson has said, "Jesus Christ is at the center of the Abrahamic covenant."[187] So we might say that the doctrine of eternal families is subordinate to the doctrine of Christ. On the other hand, Christ's Atonement exists in order to make it possible for us to have eternal families. The doctrine of the eternal family and the doctrine of Christ go hand in hand. In God's eternal plan of happiness, we cannot have the full benefits of one without the other, for without eternal families, formed through the sealing ordinances and covenants of the temple, "the whole earth would be utterly wasted at

---

185. Russell M. Nelson, "Decisions for Eternity," *Ensign* or *Liahona*, Nov. 2013, 108; emphasis added.

186. Joseph W. Sitati, "Patterns of Discipleship," *Liahona*, Nov. 2022, 86.

187. Russell M. Nelson, "The Everlasting Covenant," *Liahona*, Oct. 2022.

[Christ's] coming" (D&C 2:3). As President Nelson has said, "The earth was created and this Church was restored so that families could be formed, sealed, and exalted eternally."[188]

The doctrine of Christ is also called the gospel of Jesus Christ (see Jacob 7:6), and the doctrine of eternal families could also be called the gospel of Abraham.[189] In the scriptures, the term *gospel* is used in reference to only these two objectives: the gospel of Jesus Christ and the gospel of Abraham. These two doctrines of good news are eternally linked with one common purpose: "to bring to pass the immortality and eternal life of man" (Moses 1:39). Both are made possible through the Atonement of Jesus Christ. No wonder Sister Julie B. Beck declared, "Any doctrine or principle . . . that is antifamily is also anti-Christ."[190]

Understanding, accepting, and following the doctrine of eternal families will draw us nearer to Jesus Christ. We need to have hope in Christ, not hope in a change of policy or doctrine. Through Him and the power of His Atonement, we can eventually experience the joy of eternal family bonds, no matter what challenges we face. President Henry B. Eyring taught:

> Of all the gifts our loving Heavenly Father has provided to His children, the greatest is eternal life (see D&C 14:7). That gift is to live in the presence of God the Father and His Beloved Son forever in families. Only in the highest of the kingdoms of God, the celestial, will the loving bonds of family life continue. . . .
>
> For some, that eternal joy may seem a faint or even a fading hope. . . . To all of those whose personal experience or whose marriage and children—or absence thereof—cast a shadow over their hopes, I offer my witness: Heavenly Father knows and loves you as His spirit child. While you were with Him and His Beloved Son before this life, They placed in your heart the hope you have

---

188. Russell M. Nelson, "Celestial Marriage," *Ensign* or *Liahona*, Nov. 2008, 93.

189. The gospel of Abraham refers to the Abrahamic covenant, the blessings of which are bestowed upon a couple during their temple marriage. For a full discussion of this, see the section titled "Elias and the Dispensation of the Gospel of Abraham" in chapter 2 of this book.

190. Julie B. Beck, "Teaching the Doctrine of the Family," *Ensign*, Mar. 2011, 15.

of eternal life. With the power of the Atonement of Jesus Christ working and with the Holy Spirit guiding, you can feel now and will feel in the world to come the family love your Father and His Beloved Son want so much for you to receive.[191]

Those who struggle with the doctrine of the family are invited to lean on its sister doctrine, the doctrine of Christ, and the hope it brings. President Nelson said, "What does it mean to overcome the world? . . . It means trusting the doctrine of Christ more than the philosophies of men."[192] The next chapter will discuss how following the doctrine of Christ can bless those who experience same-sex attraction.

As Latter-day Saints, we should all strive to help one another progress along the covenant path until that day when God will welcome eternal families into the celestial kingdom. There, all who qualify will receive the blessings of the Atonement of Jesus Christ that come from the gospel of Jesus Christ along with the blessings of Abraham, Isaac, and Jacob that come from the gospel of Abraham. "And God shall wipe away all tears from [our] eyes; and there shall be no more death, neither sorrow, nor crying, neither shall there be any more pain" (Revelation 21:4).

---

191. Henry B. Eyring, "The Hope of Eternal Family Love," *Ensign*, Aug. 2018, 4–5.
192. Russell M. Nelson, "Overcome the World and Find Rest," *Liahona*, Nov. 2022, 96.

4

Support for Sexual Minorities through the Doctrine of Christ

The preceding chapter presented the doctrine of the Church regarding eternal families and showed that it is based on eternal principles. Only a husband and wife, sealed for eternity and resurrected with celestial bodies, will be able to enjoy the continuation of seed eternally. This doctrine resonates warmly with many Latter-day Saints; however, for those who experience same-sex attraction (SSA) or related sexual minority challenges,[193] it may seem inaccessible.

What can we do to help these faithful Latter-day Saints reconcile their real-life experiences with our doctrinal beliefs regarding eternal family arrangements? The Church agrees that "individuals do not

---

193. This chapter focuses primarily on supporting Latter-day Saints who experience same-sex attraction. Some aspects may be extrapolated to those who identify as transgender or other challenges in the LGBT+ constellation of experiences; however, those additional challenges will not be addressed directly.

choose to have such attractions."[194] What can be done to help them live the gospel while experiencing their unsought-for challenges? And is there any hope in the next life for those who live contrary to our doctrinal understanding of the commandments of God?

This chapter will address these questions. The experiences and testimonies of several faithful Latter-day Saints and other Christians who experience same-sex attraction will be presented, showing that help can be found by applying the doctrine of Christ. In addition, our Church doctrine on the possibility of repentance and change in the spirit world will be presented, showing that although there are limitations, this doctrine can bring hope for people who have not kept all the commandments of God in mortality due to a variety of challenges, including same-sex attraction.

This chapter is meant as a companion to the previous chapter on eternal marriage. Together, they are intended as a faithful response to a talk given by President Jeffrey R. Holland at Brigham Young University in August 2021. While addressing the conflict between same-sex marriage concerns and Church doctrine, President Holland admonished the BYU community to do better in teaching our doctrine, encouraging them to find "better ways to move toward crucially important goals in these very difficult matters—ways that show empathy and understanding for everyone while maintaining loyalty to prophetic leadership and devotion to revealed doctrine." He then spoke of a "need to define, document, and defend the faith."[195]

I hope that the concepts in these two chapters contribute in positive ways to President Holland's request. The previous chapter focused primarily on "loyalty to prophetic leadership and devotion to revealed doctrine," while this chapter will focus primarily on "ways that show empathy and understanding for everyone."

---

194. "Is Same-Sex Attraction a Sin?," Life Help | Same-Sex Attraction, Gospel Library; see also M Russell Ballard, "The Lord Needs You Now!," *Ensign*, Sept. 2015, 26–31.
195. Jeffrey R. Holland, "The Second Half of the Second Century of Brigham Young University" (Brigham Young University devotional, Aug. 23, 2021), 5, speeches.byu.edu.

The Two Dimensions of the Doctrine of Christ

One of the covenants of the temple endowment is called the law of the gospel of Jesus Christ. The gospel of Jesus Christ is also called the doctrine of Christ (see Jacob 7:6). It focuses on the Resurrection of Jesus Christ and the redeeming power of His Atonement that will not only justify His faithful followers at the Final Judgment but also strengthen them through the challenges of mortality. It also specifies a path for engaging Christ's redeeming power in our lives. This path requires us to come unto Christ and exercise faith in Him, repent of our sins, make or renew with God our covenant of baptism, and receive and follow the guidance of the Holy Ghost. We should then endure to the end by regularly repeating this cycle with the help of prayer and scripture study. This doctrine is taught in the temple endowment and in many passages of scripture.[196]

The doctrine of Christ proclaims, in the words of the Apostle Paul, "I can do all things through Christ who strengthens me" (Philippians 4:13, NKJV). Those who follow this doctrine develop a personal relationship with the Father and the Son by learning to tap into the power that comes from the Atonement of Jesus Christ—His grace.

There is, however, another dimension to the law of the gospel or doctrine of Christ from which we can draw power. God does not expect us to receive support, help, and strength exclusively from our relationship with Him and His Son, as powerful as Their help is. God invites us to also tap into the power that comes from our relationships with one another as fellow disciples in His Church and kingdom. The Apostle Paul explained that the followers of Christ are the body of Christ—His hands, ears, eyes, and feet (see 1 Corinthians 12:12–27). As such, we need to assist in His work.

Dr. Christopher Yuan was once a gay drug addict who discarded those identities after finding wholeness in Jesus Christ and strength through fraternal relationships in his evangelical Christian community. He summarized the two dimensions in which the doctrine of

---

196. For a full discussion of the doctrine or gospel of Jesus Christ, including citations of many defining scriptures, see chapter 3 of Valiant K. Jones, *The Covenant Path: Finding the Temple in the Book of Mormon* (Cedar Fort, 2020).

Christ functions by saying, "The answer is Christ. And if Christ is the answer, then that also means that the body of Christ is part of that answer."[197] As disciples of Jesus Christ, we are His body, and we are not fully living the doctrine of Christ unless we are supporting one another in the community of believers.

In the spring of 1834, the fledgling new Church of Christ in the Kirtland area was inundated with many new members whose needs were greater than their personal resources. During this time, the Lord revealed, "And it is my purpose to provide for my saints, for all things are mine. But it must needs be done in mine own way. . . . Therefore, if any man shall take of the abundance which I have made, and impart not his portion, *according to the law of my gospel,* unto the poor and the needy, he shall, with the wicked, lift up his eyes in hell, being in torment" (D&C 104:15–18; emphasis added).

This passage describes how the Lord provides for the needs of His Saints: It is usually through each other! This approach is "according to the law of my gospel" and thus according to the doctrine of Christ. And it applies not only to meeting physical needs but also to meeting social and emotional needs. As members of Christ's kingdom, each of us should "take of the abundance" of emotional strength that God has placed within us "and impart . . . his portion . . . unto the needy." When we do so, we are living "according to the law of [the] gospel," which is according to the doctrine of Christ.

Alma understood both dimensions of the law of the gospel. His description of our baptismal covenant includes a call "to come into the fold of God, and to be called his people, . . . and to stand as witnesses of God at all times and in all things, and in all places that ye may be in, even until death, that ye may be redeemed of God" (Mosiah 18:8–9). That connection with God describes the first dimension. In addition, Alma said the baptismal covenant includes being "willing to bear one another's burdens, that they may be light; yea, and . . . willing to mourn with those that mourn; yea, and comfort those that

---

197. Husband Material with Drew Boa, "Holy Sexuality and Singleness (with Dr. Christopher Yuan)," YouTube, Feb. 22, 2021, 39:25, https://www.youtube.com/watch?v=-GdyNBKsrNA.

stand in need of comfort" (Mosiah 18:8–9). That connection with fellow Saints describes the second dimension.

Paul also taught both aspects of the law of the gospel of Jesus Christ. For example, he taught the Romans that "the gospel of Christ . . . is the power of God unto salvation to every one that believeth [in Christ]" (Romans 1:16). This focus on Christ as the source of salvation is balanced by the following instructions that Paul also wrote to these Saints of Rome: "Be kindly affectioned one to another with brotherly love; in honour preferring one another; not slothful in business; fervent in spirit; . . . distributing to the necessity of saints; given to hospitality. . . . Rejoice with them that do rejoice, and weep with them that weep" (Romans 12:10–15). Paul also admonished the Galatians to "bear ye one another's burdens, and so fulfil the law of Christ" (Galatians 6:2). The gospel of Jesus Christ, the law of Christ, and the doctrine of Christ are different titles for the same doctrine, and this doctrine has two dimensions—one vertical and one horizontal.

Just as the gospel or doctrine of Christ requires that we engage with Christ in the steps of faith, repentance, covenants, and the Holy Ghost, so also this doctrine requires that we engage with the body of Christ in these same steps. We lean on the example of other faithful Saints to increase our own faith, and it is usually through missteps and occasional messy interactions with fellow Church members and family members that we learn repentance. We also join with other Saints in weekly sacrament meetings to renew our baptismal covenants so we can receive a rejuvenation of the Holy Ghost.

Sometimes when I partake of the sacrament, I not only think about the Savior, but I also look around the chapel at the other Saints I am worshipping with and think about the times so many of them have shown me love and helped me grow in the gospel. They truly are the body of Christ. There is a reason that we partake of the sacrament communally. In fact, some Christian denominations call their version of this ordinance *the communion*.

The two dimensions of the doctrine of Christ, or the law of the gospel of Jesus Christ, are seen in the revealed name of the Church: The Church (1) of Jesus Christ (2) of Latter-day Saints. These two dimensions can also be summarized by the two great commandments:

(1) love God, and (2) love your neighbor. However, the doctrine of Christ expands these to say that we should not only extend love to God and to our neighbors, but we should also *receive* love from God and *receive* love from our neighbors so we can be fortified by them. It is through the giving and receiving of love in our interactions with Deity and with others in our Church community that the doctrine of Christ has the power to change us.

This explanation of the doctrine of Christ is consistent with the following description of the temple covenant called the law of the gospel of Jesus Christ, which is given in the Church's *General Handbook*:

- Exercising faith in Jesus Christ.
- Repenting daily.
- Making covenants with God by receiving the ordinances of salvation and exaltation.
- Enduring to the end by keeping covenants.
- Striving to live the two great commandments. These are to "love the Lord thy God with all thy heart, and with all thy soul, and with all thy mind" and to "love thy neighbor as thyself" (Matthew 22:37, 39).[198]

It is in that final bullet point that we see the two dimensions of the law of the gospel or the doctrine of Christ in this *General Handbook* description. As Elder Gary E. Stevenson taught, "There is an important interdependency between loving the Lord and loving one another. . . . Our ability to follow Jesus Christ depends upon our strength and power to live the first and second commandments with balance and equal devotion to both."[199]

It is not possible to fully live the gospel of Jesus Christ in isolation. The doctrine of Christ requires engagement with the Atonement of Jesus Christ and engagement with the body of Christ—the members of His Church. Both aspects of the doctrine of Christ focus on

---

198. *General Handbook: Serving in The Church of Jesus Christ of Latter-day Saints*, 27.2, Gospel Library.

199. Gary E. Stevenson, "Bridging the Two Great Commandments," *Liahona*, May 2024, 107.

relationships. The doctrine of Christ is experienced through connections in both directions, providing two-dimensional support for any struggle.

Connections Strengthen SSA Saints

We can strengthen those who experience same-sex attraction and want to remain faithful by helping them engage the doctrine of Christ in both of its dimensions: a vertical connection with Jesus Christ and a horizontal connection with fellow Saints who are the body of Christ. These provide connections upward and outward.

Consider first the need for connections outward. We can all help anyone with any challenge, including individuals with same-sex attraction, by befriending them personally. We can invite others into our lives, engaging with them in authentic conversations and shared activities. We can show love to others, putting our arms around them and encouraging them to join us at our family and social events. We can ask them about their lives and tell them about our own. We need to validate others as children of God and listen to their stories with empathy and compassion. We should be open and vulnerable in sharing our own struggles, even if our challenges are quite different from those of our new friends. The connection that comes from opening a window to our own soul in a personal way will help fill a need for emotional intimacy in others and in ourselves. In short, we can bless others by being their friend. For those who experience same-sex attraction, same-gender connections can be especially helpful (as will be seen in coming examples). Even if our struggling friends leave the Church, we should still love them, for that is what Christ would have us do.

Consider also the need for connections upward. We can help anyone, including those with same-sex attraction, connect to Jesus Christ and the power of His Atonement by talking about our own personal experiences with the Savior. We can pray with and for anyone who faces complex challenges in their unique lives. We can encourage them as they seek personal revelation on how to best navigate those challenges. We can share our own stories about receiving guidance through the Holy Ghost and how that guidance has formed a conduit to Jesus Christ. We can encourage our friends to reconsider any views that are not aligned with the teachings and doctrine of the Church but continue to love them even if they embrace those views.

I believe that stronger peer relationships and stronger divine relationships are the keys to strengthening our sexual-minority brothers and sisters who desire to live within the boundaries of their covenants. These relationships will provide engagement with the doctrine of Christ in both of its dimensions—the horizontal and the vertical.

In my research on this topic, I have found many examples of faithful Latter-day Saints with same-sex attraction who bear testimony of the value of outward and upward connections. Following are stories from two men who are managing their lives in mixed-orientation marriages and a third who is single. All three are members of North Star International, an organization whose mission is "to be a faith affirming resource for Latter-day Saints addressing sexual orientation and gender identity who desire to live in harmony with the teachings of Jesus Christ and the doctrine and values of The Church of Jesus Christ of Latter-day Saints."[200]

In the first example, Garrett Ferguson, alongside his wife, Sallie, described in a video interview the strength he gained from emotional connections with other men in a support group and at a weekend retreat:

> I started attending this group, and it felt so life-changing. I remember walking taller after the first meeting—walking out, and I didn't feel alone anymore. There were all these other great guys that experienced the exact same things I did—some married, some not. I felt like it was life-changing. I started working on it, talking about it, and trying to understand it. And then three months later, I went to this weekend retreat with other men who experience SSA, and I came back so much better—more confident. I could be who I am, and I like who I am. I wasn't afraid anymore. I wasn't afraid to talk about it.
>
> I still attend the men's group, and it still feels life-changing often, where I just feel more whole than I ever have before. I just

---

200. "Welcome to North Star," North Star Saints, accessed Oct. 20, 2024, https://www.northstarsaints.org/north-star-intro.

feel more put together—I feel better. . . . I come home and immediately I feel more masculine than I had before the meeting. And I feel stronger, and intimacy becomes so much easier. We can tell when I haven't been to the group [for a while]. . . . Sallie will say, "You need to go spend some time with your group. You need some guy time." . . .

It took me a long time, but I finally figured out a way that I could accept [my SSA] and still live in harmony with the principles of the gospel that are so important to me. . . . I know I'm a worthy Church member, and I have a strong testimony of the gospel, and it makes me so happy and brings me so much joy every day. And I still have SSA.[201]

Garrett's efforts to emotionally connect with other men lifted him and made him feel more masculine. Clearly, some fundamental need is being met through intimate, non-sexual connections with same-gender friends.

Garrett has also found help through the grace of Jesus Christ. In his written profile, he stated the following about his connection to the Lord:

> I've often wondered why I experience same-sex attraction. Why would God give me such a difficult thing to deal with? While I don't know all the answers, I can tell you that I have learned to remain close to Him in order to stay strong. My weakness has become strength through the grace of Jesus Christ. I strive to remain close to Him by reading my scriptures every day and maintaining an eternal perspective, and I know that one day, if I remain faithful, I will be able to stand before God and tell Him that I am worthy and that I gave Him all I have. This struggle has actually brought me closer to God and helped me remain humble in His presence. I love the Lord, and while I don't understand this struggle completely, I

---

201. North Star International, "Voice(s) of Hope • Garrett & Sallie Ferguson (Full Interview)," YouTube, Nov. 4, 2013, 49:15–55:07, https://www.youtube.com/watch?v=s36K2ilFsnY; some editing liberties were taken to consolidate and incorporate comments by Sallie that Garrett confirmed.

do know that He loves me and that I am closer to Him because of it.[202]

In another North Star video, Spencer Thompson described how a connection to the Savior carried him through his struggles with same-sex attraction. He said:

> One of the most spiritual experiences I've had in dealing with [my SSA], where I felt that the Savior was so aware of me, was in a counseling session. My therapist works on a lot of visualization techniques, and one of [the sessions] was working through some of my . . . deepest pains on this issue, . . . surrendering it all over to God, to Jesus—letting Him take it all from me. [I visualized this.] And then I've never felt so close to the Savior when I imagined Him. It was palpable. It was real to me. I felt Him embracing me, kissing me on my head, wiping the tears off my cheeks and saying, "Spencer, let me have it. I love you. It's all worth it. And you're okay just as you are. You are loved."
>
> Feeling that embrace of the Savior . . . it's real. When I say I've experienced the Atonement, . . . to me it's feeling the love of the Savior. And to me, the love of the Savior can carry us through anything. I've experienced that. It took me a while to get there—to really realize what it was—but I'm here to say that the Savior is not just there cheering us on from the sidelines. He gets down there in the dirt and the grit with us and carries us through it. And to me, that's the biggest thing that I'm experiencing and that I'm gaining through all of this: that the Savior is real; that I know that He died for me, and that I'm worth it.[203]

Mitchell Clark, the third North Star member I will highlight, concluded his personal story with this testimony:

> I started to turn to God, and I really began to understand . . . that my relationship with God was more important to me than anything

---

202. Garrett Ferguson, "All That I Have," Voices of Hope: Garrett & Sallie, North Star, accessed Oct. 20, 2024, https://static1.squarespace.com/static/6329059c2789477a2e256088/t/63af4ca55f6d412cfac642f9/1672432805941/All+That+I+Have+garrett+sallie.pdf

203. North Star International, "Voice(s) of Hope • Spencer & Mary Thompson (Full Interview)," YouTube, Mar. 27, 2013, 25:59–27:51, https://www.youtube.com/watch?v=K_JVKctAuOY.

a sexual or romantic relationship with a man could bring me. This was a big turning point for me, to be able to finally realize that I could get my needs met in healthy ways—in platonic relationships with other males and through God—and that I did not have to turn from God. I didn't have to turn from the Church.[204]

I consider Garrett Ferguson, Spencer Thompson, and Mitchell Clark to be giants, along with the many other valiant men and women whose personal stories are documented at NorthStarSaints.org. In researching this issue, I have been amazed by these faithful Saints who are striving to keep their covenants while living with same-sex attraction or related experiences. Each is an inspiration. They find strength from supportive friends and from Jesus Christ.

I personally know a faithful Latter-day Saint who experiences same-sex attraction. He told me that the more same-gender emotional connections he gets, the better he is able to deal with his unwanted attractions. He said, "I do okay as long as I stay close to the Lord and have regular interactions with other men who respect me and are good to me. I call it my man vitamins or vitamin M, and I need regular doses of it. I've been able to develop close friendships with a few good men at work and at church, and their inclusion has been very helpful for me—not curing me but strengthening me by filling a void. These heterosexual friends have no idea how much good their friendship does for me."[205]

These men with same-sex attraction have been strengthened by connections with other men and by connections with Jesus Christ. However, it is important to clarify that these stories do not show that a focus on connections outward and upward will cure anyone *from* their challenges, but rather these connections will support a person *through* their challenges. Elder Jose L. Alonso taught, "When we encounter difficulties, we naturally tend to concentrate on the obstacles we face. . . . By placing Christ at the core of our thoughts and deeds, we align ourselves with His outlook and strength. *This adjustment does*

---

204. North Star International, "Voces of Esperanza: Mitchell," YouTube, July 6, 2019, 10:28–11:15, https://www.youtube.com/watch?v=WmnBkvFulro.

205. Anonymous, personal discussion with the author.

not discount our struggles; instead, it helps us to navigate through them under divine guidance. . . . With the Savior, what seems like a major problem can become a pathway to greater spiritual progress."[206]

Our same-sex attracted brothers and sisters must be patient and not expect instant miracles. In my observations of a multitude of people facing a variety of challenges, I have seen that God would rather develop a person through a lifelong process of growth in adversity than provide a miraculous, instant change. Quick miracles do not give a person the same depth of spiritual maturity that comes when a person struggles through difficulties over a lifetime. God has never been one to avoid putting His children on a path of suffering in order to stimulate growth. As the book of Job declares, "Man is born unto trouble" (Job 5:7); however, if we, like Job, will stay connected to the Lord and find friends who will sit with us, then over time, God will help heal what needs to be healed and help endure what needs to be endured as we move forward through those troubles.

This life on earth was never meant to be easy. As President Henry B. Eyring has said, "Our mortal life is designed by a loving God to be a test and source of growth for each of us."[207] Nevertheless, by keeping our covenants, we are promised divine blessings to help us with our challenges. Sister Terry Christensen shared an experience she had after her husband passed away. He came to her in spirit and said, "It is very important to be good; keep the commandments, and keep your covenants. When you do, you'll be able to handle hard things." He then added, "Don't worry about the kids. I'll take care of them." A few days later, their son-in-law was killed in a car accident.[208]

Sister Christensen's husband did not tell her that if she kept her covenants, God would remove hard things from her life. He told her that by keeping her covenants, she would be able to handle the hard things when they came. This is true for everyone, whether those hard things include living as a widow, or living with same-sex attraction,

---

206. Jose L. Alonso, "Jesus Christ at the Center of Our Lives," *Liahona*, May 2024, 40; emphasis added.
207. Henry B. Eyring, "Try, Try, Try," *Ensign* or *Liahona*, Nov. 2018, 90.
208. Anne Hinton Pratt, "The Other Side and Back," *Meridian Magazine*, Feb. 23, 2022, https://latterdaysaintmag.com/the-other-side-and-back/.

or experiencing any of a multitude of challenges in today's world. We should not try to make life easier by campaigning for changes in Church policy and doctrine. Instead, we should keep our covenants in order to arm ourselves with the power of God that we will need to better deal with the challenges we face. It is in the fire of adversity that personal growth is forged, and as Alma the Younger taught, "Whosoever shall put their trust in God shall be supported in their trials, and their troubles, and their afflictions, and shall be lifted up at the last day" (Alma 36:3).

We all need emotionally intimate connections with friends, regardless of the nature of our struggles. Elder Joseph B. Wirthlin said, "When we work together in a bond of brotherhood, when we love each other and are loyal and faithful to the great cause to which we have been called, the impossible becomes possible."[209] Everyone also needs the divine help that comes from a connection with God and Jesus Christ. These two dimensions of the strengthening power of the doctrine of Christ are universal. Community psychologist and author Dr. Jacob Hess has written some articles discussing common themes he has found in the stories of people who have overcome struggles with pornography[210] and depression.[211] With both struggles, he found repeated references to the value of connections with supportive friends and connections with God or Jesus Christ. We all need these connections regardless of our challenges. The difference for those who experience same-sex attraction or other sexual-minority experiences is that they are often either shunned or avoided, making their need for friendship and community even greater.

I believe that Christ cannot return until those who claim to be His followers learn to embrace all people with love and compassion while living our own lives within the standards He has established.

---

209. Joseph B. Wirthlin, "Band of Brothers," *Ensign*, Feb. 2008, 33.

210. See Jacob Z. Hess, "How People Get Better from Porn Addiction," Publish Peace, Jan. 2, 2024, https://www.publishpeace.net/p/how-people-get-better-from-porn-addiction.

211. See Jacob Z. Hess, "How People Get Better from Depression," Publish Peace, Jan. 3, 2024, https://www.publishpeace.net/p/how-people-get-better-from-depression.

We all need to become more Christlike if we are going to live with Him after His Second Coming, and the rise of this challenge in recent years may be one of the ways God is trying to teach us charity in order to prepare us for His Son's return. No change in Church policy or doctrine is needed for us to show love to others. We just need to engage the doctrine of Christ more fully in both of its dimensions.

Remembering these two dimensions of the doctrine of Christ, which is also called the gospel of Jesus Christ, can bless us when we participate in temple ordinances. Whenever we covenant to live the law of the gospel of Jesus Christ, either for ourselves or as proxies for others, we commit to living it in both of its dimensions: We commit to nourish our connection upward to God and Jesus Christ and our connection outward to our neighbors. These connections will bless ourselves and our fellow Saints, no matter what our individual challenges may be.

Come unto Christ, the Light of the World

The purpose of every challenge in life is to turn our hearts to God and our eyes to the light that shines from Jesus Christ. When Jesus and His disciples passed by a man who was blind from birth, the disciples apparently thought that his difficult life situation must have come about because of sin. They asked Jesus, "Master, who did sin, this man, or his parents, that he was born blind? Jesus answered, Neither hath this man sinned, nor his parents: but that the works of God should be made manifest in him. . . . I am the light of the world" (John 9:2–5).

I believe that Christ's answer applies to those who experience same-sex attraction. God may be using the lives of many faithful same-sex attracted followers of Christ in order to make manifest the works of God. Christ is the light of the world, and He will guide them if they seek that guidance with determination and persistence. Christ will shine His light into their lives not only for their own benefit but also so that others can see the works of God made manifest in their lives.

BYU religion professor Ty Mansfield once identified as gay, but after years of struggle, he determined that he wanted to live faithful to Latter-day Saint policies and doctrine. At the time, he thought he would never be married. He felt the Lord tell him, "I want you to focus on Me and learn how to be full without being married." Professor Mansfield commented, "There is such a focus on marriage as this act of completion, [yet] the act of completion is Christ. And the most important decision we can ever make is the decision to come unto Christ."[212] He was later blessed with an eternal marriage and five children, but learning first how to live with a single-minded focus on Jesus Christ prepared him for that future step.

Jason Hill is a world-renowned professor of philosophy who lived for over twenty years in several same-sex relationships and as a self-described "intransigent atheist." However, he experienced a powerful conversion to Christianity, after which his attractions "dissipated somewhat." In an interview, he explained that since his conversion, on the rare occasions when he feels a desire to be with another man, "I just find myself running to Christ, and I just say, 'Christ, open your arms because I'm coming, and I'm going to run in there, and you're going to have to fill a void that's opening back up.' And I just surrender myself to a rich prayer life, and before I know it, I have achieved a sense of equanimity and calmness and stillness—complete stillness—again."[213]

One Christian organization that supports Christians living with same-sex attraction is called the CHANGED movement. Former lesbian Elizabeth Woning, cofounder of that organization, shared the following:

> Jesus is the factor that is most overlooked in the Christian debate around LGBT. Relationship with Him is the treasure that we are willing to sacrifice for. But, it turns out that His journey is abundant. His ways overcome theory, psychology, and philosophy. . . .

---

212. BYU Religious Education, "Y Religion Episode 97 - The Power of Stillness (Ty Mansfield)," YouTube, Feb. 1, 2024, 52:02–52:56, https://www.youtube.com/watch?v=TnBcWT85dPg.

213. Becket Cook, "And I Have Come Home—at Last: Jason Hill Testimony - The Becket Cook Show Ep. 173," YouTube, Sept. 12, 2024, 25:18–27:43, youtube.com/watch?v=XNGmoRHXvIM&t=905s; see also Jason D. Hill, "No, I Wasn't Born This Way," *Front Page Magazine*, Aug. 30, 2024, https://www.frontpagemag.com/no-i-wasnt-born-this-way/.

> Jesus saved my life. He redeemed my mental and emotional health—rescuing me from suicidality. He redeemed my identity as a woman and ultimately my sexuality. As time goes on, He continues to reveal Himself to me in life-changing ways as I aspire to live as He lived and assume His heart within my own life. I am a woman, a daughter, a wife to my husband of 16 years . . . all because of Jesus. I no longer identify as LGBT. . . .
>
> For Christians, the way forward requires acknowledgment that sanctification through a relationship with Jesus restores our common human identity. We must invite believers into a way of life that emphasizes our new identity in Christ. . . .
>
> The goal isn't "straight"; the goal is human, redeemed. Then we will be free from every life-dominating behavior that draws us away from Christ's vision for human identity, whether in singleness or marriage. Only then can we become the family and the body of Christ that brings healing to the nations—together.[214]

The faithfulness of this Christian woman is remarkable. She attributes the changes in her life to being redeemed by Jesus Christ. She has aligned her primary identity with Him. Her declaration is consistent with the three identities President Russell M. Nelson said we should embrace when he declared, "No identifier should displace, replace, or take priority over these three enduring designations: Child of God, Child of the covenant, Disciple of Jesus Christ. Any identifier that is not compatible with those three basic designations will ultimately let you down. Make no mistake about it: Your potential is divine. With your diligent seeking, God will give you glimpses of who you may become."[215] Elizabeth Woning understands this. She has been on both sides of this issue, and she has found peace through Christ. As she said, "The goal isn't 'straight'; the goal is human, redeemed." Indeed! The way forward is with Jesus Christ.

---

214. Elizabeth Woning, "A Better Way Forward with LGBTQ," Jan. 30, 2021, https://www.elizabethwoning.com/essays/2021/1/30/f2o3kflgwwj7c5ocd1oh5jnq5ra23b.

215. Russell M. Nelson (@russellmnelson), "Labels can be fun and indicate your support," Instagram, July 20, 2020, https://www.instagram.com/p/CgPQLh0OqiH/; see also, Russell M. Nelson, "Choices for Eternity" (worldwide devotional for young adults, May 15, 2022).

C. S. Lewis taught the value of wholly submitting our identity to God and Jesus Christ:

> Until you have given up your self to [God] you will not have a real self. . . . But there must be a real giving up of the self. You must throw it away "blindly" so to speak. Christ will indeed give you a real personality: but you must not go to Him for the sake of that. As long as your own personality is what you are bothering about you are not going to Him at all. The very first step is to try to forget about the self altogether. Your real, new self . . . will not come as long as you are looking for it. *It will come when you are looking for Him.* . . . Even in social life, you will never make a good impression on other people until you stop thinking about what sort of impression you are making. . . . The principle runs through all life from top to bottom. Give up your self, and you will find your real self. Lose your life and you will save it. . . . Keep back nothing. Nothing that you have not given away will ever be really yours. Nothing in you that has not died will ever be raised from the dead. Look for yourself, and you will find in the long run only hatred, loneliness, despair, rage, ruin, and decay. But look for Christ and you will find Him, and with Him everything else thrown in.[216]

This will not be easy; however, suffering and struggle are part of the price of becoming like Jesus Christ. Elder Neal A. Maxwell asked, "How can you and I really expect to glide naively through life, as if to say, 'Lord, give me experience, but not grief, not sorrow, not pain, not opposition, not betrayal, and certainly not to be forsaken. Keep from me, Lord, all those experiences which made Thee what Thou art! Then let me come and dwell with Thee and fully share Thy joy!' "[217] An easy path will not make us like Jesus Christ.

A friend of mine who experiences same-sex attraction told me that he has been blessed with many deeply spiritual experiences that have affirmed God's love for him; however, at other times, his challenges were very difficult and lonely as he faced desires that pulled at him

---

216. C. S. Lewis, *Mere Christianity* (Samizdat, 2014), 120. See https://samizdat.qc.ca/vc/pdfs/MereChristianity_CSL.pdf for a Canadian public domain version of the text.

217. Neal A. Maxwell, "Lest Ye Be Wearied and Faint in Your Minds," *Ensign*, May 1991, 88.

in ways contrary to his covenants. He recounted that during one difficult period, he complained to the Lord and asked why he had to struggle so much with same-sex attraction. In response, the Lord impressed upon him thoughts of the many early Christians in the first two or three centuries after Christ who were forced to fight lions in the Roman coliseums or experience other horrible tortures. My friend said that the Spirit whispered to him that those early Christian martyrs had come to earth knowing they would suffer these horrible fates for the sake of Christ, and they felt honored to do so. My friend felt like the Lord was telling him that his situation was similar: He had agreed to come to earth in a way that would give him an opportunity to suffer for Christ's sake. It left him feeling honored that the Lord would compare him with those early Christians, and he determined that he would move forward in faithfulness despite the unwanted sexual burden he carried.

The Apostle Paul wrote to the Philippians, "For unto you it is given in the behalf of Christ, not only to believe on him, but also to suffer for his sake" (Philippians 1:29). Similarly, Paul counseled to the Saints in Corinth, "Our light affliction, which is but for a moment, worketh for us a far more exceeding and eternal weight of glory" (2 Corinthians 4:17). That verse is worthy of long pondering, for *weight* and *glory* are words not often used together. However, both words apply in the lives of faithful Saints who experience same-sex attraction. They often feel that they carry a heavy weight of affliction, but they also experience the glory of God's abundant love for them.

Paul suffered many afflictions himself, including his own unnamed "thorn in the flesh," which he described as "the messenger of Satan to buffet me" (2 Corinthians 12:7). Paul pleaded to God multiple times to take this personal burden from him, but the Lord would not, explaining, "My grace is sufficient for thee: for my strength is made perfect in weakness" (2 Corinthians 12:9). In response, Paul declared, "Most gladly therefore will I rather glory in my infirmities, that the power of Christ may rest upon me. Therefore I take pleasure in infirmities, in reproaches, in necessities, in persecutions, in distresses for Christ's sake: for when I am weak, then am I strong" (2 Corinthians 12:9–10).

Paul's words can help those who experience same-sex attraction find their own purpose and value through Jesus Christ. However, the lives of those who carry such challenges are not all suffering and struggle. The stories I have discovered of faithful followers of Jesus Christ who experience same-sex attraction tell of struggles, but they are also filled with hope and much happiness. The world is a better place because of their talents and perspective, and while some of their strengths and abilities may not be conventional for their gender, when we celebrate their gifts and encourage these brothers and sisters to share their talents with others, we all benefit. They are trying to follow the light of Jesus Christ.

That light will guide us all. President Russell M. Nelson declared, "Whatever questions or problems you have, the answer is always found in the life and teachings of Jesus Christ. Learn more about His Atonement, His love, His mercy, His doctrine, and His restored gospel of healing and progression. Turn to Him! Follow Him!"[218] He is the Light of the world.

A Three-Act Play

Thus far, this chapter has focused on how faithful individuals who experience same-sex attraction or related challenges can be fortified by focusing on Jesus Christ and engaging the support of friends and fellow Saints who make up the body of Christ. However, there are many in the LGBT+ community who have separated themselves from the Church and embraced a lifestyle contrary to the doctrine of the family and the doctrine of Christ. Sadly, others have ended their mortal lives because of the pain and internal conflict they experience. Is there any hope for these souls? How can family members of those who have rejected the covenant path find consolation and peace?

We can look to our temple doctrine and the plan of salvation taught therein for answers to these questions. The entire basis for doing proxy ordinances for those who have died is predicated on the possibility of changes within the souls of those who reside in the

---

218. Russell M. Nelson, "The Answer Is Always Jesus Christ," *Liahona*, May 2023, 127.

spirit world. Although there are boundaries and limitations, this temple-centered doctrine can bring hope to the family members of those who have lost their way during their mortal lives. The doctrine of Christ is as viable in the spirit world as it is in mortality.

Elder Neal A. Maxwell said, "Trying to comprehend the trials and meaning of this life without understanding Heavenly Father's marvelously encompassing plan of salvation is like trying to understand a three-act play while seeing only the second act."[219] In an earlier talk, President Boyd K. Packer similarly said, "The plan of redemption, with its three divisions, might be likened to a grand three-act play. Act One is entitled 'Premortal Life.' The scriptures describe it as our first estate (see Jude 1:6; Abraham 3:26, 28). Act Two, from birth to the time of resurrection, is the 'Second Estate.' And Act Three is called 'Life After Death' or 'Eternal Life.'"[220]

In most three-act plays, Act Two includes a lot of conflict and confusion with uncertainty of outcome. Resolution and reconciliation do not happen until Act Three. This can be unsettling; however, one of the blessings of the Restoration is a deeper understanding of what happens in the final scenes of Act Two—in the spirit world, prior to Resurrection and Judgment, which are events that open the curtain to Act Three. In his vision of the redemption of the dead, President Joseph F. Smith learned the following about opportunities awaiting those who were sinful during the first part of Act Two:

> Thus was the gospel preached to those who had died in their sins, without a knowledge of the truth, or in transgression, having rejected the prophets.
>
> These were taught faith in God, repentance from sin, vicarious baptism for the remission of sins, the gift of the Holy Ghost by the laying on of hands,
>
> And all other principles of the gospel that were necessary for them to know in order to qualify themselves that they might be

---

219. Neal A. Maxwell, "Enduring Well," *Ensign*, Apr. 1997, 7.
220. Boyd K. Packer, "The Play and the Plan" (Church Education System fireside, May 7, 1995); quoted in "The Great Plan of Happiness," *Book of Mormon Teacher Resource Manual* (2004), 290; some style changes made.

judged according to men in the flesh, but live according to God in the spirit. (D&C 138:32–34)

What a glorious truth it is to know that those who "died in their sins," and even those who had "rejected the prophets" will be taught the principles of the gospel in the spirit world and given the opportunity to receive proxy saving ordinances "in order to qualify themselves" to "live according to God in the spirit." This is a witness of the grace and mercy of Jesus Christ, who provides for the possibility of repentance in the spirit world.

In what seems like a contradiction to this doctrine, the prophet Amulek taught, "For behold, this life is the time for men to prepare to meet God; yea, behold the day of this life is the day for men to perform their labors" (Alma 34:32). However, this is not inconsistent with President Smith's vision if we interpret Amulek's reference to "this life" to include both mortality and the spirit world.

In Doctrine and Covenants 19, the Lord explains that He sometimes uses words in a way that will increase their expression and have a greater impact on the hearts of mankind:

> And surely every man must repent or suffer, for I, God, am endless. . . .
>
> Nevertheless, it is not written that there shall be no end to this torment, but it is written endless torment.
>
> Again, it is written eternal damnation; wherefore *it is more express than other scriptures, that it might work upon the hearts of the children of men, altogether for my name's glory.*
>
> Wherefore, I will explain unto you this mystery. . . .
>
> For, behold, I am endless, and the punishment which is given from my hand is endless punishment, for Endless is my name. Wherefore—
>
> Eternal punishment is God's punishment.
>
> Endless punishment is God's punishment. (D&C 19:4, 6–8, 10–12; emphasis added)

We see that the Lord uses the terms "Eternal punishment" and "Endless punishment" precisely because they have a double meaning. Apparently, He wants us to feel in our hearts the impact of the usual meaning of these words so that we will feel motivated to adjust our behavior as soon as possible. At the same time, His higher definition of these terms gives God leeway to show mercy when Judgment Day comes, without going back on His decrees.

I believe that Amulek's use of the phrase "this life" is similar. The Lord wants this term to weigh on our hearts and motivate us to repent as early as possible on earth so we can receive His blessings sooner in our lives. However, considering the merciful statements in Doctrine and Covenants 138, it seems that the Lord defines "this life" more broadly to include the spirit world, for why would the Lord state that those in the spirit world are taught repentance if they cannot repent there? In fact, they can. The Prophet Joseph Smith taught, "There is never a time when the spirit is too old to approach God. All are within the reach of pardoning mercy, who have not committed the unpardonable sin, which hath no forgiveness."[221] (Notice, however, that this refers to the state of the spirit, not the state of the resurrected soul after the Judgment.)

President Dallin H. Oaks spoke of the hopeful way Doctrine and Covenants 138 allows us to interpret "this life." He said, "The Book of Mormon teaches that 'this life is the time for [us] to prepare to meet God' (Alma 43:32). But that challenging limitation to 'this life' was given a hopeful context (at least to some extent for some persons) by what the Lord revealed to President Joseph F. Smith, now recorded in Doctrine and Covenants section 138."[222]

That hopeful context becomes clearer when we remember President Packer's description of the three-act play, quoted earlier. He said, "Act Two, from birth to the time of resurrection, is the 'Second Estate.'"[223] Elder Maxwell likewise declared, "The spirit world and paradise are part, really, of the second estate. . . . The veil of forgetfulness of the first estate . . . will continue in some key respects into the spirit world."[224]

---

221. *Teachings of the Prophet Joseph Smith*, sel. Joseph Fielding Smith (1976), 191.
222. Dallin H. Oaks, "Kingdoms of Glory," *Liahona*, Nov. 2023, 28.
223. Boyd K. Packer, "The Play and the Plan."
224. Neal A. Maxwell, *The Promise of Discipleship* (Deseret Book, 2010), 119; quoted in "Chapter 9: The Spirit World and the Redemption of the Dead," *Introduction to Family History Student Manual* (2012).

This inclusion of the spirit world as part of our second estate is also consistent with the teachings of Moroni who taught that our fate is not sealed until the Day of Judgment that follows our resurrection:

> The death of Christ bringeth to pass the resurrection, which bringeth to pass a redemption from an endless sleep, from which sleep all men shall be awakened by the power of God . . . and all shall stand before his bar, being redeemed and loosed from this eternal band of death, which death is a temporal death.
>
> And then cometh the judgment of the Holy One upon them; and *then cometh the time* that he that is filthy shall be filthy still; and he that is righteous shall be righteous still. (Mormon 9:13–14; emphasis added)

This helps us understand Amulek's statement that "if ye have procrastinated the day of your repentance even until death, behold, ye have become subjected to the spirit of the devil, and he doth seal you his; therefore, the Spirit of the Lord hath withdrawn from you, and hath no place in you, and the devil hath all power over you; and this is the final state of the wicked" (Alma 34:35). Apparently, the death Amulek is referring to is the second death, which is a death that will be suffered by those who are banished to outer darkness.[225] However, in divine, double-meaning fashion, his warning is also meant to motivate everyone to repent before death in this mortal world.

Amulek's statement may also have reference to the fact that those who die in their sins but repent in the spirit world will suffer to some degree themselves before they are cleansed by the power of Christ's Atonement. In Doctrine and Covenants 138, we read, "The dead who repent will be redeemed, through obedience to the ordinances of the house of God, And *after they have paid the penalty of their transgressions*, and are washed clean, shall receive a reward according to their works, for they are heirs of salvation" (D&C 138:58–59, emphasis added; see also Matthew 5:26). It is possible that this payment comes

---

[225] Other scripture commentators have arrived at this same conclusion. See Joseph Fielding McConkie and Robert L. Millet, *Doctrinal Commentary on the Book of Mormon* (Deseret Book, 2012), 3:257, and Richard M. Romney, "Spiritual Death," *Encyclopedia of Mormonism* (Macmillan, 1992), 832, https://eom.byu.edu/index.php/Spiritual_Death.

through temporary suffering in spirit prison, for everyone who repents from serious sin must suffer the emotional anguish of regret and remorse before experiencing the joyful cleansing of Christ's Atonement (see Alma 36, for example). We should not think that our choices in our mortal life can be overridden in the spirit world with no consequences, but we should also not think that repentance is unavailable after mortality.

Jesus Christ Will Be Our Judge

In spite of our hopeful doctrine of spirit world repentance, it is important to recognize that there is no guarantee that a person's heart will change after mortality, "for that same spirit which doth possess your bodies at the time that ye go out of this life, that same spirit will have power to possess your body in that eternal world" (Alma 34:34). There are some people who rejected the truth with hardened hearts on earth, and if pride and a spirit of rebellion remain with them in the spirit world, they will not qualify for the blessings of repentance and proxy ordinances there.

President Joseph Fielding Smith taught that those who receive a terrestrial and not a celestial glory will include "those who have lived clean lives but who, notwithstanding their membership in the Church, were not valiant, and those who refused to receive the gospel when they lived on the earth, but in the spirit world accepted the testimony of Jesus."[226] This echoes Doctrine and Covenants 76, which describes terrestrial beings as those "who received not the testimony of Jesus in the flesh, but afterwards received it. These are they who are honorable men of the earth, who were blinded by the craftiness of men. . . . These are they who are not valiant in the testimony of Jesus" (D&C 76:74–75, 79). We don't know what level of understanding is necessary before a person who rejects the gospel on earth will be limited in his or her eternal progress in the spirit world; however, we do know that the question of valiance will not be answered until the Day of Judgment, and it will be based on the progress of our souls in

---

226. Joseph Fielding Smith, *Answers to Gospel Questions*, comp. Joseph Fielding Smith Jr. (1966), 2:209.

the entirety of our second estate, including both mortality and the spirit world. Also, there is a difference between those who reject the gospel in mortality because they have been "blinded by the craftiness of men" and those who struggle to live it due to personal limitations that are beyond their control, such as might be the case for many of those who experience same-sex attraction.

Furthermore, as clarified in Joseph Smith's vision of the celestial kingdom, "All who have died without a knowledge of this gospel, who would have received it if they had been permitted to tarry, shall be heirs of the celestial kingdom of God" (D&C 137:7). I can't help but wonder if a similar opportunity applies to the dead who had left the Church while they were on earth but would have later returned if they had been permitted to tarry on earth longer. Perhaps it depends on how complete their "knowledge of the gospel" was before they left the Church and whether they actively rebelled against it.

We should also acknowledge that there will be some people who will inherit the celestial kingdom without receiving eternal marriage: "In the celestial glory there are three heavens or degrees; And in order to obtain the highest, a man must enter into . . . the new and everlasting covenant of marriage" (D&C 131:1–2). Those who inherit the lower two levels of the celestial kingdom are "appointed angels in heaven, which angels are ministering servants, to minister for those who are worthy of a far more, and an exceeding, and an eternal weight of glory. For these angels did not abide my law; therefore, they cannot be enlarged, but remain separately and singly, without exaltation, in their saved condition, to all eternity" (D&C 132:16–17). Nevertheless, these souls will be worthy to abide in the celestial kingdom where they will enjoy the society of other celestial beings, including our Heavenly Father and Mother, our Savior Jesus Christ, and other celestial family members. I believe that these single celestial

Saints will enjoy happiness in their eternal role as ministering angels; otherwise, it would not be heaven for them.[227]

It is not for us to judge who will receive what level of eternal glory. Clearly there is a balance to be found between accountability for choices made in mortality and mercy for those who experience a change of heart and humbly repent in the spirit world. Elder Gerrit W. Gong taught, "In the spirit world, even those in sin and transgression have opportunity to repent (see D&C 138:32). In contrast, those who deliberately choose wickedness, who consciously procrastinate repentance, or who in any premeditated or knowing way break the commandments, planning for easy repentance, will be judged by God and a 'bright recollection of all [their] guilt' (Alma 11:43)."[228]

There may be many members of the Church who have not fully lived the gospel in mortality due to a variety of spiritual, physical, or emotional challenges, including same-sex attraction, and these circumstances, along with a repentant attitude in the spirit world, could qualify them for a second chance to show that they are valiant in the testimony of Jesus and thus have become heirs of celestial glory. Elder Spencer J. Condie offered the following explanation to the question "Why do you perform baptisms for deceased people whose lives on earth indicated little inclination to keep the commandments of God?":

---

227. The Lord has not revealed what distinguishes the two lower levels of the celestial kingdom. However, by way of conjecture, I wonder if one sublevel might include souls who sincerely do not want to be married eternally even though they qualify for it. President Dallin H. Oaks taught, "[God] will force no one into a sealing relationship against his or her will" ("Kingdoms of Glory," *Liahona*, Nov. 2023, 29). The other sublevel might include those who would not, of themselves, qualify for the celestial kingdom but are lifted to that station by the covenant bonds of their parents for whom it would not be heaven without their children present. President Joseph Fielding Smith taught, "Children born under the covenant, who drift away, are still the children of their parents; and the parents have claim upon them; and if the children have not sinned away all their rights, the parents may be able to bring them through repentance, into the celestial kingdom, but not to receive the exaltation" (Joseph Fielding Smith, *Doctrines of Salvation*, comp. Bruce R. McConkie [1955], 2:91).

228. Gerrit W. Gong, "Happy and Forever," *Liahona*, Nov. 2022, 84.

We believe that many people are like Amulek, who once said of himself, "I did harden my heart, for I was called many times and I would not hear; therefore I knew concerning [the gospel of Jesus Christ], yet I would not know" (Alma 10:6). Amulek later became a great missionary and teacher of his people. . . .

We simply do not know who among the dead will turn their hearts to the Lord and repent. We are not in a position to judge. We must do the work and leave the matter in the hands of the deceased person and the Lord.[229]

Only Jesus Christ will be the final Judge of what each person's eternal reward will be, but we should remember that His judgment will not be based solely on our earth life. The possibility of repentance and change in the spirit world, before the Resurrection and Final Judgment, is an important part of our doctrine. This fact can give hope to the family members and friends of those who have strayed from the covenant path in mortality. President Oaks taught, "The power of the Atonement and the principle of repentance show that we should never give up on loved ones who now seem to be making many wrong choices."[230]

Brother Larry James shared an experience he had regarding his deceased younger sister. During her life, she had been married five times and had six children, each with a different man. After she passed away, Brother James did not consider doing temple work for her because she had never been active in the Church, and he had written her off as one who had already rejected the gospel. However, while helping to perform sealing ordinances in the temple, he had an unexpected experience. He wrote, "I was sitting in one of the witness chairs when the sound in the room became very still. I heard a female voice speak to my mind. She said, 'DON'T FORGET ME!' It was the voice of my younger sister." Within one week, Brother James and his

---

229. Spencer J. Condie, "The Savior's Visit to the Spirit World," *Ensign*, July 2003, 36.
230. Dallin H. Oaks, "The Challenge to Become," *Ensign*, Nov. 2000, 34.

wife completed the temple work for his sister, confident that she had been able to repent and had qualified for exaltation.[231]

Elder Orson F. Whitney taught:

> The Prophet Joseph Smith declared—and he never taught more comforting doctrine—that the eternal sealings of faithful parents and the divine promises made to them for valiant service in the Cause of Truth, would save not only themselves, but likewise their posterity. Though some of the sheep may wander, the eye of the Shepherd is upon them, and sooner or later they will feel the tentacles of Divine Providence reaching out after them and drawing them back to the fold. *Either in this life or the life to come, they will return.* They will have to pay their debt to justice; they will suffer for their sins; and may tread a thorny path; but if it leads them at last, like the penitent Prodigal, to a loving and forgiving father's heart and home, the painful experience will not have been in vain. Pray for your careless and disobedient children; hold on to them with your faith. Hope on, trust on, till you see the salvation of God.[232]

We cannot judge the hearts of those who have faced difficult life circumstances that may have limited their perspective on the gospel during mortal life. We also need to realize that our personal attitudes on certain aspects of mortality may change when we gain a broader perspective in the next life. We have each been given unique challenges in mortality, customized for the development of our eternal souls, and we may find that those who lived with same-sex attraction on earth will have learned some things and gained some growth that will benefit them eternally in ways that we will admire. Once they have aligned themselves with Christ's atoning powers, as all must do, we may discover that these select souls have gained many Christlike attributes much faster and in a deeper measure than those who have not faced similar life challenges on earth.

---

231. Anne Hinton Pratt, "Becoming 'Angels' to Angels: Setting the Prisoners Free," *Meridian Magazine*, Jan. 12, 2022, https://latterdaysaintmag.com/becoming-angels-to-angels-setting-the-prisoners-free/.
232. Orson F. Whitney, in Conference Report, Apr. 1929, 110; emphasis added. See also Harold C. Brown, "I Have a Question," *Ensign*, Mar. 1993, 53–54.

It is worth emphasizing once more that even though our doctrine of repentance and change in the spirit world can give hope, this does not mean that the choices a person makes in mortality do not matter or that all our wrongs can be corrected in the spirit world. President Oaks taught the following:

> To assure that we will be clean before God, we must repent before the Final Judgment. . . . Although we are taught that some repentance can occur in the spirit world, that is not as certain. Elder Melvin J. Ballard taught: "It is much easier to overcome and serve the Lord when both flesh and spirit are combined as one. This is the time when men are more pliable and susceptible. . . . This life is the time to repent" (Melvin J. Ballard, in *Melvin J. Ballard: Crusader for Righteousness* [Bookcraft, 1966], 212–13).[233]

> We will be judged according to our actions, the desires of our hearts, and the kind of person we have become. This judgment will cause all of the children of God to proceed to a kingdom of glory for which their obedience has qualified them and where they will be comfortable. The judge of all this is our Savior, Jesus Christ. His omniscience gives Him a perfect knowledge of all of our acts and desires, both those unrepented or unchanged and those repented or righteous. Therefore, after His judgment we will all confess "that his judgments are just" (Mosiah 16:1).[234]

The bottom line is that we can and should hope that all souls will access the power of Christ's Atonement in whatever state they are in, prior to the Final Judgment. We who are living on the earth should choose to follow the gospel path while we live in mortality. And for those who are in the spirit world, we should do their temple work with the hope and expectation that they will exercise faith in Jesus Christ, repent of their sins, and qualify for both salvation and exaltation. Hope in Christ applies on both sides of the veil.

What a blessing it is to have such an extensive knowledge of the plan of salvation and exaltation, including the possibility of repentance

---

233. Dallin H. Oaks, "Cleansed by Repentance," *Ensign* or *Liahona*, May 2019, 94.
234. Dallin H. Oaks, "The Great Plan," *Ensign* or *Liahona*, May 2020, 96.

and continued progress in the spirit world prior to the Resurrection and Final Judgment. It is with this faith and knowledge that we perform proxy ordinances of salvation and exaltation in the temples of God for our ancestors and loved ones without judgment regarding the challenges they faced in mortal life. We leave that judgment to our loving Advocate and Savior, Jesus Christ, who loves and understands us individually because of His Atonement.

Love and Law: Leave Not the Other Undone

As children of God, everyone deserves to be treated with kindness and love, regardless of the inclinations or other challenges they experience and the life path they choose to follow. Joseph Smith advocated for kindness, saying, "Nothing is so much calculated to lead people to forsake sin as to take them by the hand and to watch over them in tenderness. When persons manifest the least kindness and love to me, O what power it has over my mind, while the opposite course has a tendency to harrow up all the harsh feelings and depress the human mind."[235] This does not mean that our kindness should be motivated only by a desire to get other people to change, for Christlike love, which is charity, "seeketh not her own" (1 Corinthians 13:5). Charity allows for differences.

The *General Handbook* of the Church specifies the loving, respectful approach all members should take toward those who experience same-sex attraction:

> The Church encourages families and members to reach out with sensitivity, love, and respect to persons who are attracted to others of the same sex. The Church also promotes understanding in society at large that reflects its teachings about kindness, inclusiveness, love for others, and respect for all human beings. . . .
>
> All members who keep their covenants will receive all promised blessings in the eternities whether or not their circumstances allow them to receive the blessings of eternal marriage and parenthood in this life (see Mosiah 2:41).[236]

---

235. *Teachings of the Prophet Joseph Smith*, 240.
236. *General Handbook*, 38.6.15.

On the other hand, the *General Handbook* also says the following regarding the same issue:

> God's commandments forbid all unchaste behavior, either heterosexual or same-sex. Church leaders counsel members who have violated the law of chastity. Leaders help them have a clear understanding of faith in Jesus Christ and His Atonement, the process of repentance, and the purpose of life on earth. Behavior that is inconsistent with the law of chastity may be cause for holding a Church membership council. It can be forgiven through sincere repentance.[237]

There is a balance to be found between emphasizing empathy and compassion on the one hand and teaching the boundaries of God's laws and commandments on the other. That balance cannot be achieved by teaching only one of these principles while ignoring the other. We must teach both love and law. President Dallin H. Oaks said, "The love of God does not supersede His laws and His commandments, and the effect of God's laws and commandments does not diminish the purpose and effect of His love."[238] Love and law are both needed.

Jesus reprimanded the Pharisees who focused only on the law while ignoring principles such as mercy and faith. He said, "These ought ye to have done, and not to leave the other undone" (Matthew 23:23). He wasn't saying to forget the law and only show mercy. He was saying that both principles must be lived. He took a similar approach with the woman caught in adultery: He showed her love and mercy while directing her to "go, and sin no more" (John 8:11). As President Jeffrey R. Holland said of Jesus, "He is one who could administer grace and insist on truth at the same time. . . . His love allows an encouraging embrace when it is needed and a bitter cup when it has to be swallowed."[239] Jesus emphasized both love and law, declaring, "He that hath my commandments, and keepeth them, he it is that

---

237. *General Handbook*, 38.6.15.
238. Dallin H. Oaks, "Love and Law," *Ensign* or *Liahona*, Nov. 2009, 26.
239. Jeffrey R. Holland, "I Am He," *Liahona*, Nov. 2024, 78.

loveth me: and he that loveth me shall be loved of my Father" (John 14:21).

Our modern prophets and apostles have demonstrated this balance between law and love in their teachings. The following quotes give statements of love balanced by statements of law from discourses presented by several of our leaders as they have addressed the sexual and gender challenges of our day.

Discourse	Love Statement	Law Statement
Russell M. Nelson, "Decisions for Eternity," Oct. 2013[240]	"We are to emulate our Savior's kindness and compassion, [and] we are to value the rights and feelings of all of God's children."	"The doctrine of the Lord regarding marriage and morality *cannot be changed*. Remember: sin, even if legalized by man, is still sin in the eyes of God! . . . We cannot change His doctrine. It is not ours to change. His doctrine is ours to study, understand, and uphold."
M. Russell Ballard, "Questions and Answers," Nov. 2017[241]	"We need to listen to and understand what our LGBT brothers and sisters are feeling and experiencing. Certainly we must do better than we have done in the past so that all members feel they have a spiritual home where their brothers and sisters love them and where they have a place to worship and serve the Lord."	"When we love God, we make and strive to keep our sacred covenants. I testify that living gospel commandments brings anyone untold blessings, allowing us to become our very best selves—exactly who God wants us to be."

---

240. Russell M. Nelson, "Decisions for Eternity," *Ensign*, Nov. 2013, 108.
241. M. Russell Ballard, "Questions and Answers" (Brigham Young University devotional, Nov. 14, 2017), 3, speeches.byu.edu.

Discourse	Love Statement	Law Statement
Dallin H. Oaks, "Two Great Commandments," Oct. 2019[242]	"We seek to persuade our members that those who follow lesbian, gay, bisexual, or transgender teachings and actions should be treated with the love our Savior commands us to show toward all our neighbors. . . . Further, we must never persecute those who do not share our beliefs and commitments. Regretfully, some persons facing these issues continue to feel marginalized and rejected by some members and leaders in our families, wards, and stakes. We must all strive to be kinder and more civil."	"The work of The Church of Jesus Christ of Latter-day Saints is ultimately concerned with preparing the children of God for the celestial kingdom, and most particularly for its highest glory, exaltation or eternal life. That highest destiny is possible only through marriage for eternity. Eternal life includes the creative powers inherent in the combination of male and female—what modern revelation describes as the 'continuation of the seeds forever and ever' (D&C 132:19)."
Jeffrey R. Holland, "The Second Half of the Second Century of BYU," Aug. 2021[243]	"Let me go no farther before declaring unequivocally my love and that of my Brethren for those who live with this same-sex challenge and so much complexity that goes with it. Too often the world has been unkind—in many instances crushingly cruel—to these, our brothers and sisters. Like many of you, we have spent hours with them, and we have wept and prayed and wept again in an effort to offer love and hope."	"We have to be careful that love and empathy do not get interpreted as condoning and advocacy or that orthodoxy and loyalty to principle not be interpreted as unkindness or disloyalty to people. As near as I can tell, Christ never once withheld His love from anyone, but He also never once said to anyone, 'Because I love you, you are exempt from keeping my commandments.' We are tasked with trying to strike that same sensitive, demanding balance in our lives."

---

242. Dallin H. Oaks, "*Two* Great Commandments," *Ensign* or *Liahona*, Nov. 2019, 74–75.

243. Jeffrey R. Holland, "The Second Half of the Second Century of Brigham Young University" (Brigham Young University devotional, Aug. 23, 2021), 4, speeches.byu.edu.

Discourse	Love Statement	Law Statement
D. Todd Christofferson, "The Love of God," Oct. 2021[244]	"Our Heavenly Father loves us profoundly and perfectly. . . . Jesus Christ shares with the Father this same perfect love. . . . This divine love should give us abundant comfort and confidence as we pray to the Father in the name of Christ. Not one of us is a stranger to Them. We need not hesitate to call upon God, even when we feel unworthy. We can rely on the mercy and merits of Jesus Christ to be heard. (See 2 Nephi 2:8; Moroni 6:4.)"	"Because God's love is all-embracing, some speak of it as 'unconditional,' and in their minds they may project that thought to mean that God's *blessings* are 'unconditional' and that *salvation* is 'unconditional.' They are not. Some are wont to say, 'The Savior loves me just as I am,' and that is certainly true. But He cannot take any of us into His kingdom just as we are, 'for no unclean thing can dwell there, or dwell in his presence' (Moses 6:57). Our sins must first be resolved."
Dallin H. Oaks, "Divine Love in the Father's Plan," Apr. 2022[245]	"As followers of Christ who should love our fellow men, we should live peacefully with those who do not believe as we do. We are all children of a loving Heavenly Father. For all of us, He has destined life after death and, ultimately, a kingdom of glory. . . . We must seek to share these truths of eternity with others. But with the love we owe to all of our neighbors, we always accept their decisions. As a Book of Mormon prophet taught, we must press forward, having 'a love of God and of all men' (2 Nephi 31:20)."	"Fundamental to us is God's revelation that exaltation can be attained only through faithfulness to the covenants of an eternal marriage between a man and a woman. That divine doctrine is why we teach that 'gender is an essential characteristic of individual premortal, mortal, and eternal identity and purpose.' That is also why the Lord has required His restored Church to oppose social and legal pressures to retreat from His doctrine of marriage between a man and a woman, to oppose changes that homogenize the differences between men and women or confuse or alter gender.

---

244. D. Todd Christofferson, "The Love of God," *Liahona*, Nov. 2021, 16.

245. Dallin H. Oaks, "Divine Love in the Father's Plan," *Liahona*, May 2022, 103.

As exemplified in the teachings above, we need to address both love and law in a balanced way in our public discourse and in teaching situations. Certainly, our personal communications with individuals may emphasize one side or the other, as directed by the Spirit in specific circumstances; however, our general communications and personal behaviors should always demonstrate adherence to both love and law.

Elder Neal A. Maxwell taught, "All the doctrines of the gospel of Jesus Christ are weaved together to give it the necessary strength and totality. Any one of these doctrines by itself could go mad. Love without justice and truth goes wild. And mercy without the elements of the gospel that bring discipline to bear becomes maudlin and sentimental. Each doctrine needs each other doctrine. Just as the people of the Church need each other, the doctrines need each other."[246]

President Oaks echoed this idea when he taught, "To balance our commitments to love and law we must continually show love even as we continually honor and keep the commandments. We must strive to preserve precious relationships and at the same time not compromise our responsibilities to be obedient to and supportive of gospel law."[247] He later followed his own counsel when he admonished, "Anyone who does not treat individuals who face gender identity challenges with love and dignity is not aligned with the teachings of the first and second great commandments. Thus, on the subject of God's law, we need to remember that God has revealed again and again that He created male and female. And on the subject of our duty to love our neighbor, we need to remember that God has commanded us to love even those who do not keep all of the commandments."[248]

---

246. Neal A. Maxwell, "The Simplicity of the Gospel" (Brigham Young University devotional, May 4, 1969, 8, https://radiobeloved.wordpress.com/wp-content/uploads/2012/04/maxwellsimplicityofgospel.pdf.

247. Dallin H. Oaks, "The Paradox of Love and Law" (Brigham Young University–Idaho devotional, Oct. 30, 2018), byui.edu.

248. The Church of Jesus Christ of Latter-day Saints, "May 2023 Worldwide Devotional for Young Adults with President and Sister Oaks," YouTube, May 21, 2023, 42:06, https://www.youtube.com/watch?v=wull4cTXUTk; see also "Combine and Apply Both Law and Love, President and Sister Oaks Encourage Young Adults," *Church News*, May 21, 2023.

President Oak's counsel shows that the balancing principles of law and love correspond to the two dimensions of the law of the gospel discussed earlier, which are to love God and to love our neighbors. When we demonstrate both principles, we are abiding by our temple covenant to keep the law of my gospel of Jesus Christ.

As lay leaders and covenant members of the Church, we are obligated to teach true doctrine, including the laws and covenants set forth by God. These are not up for negotiation. And at the same time, we have an equal obligation, as well as an opportunity and blessing, to respond in love and empathy to those who, through no choice of their own, experience same-sex attraction or other related challenges. Our love and compassion toward others need to be as broad as the many life experiences of those who must tread these difficult life paths. We can sit with others in their pains and celebrate with them in their joys while making clear our love for and allegiance to the laws of God and the doctrines of His Church. We can show love and compassion while also living our covenants and supporting the doctrine of the eternal family. These covenants and doctrines are eternal and will never change. Likewise, our love toward others should be eternal and unchanging. We can teach both, and we can live both. Our faith requires this.

President Nelson taught:

> Because the Father and the Son love us with infinite, perfect love and because They know we cannot see everything They see, They have given us laws that will guide and protect us.
>
> There is a strong connection between God's love and His laws. . . . Just as the rules that my wife and I developed for our children were motivated by love, God's laws reflect His perfect love for each of us. His laws keep us spiritually safe and help us to progress eternally. . . . Divine laws are God's gifts to His children. . . . Abiding by God's laws will keep you safe as you progress toward eventual exaltation. . . . God's greatest blessings are reserved for those who obey His laws, as He explained: "For all who will have a blessing at my hands shall abide the law which was appointed for that blessing" (D&C 132:5). God's laws are motivated entirely by

His infinite love for us and His desire for us to become all we can become.[249]

The Doctrine of Christ Leads to Exaltation

This chapter has described how the seeming exclusivity of Latter-day Saint doctrine of the family and temple marriage can be overcome by the inclusivity of the doctrine of Christ. After teaching His doctrine, the Savior declared, "Verily, verily, I say unto you, that this is my doctrine, and whoso buildeth upon this buildeth upon my rock, and the gates of hell shall not prevail against them" (3 Nephi 11:39). As quoted earlier, President Nelson similarly declared, "Whatever questions or problems you have, the answer is always found in the life and teachings of Jesus Christ."[250] The doctrine of Christ is also called the law of the gospel of Jesus Christ, and our promise to live it is a central covenant of the temple.

We have reviewed testimonies from some individuals who, while living with same-sex attraction, have formed a deep connection with Jesus Christ as an anchor to their souls to help them remain true to their covenants. They have been further strengthened through personal connections with loving friends. We can all join that cadre of support by inviting those who face sexual or gender challenges into our circle of brotherhood or sisterhood in an emotionally intimate way. This does not mean that their challenges will go away, but with connections to Christ and connections to friends, their burdens will be lighter. We can remember these two dimensions of the doctrine of Christ whenever we go to the temple and commit to follow the law of the gospel of Jesus Christ.

We have also seen that this law or doctrine of Christ is viable not only in mortality but also in the spirit world. This truth can bring hope and comfort to the loved ones of those who have made choices in mortal life that do not align with the covenant path God has defined. Finally, we have reviewed the teachings on love and law from

---

249. Russell M. Nelson, "The Love and Laws of God" (Brigham Young University devotional, Sept. 17, 2019), 2, speeches.byu.edu (formatting modified).
250. Russell M. Nelson, "The Answer Is Always Jesus Christ," 127.

latter-day apostles and prophets. These teachings have influenced the approach of this book in dealing with sexual minority issues: The previous chapter focuses primarily on law, while this chapter focuses primarily on the need for love. Together, the two chapters have tried to provide a balanced approach within the boundaries of our doctrine.

Like the ancient Israelites, we Latter-day Saints are a people of prophets, scriptures, temples, and covenants who follow the Lord God, Jehovah, who is Jesus Christ, toward the goal of entering into His divine presence and gaining our eternal exaltation. When we commit to keep the law of the gospel of Jesus Christ, also called the doctrine of Christ, in both of its dimensions, we affirm that we will follow Jesus Christ on the covenant path, arm in arm with our fellow Saints, as together we face the challenges and adversities of this mortal life. By supporting one another and staying focused on the Son of God, with an eye single to His glory, we will eventually find eternal joy and happiness in the presence of our heavenly parents and our Savior Jesus Christ, with beloved family members and friends at our side.

President Russell M. Nelson taught:

> God . . . sent His Only Begotten Son to atone for us and to show us the way. The godly power available to all who love and follow Jesus Christ is the power to heal us, strengthen us, cleanse us from sin, and magnify us to do things we could never do on our own. Our Savior is the Divine Exemplar who marked the path that we are to follow. . . .
>
> There is always a way back. Jesus Christ (and His gospel) is the way. You have not committed any sin so serious that you are beyond the reach of the Savior's love and atoning grace. As you take steps to repent and follow God's laws, you will begin to feel just how much Heavenly Father and His Beloved Son want you back home with Them! They want you to be happy. They will do anything within Their power that does not violate your agency or Their laws to help you come back. . . .
>
> Exaltation is not easy. Requirements include a focused and persistent effort to keep God's laws, rigorously repenting when we don't. But the reward for doing so is far greater than anything we

can imagine, because it brings us joy here and "never-ending happiness" (Mosiah 2:41) hereafter.[251]

Armed with power from the Atonement of Jesus Christ and with the loving support of fellow Saints who are His body, we will be able to return to the presence of our loving heavenly parents and partake of that never-ending happiness. This is what is modeled in the temple and is the purpose of our covenants there. By focusing on Jesus Christ and our covenants with Him, we will be able to gain that eternal happiness.

---

251. Russell M. Nelson, "The Love and Laws of God," 2.

5

Sustaining the Lord's Imperfect Leaders

THE TEMPLE ENDOWMENT TEACHES THE IMPORTANCE OF FOLLOWING living apostles and prophets. One way it does this is by including Peter, James, and John in a drama alongside Adam and Eve.[252] Because we are instructed to see ourselves in the role of Adam or Eve, this anachronistic inclusion of the Apostles is not likely meant to convey historical events but rather to teach us the importance of following the counsel of living prophets and apostles in our day. The endowment also includes a charge associated with the law of the gospel that pertains to our leaders: In order to ensure that we always have the Holy Ghost with us, we are directed, among other things, to avoid speaking evil of the Lord's anointed.

In the preface to the Doctrine and Covenants, the Lord is even more emphatic about the need to follow the direction of His prophets and apostles: "The day cometh that they who will not hear the voice

---

252. As stated in the introduction, the discussion of temple ordinances in this book tries to follow the guidelines presented by Elder David A. Bednar in His April 2019 general conference talk "Prepared to Obtain Every Needful Thing."

of the Lord, neither the voice of his servants, neither give heed to the words of the prophets and apostles, shall be cut off from among the people; for they have strayed from mine ordinances, and have broken mine everlasting covenant; they seek not the Lord to establish his righteousness, but every man walketh in his own way, and after the image of his own god" (D&C 1:14–16).

The statement that those who do not follow the voice of the Lord or His servants have "strayed from mine ordinance, and have broken mine everlasting covenant" includes straying from the ordinances and covenants of the temple. As Saints of God, we are under a covenant obligation to follow those who are called to lead us, especially those called as prophets and apostles.

At the same time, the Lord acknowledges that His servants are not perfect. In the same revelation, the Lord explained, "These commandments are of me, and were given unto my servants *in their weakness*, after the manner of their language, that they might come to understanding. And *inasmuch as they erred* it might be made known; And inasmuch as they sought wisdom they might be instructed; And *inasmuch as they sinned* they might be chastened, that they might repent; And inasmuch as they were humble they might be made strong, and blessed from on high, and receive knowledge from time to time" (D&C 1:24–28; emphasis added).

The Lord says that He knows His servants will make mistakes, but He expects them to learn from their errors and repent. However, their errors do not release us from our obligation to follow these chosen servants. At the end of this revelation, the Lord reaffirms His confidence in them, proclaiming, "Though the heavens and the earth pass away, my word shall not pass away, but shall all be fulfilled, whether by mine own voice or by the voice of my servants, it is the same" (D&C 1:38).

It is remarkable how much trust and confidence the Lord places in His prophets and apostles while acknowledging their weaknesses, errors, and even their sins. It is equally remarkable that He would instruct us to follow the voice of these flawed leaders as if it were God's own voice. This chapter will review this doctrine and give encouragement on how to follow it in today's world where the flaws of our leaders that we might not observe on our own are quickly broadcast across the internet for all to comment on and criticize.

The inclusion of Peter, James, and John in the temple drama provides interesting examples of faithful yet imperfect leadership. Peter denied knowing Jesus (see Matthew 26:69–75) and James and John sought special recognition from Jesus, upsetting the other Apostles (see Matthew 20:20–24; Mark 10:35–41). Yet these three are the men to whom Christ entrusted the leadership of His Church. They were imperfect, yet they were chosen to receive the keys of the priesthood on the Mount of Transfiguration (see Matthew 17; Mark 9; Luke 9). They were flawed, yet Christ turned over the leadership of His kingdom on earth to their care after His ascension.

Prophets Are Not Infallible

There is a joke that goes something like this: Catholics teach that their popes are infallible, yet their members don't believe it; Latter-day Saints teach that their prophets are fallible, yet their members also don't believe that.

A difficulty with our Church's doctrine on the fallibility of its leaders is that, while we do believe that our leaders can make mistakes, we also believe that we should sustain, follow, and uphold them. Logically, this does not add up. How can we be expected to follow leaders who are known to make mistakes? Nevertheless, the scriptures give many examples of fallible prophets, and we know that God's people were expected to follow them—not to repeat their personal mistakes but to obey their counsel.

There are many scriptural examples of imperfect prophets. Moses was kept from entering the promised land with the children of Israel because of disobedience. He chose to do things his own way instead of the Lord's way when he needed to get water from a rock for the thirsty Israelites. The prophet Nathan also made a mistake. When David sought Nathan's approval to build a temple, the prophet initially gave that approval, but then the Lord visited Nathan and told him that he had been wrong to do so and that David's son, Solomon, would build the temple.

The prophet Jonah is well known for fleeing from a missionary assignment given by God and then being swallowed by a whale as a consequence. Another scriptural example of a leader's mistake comes from Peter. Before ascending up into heaven, Christ told his disciples, "Go ye into all the world, and preach the gospel to every creature" (Mark 16:15). Yet Peter had to receive a separate revelation to correct an apparent cultural bias that this instruction meant they should go only to the Jews who were scattered in the world.

Joseph Smith also made mistakes. Repeatedly in the Doctrine and Covenants, the Lord reprimanded Joseph or said He forgave Joseph of his sins.[253] No wonder Joseph Smith taught that "a prophet was a prophet only when he was acting as such."[254]

Joseph was given gifts in spiritual matters much more than in temporal matters. In Kirtland, he supported the formation of a financial institution called the Kirtland Safety Society, but it turned out not to be very safe and failed during a nationwide financial crisis. At the time, many considered Joseph to be a fallen prophet, and some brethren met secretly to scheme about how they could remove him as leader of the Church. They made the mistake of inviting Brigham Young to one of their clandestine meetings. He later described what happened: "I rose up, and in a plain and forcible manner told them that Joseph was a Prophet, and I knew it, and they might rail and slander him as much as they pleased, they could not destroy the appointment of the Prophet of God, they could only destroy their own authority, cut the thread that bound them to the Prophet and to God and sink themselves to hell."[255] Brigham sustained Joseph in spite of Joseph's shortcomings.

Sister Sheri Dew explained, "Prophets are mortal and are being tested just as we are. Being ordained as special witnesses of Jesus Christ gives them unique spiritual privileges, but it does not magically absolve them of human weakness. Further, I've never heard a

---

253. See D&C 3:6–8; 64:5–7; 90:1; 93:47; 110:5; 132:48–50. On more than twenty other occasions, the Lord also declared forgiveness for other early Church leaders.
254. Joseph Smith, in *History of the Church*, 5:265.
255. *Teachings of Presidents of the Church: Brigham Young* (1997), 79.

prophet claim perfection. Have you? Can you think of any scriptural prophet who didn't demonstrate some weakness? (See Mormon 9:31.) Moroni even acknowledged 'imperfections' in the Book of Mormon (see Mormon 8:12)."[256]

Elder Bruce R. McConkie said, "With all their inspiration and greatness, prophets are yet mortal men with imperfections common to mankind in general. They have their opinions and prejudices and are left to work out their problems without inspiration in many instances. . . . Thus the opinions and views, even of a prophet, may contain error, unless those opinions and views were inspired by the Spirit."[257]

President George Q. Cannon said, "If men whom [the Lord] chooses are fallible, that is His business. He requires on our part obedience to His will, as it is made manifest through the man whom He has chosen."[258] And Joseph Smith himself stated, "I never told you I was perfect; but there is no error in the revelations which I have taught."[259] There is a key in that statement: We should look primarily at the inspired teachings and revelations of the prophets as we seek guidance for our own lives.

Moroni advised, "Condemn me not because of mine imperfection, neither my father . . . ; but rather give thanks unto God that he hath made manifest unto you our imperfections, that ye may learn to be more wise than we have been" (Mormon 9:31). Sometimes we rightfully do see imperfections in our Church leaders; however, giving them the time and grace to take missteps and then correct themselves can give us faith in our own ability to be guided by God, to make mistakes, and then to correct ourselves. Elder Allen D. Haynie said, "A prophet is someone God has personally prepared, called, corrected,

---

256. Sheri Dew, "Prophets Can See Around Corners" (Brigham Young University–Hawaii devotional, Nov. 2, 2022), speeches.byuh.edu.

257. Bruce R. McConkie, "Are General Authorities Human?," *New Era*, Jan. 1973.

258. George Q. Cannon, in *Journal of Discourses*, 24:276.

259. *Teachings of the Prophet Joseph Smith*, sel. Joseph Fielding Smith (1976), 368.

inspired, rebuked, sanctified, and sustained. That is why we are never spiritually at risk in following prophetic counsel."[260]

In spite of their imperfections, the Lord still uses prophets to achieve His purposes, and He commands His Saints not to criticize them. President Ezra Taft Benson told this story about Brigham Young:

> President Brigham Young revealed that on one occasion he was tempted to be critical of the Prophet Joseph Smith regarding a certain financial matter. He said that the feeling did not last for more than perhaps thirty seconds. That feeling, he said, caused him great sorrow in his heart. The lesson he gave to members of the Church in his day may well be increased in significance today because the devil continues more active:
>
> "I clearly saw and understood, *by the spirit of revelation manifested to me*, that if I was to harbor a thought in my heart that Joseph could be wrong in anything, I would begin to lose confidence in him, and that feeling would grow from step to step, and from one degree to another, until at last I would have the same lack of confidence in his being the mouthpiece for the Almighty. . . .
>
> "I repented of my unbelief, and that too, very suddenly; I repented about as quickly as I committed the error. It was not for me to question whether Joseph was dictated by the Lord at all times and under all circumstances. . . .
>
> "It was not my prerogative to call him in question with regard to any act of his life. He was God's servant, and not mine. He did not belong to the people but to the Lord, and was doing the work of the Lord." (In *Journal of Discourses*, 4:297.)[261]

When President Wilford Woodruff was criticized by some members of the Church for ending plural marriage, he defended his actions, saying, "The Lord will never permit me or any other man who stands as President of this Church to lead you astray. . . . It is not in the mind of God" (Official Declaration 1). Similarly, President Dieter F. Uchtdorf has said, "This is the Church of Jesus Christ. God will not

---

260. Allen D. Haynie, "A Living Prophet for the Latter Days," *Liahona*, May 2023, 25.
261. Ezra T. Benson, "Valiant in the Testimony of Jesus," *Ensign*, May 1982, 64.

allow His Church to drift from its appointed course or fail to fulfill its divine destiny."[262]

This doesn't mean that there won't be some challenges along the way. The Lord warned us that following the prophet will sometimes test our patience and faith. Speaking of how Church members are to treat the prophet's counsel, the Lord said, "Thou shalt give heed unto all his words and commandments which he shall give unto you as he receiveth them, walking in all holiness before me; For his word ye shall receive, as if from mine own mouth, in all patience and faith" (D&C 21:4–5).

Following the prophet "in all patience and faith" implies that we may not understand the reasons for everything that he tells us. In fact, it may be that the prophet himself does not fully understand the reasons behind the direction he receives. Nevertheless, the Lord said we should treat the prophet's counsel as if it came from the Lord's own mouth. He then added this promise: "For by doing these things the gates of hell shall not prevail against you; yea, and the Lord God will disperse the powers of darkness from before you, and cause the heavens to shake for your good, and his name's glory" (D&C 21:6). What a powerful promise! I want to be a recipient of that promise.

We can accept that our leaders make mistakes, *and* we can follow their counsel and direction. If we think that something they have said might not be inspired by God, then I believe that the wisest course of action is to nonetheless follow their direction until mistakes or misunderstandings come to light—theirs or our own. They are honest and good men doing their best in their callings, and we can trust that they have the best interests of God's kingdom and His children at heart. Sometimes we simply need to follow the counsel the Lord once gave to Joseph Smith: "Hold your peace until I shall see fit to make all things known unto the world concerning the matter" (D&C 10:37).

In 1970 President Harold B. Lee said, "We have some tight places to go before the Lord is through with this church and the world in this dispensation, which is the last dispensation, which shall usher in the coming of the Lord. The gospel was restored to prepare a people ready

---

262. Dieter F. Uchtdorf, "Come Join With Us," *Ensign* or *Liahona*, Nov. 2013, 23.

to receive him. The power of Satan will increase; we see it in evidence on every hand. There will be inroads within the Church. . . . We will see those who profess membership but secretly are plotting and trying to lead people not to follow the leadership that the Lord has set up to preside in this church."[263]

More than fifty years later, we are seeing this prophecy being fulfilled. The internet is full of criticism from members and former members who try to change or tear down the Church. They frequently attack our Church leaders, and therefore they do not qualify for the blessing promised to those who follow the counsel of the Lord's prophets and apostles "in all patience and faith." We should be careful not to get drawn into their mindset.

Disagreeing without Being Disagreeable

Does our doctrine mean that we cannot disagree with our Church leaders? No. In fact, the Lord has instructed His Saints that they should judge all things related to the Church. He said, "For it shall come to pass that the inhabitants of Zion shall judge all things pertaining to Zion. And liars and hypocrites shall be proved by them, and they who are not apostles and prophets shall be known. And even the bishop, who is a judge, and his counselors, if they are not faithful in their stewardships shall be condemned, and others shall be planted in their stead" (D&C 64:38–40).

Brigham Young expressed a concern that Church members will accept everything their leaders say without question:

> I am more afraid that this people have so much confidence in their leaders that they will not inquire for themselves of God whether they are led by Him. I am fearful they settle down in a state of blind self-security, trusting their eternal destiny in the hands of their leaders with a reckless confidence that in itself would thwart the purposes of God in their salvation, and weaken that influence they could give to their leaders, did they know for themselves, by the revelations of Jesus, that they are led in the right way. Let every man and woman know, by the whispering of the Spirit of God to

---

263. Harold B. Lee, in Conference Report, Oct. 1970, 152; punctuation updated.

themselves, whether their leaders are walking in the path the Lord dictates, or not.[264]

On another occasion, President Young said, "I say to all, to my brethren and sisters and to strangers, if we teach anything that is good, receive it, I beseech you. If we have any good in our doctrine, believe it and embrace it, it will do you good. If we have errors, do not embrace them."[265]

In more recent times, Elder D. Todd Christofferson was asked by a reporter, "Can members of the church, say, support gay marriage, or other things that . . . the Church teaches against?" The Apostle responded:

> Well, there is a diversity of opinion among church members [regarding same-sex marriage]. And that's always been true, I guess, on many subjects over the years, and we don't have qualms about that. I mean we urge people to take part, for example, in the political process, and we don't tell them how to vote or who to vote for, but that they exercise their own good judgment and make their decisions. Obviously, that's different than when somebody attacks the Church, per se, or tries to hinder its work. But anybody pursuing their view of what ought to happen in the community—that's what we hope to see, frankly.[266]

Elder Christofferson later talked about the ways we can disagree, saying, "Unity does not require sameness, but it does require harmony. We can have our hearts knit together in love, be one in faith and doctrine, and still cheer for different teams, disagree on various political issues, debate about goals and the right way to achieve them, and many other such things. But we can never disagree or contend with anger or contempt for one another."[267] Anger and contempt are im-

---

264. Brigham Young, in *Journal of Discourses*, 9:150.
265. Brigham Young, in *Journal of Discourses*, 13:335.
266. J. Max Wilson, "LDS Apostle D. Todd Christofferson on Disagreeing with the Church about Same-Sex Marriage," Sixteen Small Stones, last modified June 28, 2015, https://www.sixteensmallstones.org/lds-apostle-d-todd-christofferson-on-disagreeing-with-the-church-about-same-sex-marriage/; minor edits made.
267. D. Todd Christofferson, "One in Christ," *Liahona*, May 2023.

portant qualifiers. As President Gordon B. Hinckley once said, "We can politely disagree without being disagreeable."[268]

As affirmed earlier, in the temple we promise to avoid evil speaking of the Lord's anointed. The Guide to the Scriptures defines "Evil Speaking" as "saying things that are wrong, hurtful, and wicked. Often in scripture such speaking is directed at a person with the specific intent to cause pain."[269] So evil speaking is not merely voicing disagreement; it involves language intended to cause harm. Also, although "the Lord's anointed" refers primarily to our Church leaders, in a broader sense it can include any who have received their washings and anointings in the temple. Everyone deserves to be treated respectfully. In fact, the following scriptures prohibit evil speaking of anyone:

- "Wherefore laying aside all malice, and all guile, and hypocrisies, and envies, all evil speakings, As newborn babes, desire the sincere milk of the word, that ye may grow thereby" (1 Peter 2:1–2).
- "And see that there is no iniquity in the church, neither hardness with each other, neither lying, backbiting, nor evil speaking" (D&C 20:54).
- "Thou shalt not speak evil of thy neighbor, nor do him any harm" (D&C 42:27).

So we should not speak evil of any person. However, speaking evil of our Church leaders is especially harmful because it attacks not only the individuals but also the institution. Our Church leaders are not so much concerned about their personal social stature as they are concerned about the stature of the Church and a need to encourage respect for the callings and keys they hold. This doctrine is not in place because our leaders cannot handle criticism. Anyone who has served in any leadership calling has learned the value of developing a thick skin. Our general Church leaders have enough emotional maturity to not take critical remarks personally but rather as opportunities for greater understanding or improvement. The kingdom of God is their primary concern.

---

268. *Teachings of Presidents of the Church: Gordon B. Hinkley* (2016), 278.
269. Guide to the Scriptures, "Evil Speaking," Gospel Library.

Paul admonished the early Saints: "And we beseech you, brethren, to know [i.e., acknowledge or respect[270]] them which labour among you, and are over you in the Lord, and admonish you; And to esteem them very highly in love *for their work's sake*" (1 Thessalonians 5:12–13; emphasis added). Paul's point is that we need to respect those who preside over us for the sake of the work of God, not for their personal aggrandizement.

Miriam and Aaron learned a hard lesson directly from God about the importance of treating their prophet brother, Moses, with respect. They did more than disagree with Moses—they spoke against him and tried to place themselves in a leadership status equal to him. By so doing, Miriam and Aaron actively sought to diminish the standing of Moses before all of Israel. God used this episode to teach a lesson in typical, dramatic, Old Testament fashion. The story is told in Numbers 12:

> And Miriam and Aaron spake against Moses because of the Ethiopian woman whom he had married: for he had married an Ethiopian woman.
>
> And they said, Hath the Lord indeed spoken only by Moses? hath he not spoken also by us? And the Lord heard it.
>
> (Now the man Moses was very meek, above all the men which were upon the face of the earth.)
>
> And the Lord spake suddenly unto Moses, and unto Aaron, and unto Miriam, Come out ye three unto the tabernacle of the congregation. And they three came out.
>
> And the Lord came down in the pillar of the cloud, and stood in the door of the tabernacle, and called Aaron and Miriam: and they both came forth.
>
> And he said, Hear now my words: If there be a prophet among you, I the Lord will make myself known unto him in a vision, and will speak unto him in a dream.
>
> My servant Moses is not so, who is faithful in all mine house.
>
> With him will I speak mouth to mouth, even apparently [i.e., clearly], and not in dark speeches [i.e., not in riddles]; and the

---

270. The terms *acknowledge* and *respect* come from the New International Version and the Thomas Wayment translation, respectively.

similitude of the Lord shall he behold: wherefore then were ye not afraid to speak against my servant Moses?

And the anger of the Lord was kindled against them; and he departed.

And the cloud departed from off the tabernacle; and, behold, Miriam became leprous, white as snow. (Numbers 12:1–10)

Aaron then acknowledged their sin and asked Moses to forgive them and to seek healing from God for Miriam. Moses did so, but the Lord required that the journey of Israel be halted while Miriam was shut out of the camp for seven days of purification. It is likely that all of the camp of Israel spoke of little else during those seven days. It was a dramatic lesson about not speaking evil of the Lord's anointed.

I believe that God reprimanded Miriam and Aaron not merely because they disagreed with Moses but because of *how* they disagreed. It is acceptable to differ with leaders of the Church, both local and general, but we must not speak against them in ways that are insulting, malicious, or spoken with contempt. And we should never seek to undermine the Church and its mission. We are covenant-bound to sustain our leaders in ways that will strengthen the Church.

The Purposes of Prophets and Apostles

The primary purpose of prophets and apostles is to testify of Jesus Christ. Even Jesus Himself was called a prophet, and He testified of His own mission. When He appeared to the Nephites, He said, "Behold, I am he of whom Moses spake, saying: A prophet shall the Lord your God raise up unto you of your brethren, like unto me; . . . Verily I say unto you, . . . all the prophets . . . , as many as have spoken, have testified of me" (3 Nephi 20:23–24). Nephi's brother Jacob similarly declared, "Behold, I say unto you that none of the prophets have written, nor prophesied, save they have spoken concerning this Christ" (Jacob 7:11).[271]

Elder Neil L. Andersen affirmed that "a prophet's greatest responsibility and most precious gift to us is his sure witness, his certain

---

271. See also Alma 34:6–7; Helaman 8:14–19; 3 Nephi 10:15–16.

knowledge, that Jesus is the Christ."[272] No wonder John the Beloved wrote that "the testimony of Jesus is the spirit of prophecy" (Revelation 19:10).

The Apostle Paul instructed the Ephesians more generally about the importance of prophets and apostles: "Now therefore ye are no more strangers and foreigners, but fellowcitizens with the Saints, and of the household of God; And are built upon the foundation of the apostles and prophets, Jesus Christ himself being the chief corner stone; In whom all the building fitly framed together groweth unto an holy temple in the Lord: In whom ye also are builded together for an habitation of God through the Spirit" (Ephesian 2:19–22).

Paul was saying that prophets and apostles, aligned with Christ as the cornerstone, are "fitly framed together" to form the foundation of a metaphorical temple. As fellow Saints, our lives should be built within the superstructure of this temple, which becomes the habitation of God when the Spirit is in us. Paul's metaphor makes a connection between temple worship and the need to build our lives on the foundation of prophets and apostles. It is no wonder that following Peter, James, and John is modeled in the temple drama!

Later in the same epistle, Paul explained why the Lord calls prophets, apostles, and other priesthood officers: "And he gave some, apostles; and some, prophets; and some, evangelists; and some, pastors and teachers; For the perfecting of the saints, for the work of the ministry, for the edifying of the body of Christ: Till we all come in the unity of the faith, and of the knowledge of the Son of God, unto a perfect man, unto the measure of the stature of the fulness of Christ: That we henceforth be no more children, tossed to and fro, and carried about with every wind of doctrine" (Ephesians 4:11–14).

This passage outlines several of the purposes of prophets and apostles:

1. Prophets and apostles are called "for the perfecting of the saints, for the work of the ministry, for the edifying of the body of Christ." We fellow Saints are that body of Christ (see 1 Corinthians 12:12–27), and the purpose of "the work of

---

272. Neil L. Andersen, "The Prophet of God," *Ensign* or *Liahona*, May 2018, 27.

the ministry" is to edify us (meaning to build us up) and to perfect us (meaning to improve us). We must be willing to follow the counsel of prophets and apostles if those outcomes are to be achieved.

2. Prophets and apostles are called to bring us to a "unity of the faith." This is why we have one head apostle, who is also our prophet, with a hierarchical Church organization under him. This structure brings unity to the Church, and with that unity comes strength. It keeps us from going in different directions.

3. Prophets and apostles are called to bring us to "the knowledge of the Son of God." This confirms the primary purpose for these leaders, already discussed: All prophets and apostles testify of Jesus Christ.

4. Prophets and apostles are called "unto a perfect man, unto the measure of the stature of the fulness of Christ." In this statement, Paul emphasizes the desired outcome for the work of all priesthood leaders, which is to guide us all to become perfect like Christ, or, as Moroni said, to help us to "come unto Christ, and be perfected in him" (Moroni 10:32).

The first and final points are connected. They emphasize that we still need to progress, both individually and institutionally. We all need perfecting, whether we are a leader or a follower. Sister Sheri Dew observed, "Prophets, seers, and revelators continue to learn, just as we do. For that reason, some may wonder about Church policies that change. Were the earlier policies wrong? Honestly, I don't know. But it seems just as likely that changes in policy reflect the maturing of the Church itself, not to mention our maturing as its members. President Nelson has repeatedly stressed that the Restoration is on-going."[273]

As we, the body of the Church, progress, adjustments in Church policy will naturally happen in ways that reflect this maturing. At the same time, our leaders themselves are also progressing. Nevertheless,

---

273. Sheri L. Dew, "Celestial Training in a Telestial World" (BYU Women's Conference address, May 5, 2023), https://womensconference.ce.byu.edu/sites/womensconference.ce.byu.edu/files/sheri_dew_-_celestial_training_in_a_telestial_world_-_may_5_2023-1.pdf.

they are some of the best men alive on the earth, and I consider it an honor to follow their leadership. They are good and honorable men and are more worthy to receive direction from God than I will ever be. I trust them, and I am comfortable following their leadership as we all grow together "unto the measure of the stature of the fulness of Christ."

The second point above deserves further discussion. Unity in the Church is a paramount reason we have prophets and apostles. By following these leaders, we will not be scattered in our thinking, each of us "carried about with every wind of doctrine" according to our individual interests and biases. Unity in any organization is best achieved when a leader or a leading body sets the direction and vision and everyone else in that organization aligns their actions with that direction.

In my career in corporate America, every year my company presented new business goals established by top company leaders, and I was required to establish my own personal engineering goals in support of those broader business goals. A hierarchical structure like this fosters unity because it helps everyone align with the direction specified from above. It enables faster progress toward the company goals because everyone's actions are aligned in the same direction.

Sometimes the leaders of a company discover that adjustments to their goals need to be made mid-year. In other words, they see that they made some errors in judgment or that factors around them changed, so they need to modify their goals. If their employees make similar adjustments in a unified way, then the corrections at the top level quickly steer the entire company in a better direction. If the company has a culture where everyone consistently follows the direction of top leadership, then the entire company can shift with agility, unity, and focus.

This analogy to the business world is not perfect, but it illustrates the value of being united under the direction of our Church leaders. It is not an issue of blind obedience. We are talking about following righteous leaders who hold priesthood keys. It is only in this context that a covenant to follow our leaders makes sense in the first place. There are some business leaders in the world that I would never want to follow; however, within the kingdom of God, I have full confidence that our leaders are sincerely trying to follow Jesus Christ. If they ever steer us in a direction where a course correction is needed, I am confident that the Lord will guide them to make the appropriate adjustments. President James E. Faust said, "We make no claim of infallibility or perfection in the prophets, seers, and revelators. Yet I humbly state that I have sat in the company of these men, and I believe their greatest desire is to know and do the will of our Heavenly Father."[274]

Speaking of New Testament times, President Henry B. Eyring taught, "The ministry of the apostles and prophets in that day, as it is today, was to bring the children of Adam and Eve to a unity of the faith in Jesus Christ. The ultimate purpose of what they taught, and of what we teach, is to unite . . . all of the family of Adam and Eve who will choose it."[275] We all need to be united, and following the leadership of prophets and apostles helps us achieve this.

How God Guides His Prophets and Apostles

Prophets do not serve in isolation. The Lord often provides inspiration to prophets through counsel from other people. For example, Jethro counseled his son-in-law Moses, "This thing is too heavy for thee; thou art not able to perform it thyself alone. Hearken now unto my voice, I will give thee counsel, and God shall be with thee" (Exodus 18:18–19). Jethro then suggested to Moses that he appoint lower judges and added, "If thou shalt do this thing, *and God command thee so*, then thou shalt be able to endure" (Exodus 18:23; emphasis added). This was Jethro's way of saying, "Here is my counsel, but you need to confirm with the Lord that it is right." Moses later called "seventy men of the elders of Israel" to further assist him (see Numbers 11:16–17). We might call this the original Council of the Seventy, and this body provided an additional source of counsel for the prophet as well as for all the children of Israel.

When Jesus Christ began His ministry, he instituted this same method of leadership by council with the calling of His Twelve

---

274. James E. Faust, "Continuous Revelation," *Ensign*, Nov. 1989, 10.
275. Henry B. Eyring, "That We May Be One," *Ensign*, May 1998, 66.

Apostles. This council led the Church after Christ's ascension. Today we are led by a council formed by the First Presidency and the Quorum of the Twelve Apostles, and they are supported by the Seventies. The president of the Church does not decide things on his own.

While serving as an Apostle, President Russell M. Nelson explained:

> The calling of 15 men to the holy apostleship provides great protection for us as members of the Church. Why? Because decisions of these leaders must be unanimous. Can you imagine how the Spirit needs to move upon 15 men to bring about unanimity? These 15 men have varied educational and professional backgrounds, with differing opinions about many things. Trust me! These 15 men—prophets, seers, and revelators—know what the will of the Lord is when unanimity is reached! They are committed to see that the Lord's will truly will be done. . . . They learn how to hear the voice of the Lord through the whisperings of the Spirit.[276]

President Boyd K. Packer taught that this council brings a mixture of wisdom and human frailty. He said, "We function . . . in council assembled. That provides safety for the Church and a high comfort level for each of us who is personally accountable. Under the plan, men of very ordinary capacity may be guided through counsel and inspiration to accomplish extraordinary things. [However,] even with the best of intentions, it does not always work the way it should. Human nature may express itself on occasion, *but not to the permanent injury of the work.*"[277] In other words, our leaders use the power of councils to provide checks and balances, but even then, they recognize that they do not always get things right. Nevertheless, the Lord will redirect them if needed, and His work will not be permanently hindered. His redeeming influence can correct any mistake over time.

This points to another principle of prophetic leadership: Prophets work by inspiration. The Lord declared, "Yea, behold, I will tell you in your mind and in your heart, by the Holy Ghost, which shall come

---

276. Russell M. Nelson, "Sustaining the Prophets," *Ensign* or *Liahona*, Nov. 2014, 75.

277. Boyd K. Packer, "I Say unto You, Be One" (Brigham Young University devotional, Feb. 12, 1991), 3–4, speeches.byu.edu; emphasis added.

upon you and which shall dwell in your heart. Now, behold, this is the spirit of revelation; behold, this is the spirit by which Moses brought the children of Israel through the Red Sea on dry ground" (D&C 8:2–3). So Moses, who spoke with God in a burning bush, did not always have such dramatic revelations. Most of the guidance he received came to his mind and heart through the Holy Ghost.

Brother John S. Tanner, former President of BYU–Hawaii, said:

> I will never forget a conversation [I had] with President Harold B. Lee. . . . [He] had talked freely that day about a new program the Church had just announced. He then remarked that he had just reread the minutes of the meetings in which the program had been formulated and that he saw now, in retrospect, that the Lord had been guiding the deliberations all along. What a remarkable description of revelation! The Lord's guidance was not fully evident, even to his prophet, until President Lee turned to survey the terrain he had traversed. The Lord led his servant, yes, but one step at a time.[278]

The inspiration that guides our prophets and apostles comes from Jesus Christ, who is the head of this Church. This is His Church, and He will ultimately guide His leaders where He wants the Church to go, even if they temporarily deviate in some way. As Sister Dew so beautifully articulated, "When we follow the prophet, we are actually following and placing our trust in Jesus Christ. For He has promised that His words will all be fulfilled, 'whether by [His] own voice or by the voice of [His] servants, it is the same' (D&C 1:38)."[279]

Elder D. Todd Christofferson explained:

> Council deliberations will often include a weighing of canonized scriptures, the teachings of Church leaders, and past practice. But in the end, just as in the New Testament Church, the objective is not simply consensus among council members but revelation from God. It is a process involving both reason and faith for obtaining the mind and will of the Lord.

---

278. John S. Tanner, "One Step at a Time" (Brigham Young University devotional, June 30, 1992), 4, speeches.byu.edu.

279. Sheri L. Dew, "Prophets Can See Around Corners."

At the same time it should be remembered that not every statement made by a Church leader, past or present, necessarily constitutes doctrine. It is commonly understood in the Church that a statement made by one leader on a single occasion often represents a personal, though well-considered, opinion, not meant to be official or binding for the whole Church.[280]

There is safety in following the united voice of the fifteen men who lead our Church. God guides these prophets and apostles through direct inspiration and through counsel with one another and with those they choose to consult regarding specific matters. They do not need the additional counsel of seventeen million Church members. As Elder Neal A. Maxwell said, "Prophets need tutoring, as do we all. However, this is something the Lord seems quite able to manage without requiring a host of helpers."[281]

Following Those with Priesthood Keys

One of the controlling principles of leadership in The Church of Jesus Christ of Latter-day Saints is the concept of priesthood keys. An earlier chapter discussed the restoration of the keys pertaining specifically to temple work; however, priesthood keys affect all areas of Church administration. The Church's Guide to the Scriptures defines priesthood keys as follows:

> Keys are the rights of presidency, or the power given to man by God to direct, control, and govern God's priesthood on earth. Priesthood holders called to positions of presidency receive keys from those in authority over them. Priesthood holders use the priesthood only within the limits outlined by those who hold the keys. The President of the Church is the only person on earth who holds and is authorized to exercise all priesthood keys (see D&C 107:65–67, 91–92; 132:7).[282]

---

280. D. Todd Christofferson, "The Doctrine of Christ," *Ensign* or *Liahona*, May 2012, 88.
281. Neal A. Maxwell, "A Brother Offended," *Ensign*, May 1982, 39.
282. Guide to the Scriptures, "Keys of the Priesthood," Gospel Library.

President Joseph Fielding Smith explained priesthood keys this way: "These keys are the right of presidency; they are the power and authority to govern and direct all of the Lord's affairs on earth. Those who hold them have power to govern and control the manner in which all others may serve in the priesthood. All of us [brethren] may hold the priesthood, but we can only use it as authorized and directed so to do by those who hold the keys."[283]

In our Church, we respect those who hold priesthood keys. These are the primary leaders we promise to follow as part of our temple covenants. Whether we agree with them or not, they carry the privilege and responsibility of directing a certain scope of the Lord's work on the earth. This is part of our organizational structure and culture, and if we choose to be covenant members, we agree to abide by this framework.

A couple of years after my mission, I was invited by a young lady to go with her to a family reunion. The year was 1980, and Elder Eldred G. Smith, Patriarch Emeritus of the Church, attended the reunion. He had brought several family heirlooms to display, and he talked about his great-great-grandfather, Hyrum Smith. After his presentation, I was able to have a personal conversation with Elder Smith. Less than one year earlier, he had been "honorably relieved of all duties and responsibilities pertaining to the office of Patriarch to the Church,"[284] and no one was sustained to replace him. I was surprised to see that he was still relatively young and seemed healthy and robust. In that personal setting, I felt comfortable asking Elder Smith about the Church's decision to retire his position, considering the references to it in Doctrine and Covenants 124. He told me that when President Kimball told him of his imminent release, he reminded the prophet of that revelation, and the prophet replied to him, "Well, we can change things, can't we?" Elder Smith then said to me conclusively, "And they can!" He did not say it with a tone of resentment or disappointment. He said it with confidence that President Spencer W. Kimball held

---

283. Joseph Fielding Smith, "Eternal Keys and the Right to Preside," *Ensign*, July 1972, 87.

284. N. Eldon Tanner, "The Sustaining of Church Officers," *Ensign*, Nov. 1979, 18.

all the keys of the priesthood and the responsibility to make changes in the Church under inspiration and revelation from God. Making changes within the scope of their calling is a prerogative of all who hold priesthood keys.

I have lived under the leadership of nine presidents of the Church, and each one of them has had his own unique style and emphasis. There is no question in my mind that all of them have been directed by the Lord, but I have also seen that He has allowed each one to contribute to the development of the Church in ways that reflected the personality and interests of the individual prophet. These chosen men of Christ are His friends, and He has trusted them with the power and authority to make changes in the Church that He validates as if the changes had been declared directly from heaven by his own voice (see D&C 1:38).

Can you imagine what it must be like for Christ to have no peers? It must feel lonely at times. No wonder Jesus was happy to call His New Testament disciples His friends (see John 15:13). Likewise, to the early leaders of this dispensation, He said, "And as I said unto mine apostles, even so I say unto you, for you are mine apostles, even God's high priests; ye are they whom my Father hath given me; ye are my friends" (D&C 84:63). Later in the same revelation, the Lord added, "And again I say unto you, my friends, for from henceforth I shall call you friends, it is expedient that I give unto you this commandment, that ye become even as my friends in days when I was with them, traveling to preach the gospel in my power" (D&C 84:77). And in another revelation, the Lord said, "I will call you friends, for you are my friends, and ye shall have an inheritance with me" (D&C 93:45).

Sometimes our friends don't do everything the way we would like, but if they do the best they can and are loyal to us, we forgive them and accept their best efforts. Christ does the same with the leaders of His Church, for they are His friends. If they don't do everything perfectly, He has the power to make up for the deficits that ensue, whether He does so in this life or in the life to come. Nevertheless, He gives to these friends the right and responsibility to direct His Church by giving them priesthood keys.

I like to think about the relationship between Jesus Christ and Brigham Young. President Young presided over the Church for thirty-three years—longer than any other prophet. He led the migration of tens of thousands of Saints across the Great Plains of North America and oversaw their colonization in scores of new towns and settlements built in the desert valleys and rocky high places of the Intermountain West. One historian wrote of him, "Brigham Young dug canals, imported plants and animals, built railways and telegraphs; established industries and banks, constructed theatres and universities; and encouraged literature, music, and art. . . . He planned and erected temples and tabernacles, still used by his people today; they are the wonder of modern architects."[285] He also reestablished missionary work to nations around the globe, growing the Church from 26,000 to 115,000 members during his tenure.[286]

Brigham Young did all this while facing tremendous political opposition from the United States government, which sent an army to restrain him. I cannot imagine another person in the history of the world who could have accomplished all that he did to build up the kingdom of God in those early days of the modern Church. Yet he clearly made some mistakes. The Church has repudiated his teachings on blood atonement[287] and the Adam-God theory.[288] In addition, the race restrictions that Brigham Young institutionalized[289] have caused immeasurable pain for many members of the Church as well as limiting the spread of the gospel for more than a century to many who could have benefited from it.

---

285. Harold J. Shepstone, quoted in Emerson Roy West, *Profiles of the Presidents* (Deseret Book, 1980), 80.

286. See *2013 Church Almanac* (Deseret Book, 2012).

287. Blood atonement was formally denied and repudiated by the Church in a statement issued in 1889. See B. H. Roberts, "Blood Atonement," *A Comprehensive History of the Church*, 4:126–137.

288. See Spencer W. Kimball, "Our Own Liahona," *Ensign*, Nov. 1976, 77–79.

289. "In 1852, President Brigham Young publicly announced that men of black African descent could no longer be ordained to the priesthood" (Gospel Topics Essays, "Race and the Priesthood," Gospel Library).

I imagine that when Brigham passed to the other side of the veil, Jesus thanked His friend for all he had done to build up the kingdom of God and then had some strong words of reprimand for his mistakes, "for whom the Lord loveth he chasteneth" (Hebrews 12:6). I can also imagine the Lord assuring Brigham that he was still His friend, and that Christ would heal all wounds and correct all the errors of His chosen servant, even if it took more than a hundred years. Christ has time on His side.

In the meantime, during Brigham's watch, the kingdom of God grew with tens of thousands of people receiving saving ordinances and entering into covenant relationships with God. Temples were built and the great work of the gathering of Israel was expanded. None of this could have happened without respect for the keys of the priesthood that Brigham Young held. And because those priesthood keys were passed on to his successors, millions more of God's children have received the ordinances and covenants of salvation since then.

President Gordon B. Hinckley has said:

> We recognize that our forebears were human. They doubtless made mistakes. But the mistakes were minor, when compared with the marvelous work which they accomplished. . . . There was only one perfect man who ever walked the earth. The Lord has used imperfect people in the process of building his perfect society. If some of them occasionally stumbled, or if their characters may have been slightly flawed in one way or another, the wonder is the greater that they accomplished so much. . . .
>
> Brethren, the Church is true. Those who lead it have only one desire, and that is to do the will of the Lord. They seek his direction in all things. There is not a decision of significance affecting the Church and its people that is made without prayerful consideration, going to the fount of all wisdom for direction. Follow the leadership of the Church. God will not let his work be led astray.[290]

Those to whom the Lord has given priesthood keys have been entrusted with the right and authority to make decisions and set the direction of the Church. Even if they make mistakes, over time God will correct those errors and heal the wounds they cause if the

---

290. Gordon B. Hinckley, "Be Not Deceived," *Ensign*, Nov. 1983, 46.

wounded will turn to Him, for, as President Hinckley said, "God will not let His work be led astray."

Facing the Racial Policies of Past Leaders

After the historical race restrictions on the priesthood and temple work were lifted in 1978, Elder Bruce R. McConkie spoke at a BYU devotional about the change in policy and past attempts to justify it doctrinally, saying, "Forget everything that I have said, or what President Brigham Young or . . . whomsoever has said in days past that is contrary to the present revelation. *We spoke with a limited understanding* and without the light and knowledge that now has come into the world. We get our truth and our light line upon line and precept upon precept. We have now had added a new flood of intelligence and light on this particular subject, and it erases all the darkness and all the views and all the thoughts of the past. They don't matter any more."[291] Elder McConkie's statement makes it clear that prophets and apostles are progressing, just like the rest of us. We need to afford them the same grace we would wish for ourselves.

In an interview in 2006 for a PBS TV special, President Jeffrey R. Holland was asked about the folklore that had been used to justify the priesthood ban for Blacks from the days of Brigham Young until 1978. President Holland said, "I have to concede to my earlier colleagues. . . . They, I'm sure, in their own way, were doing the best they knew to give shape to [the policy], to give context for it, to give even history to it. All I can say is however well intended the explanations were, I think almost all of them were inadequate and/or wrong."[292]

President Holland's efforts to strike a balance between respecting the motivations of his "earlier colleagues" and acknowledging their errors is a noteworthy example for us all. It is an example of fulfilling a covenant commitment to avoid speaking evil of the Lord's anointed while being true to one's honest opinion. His response is consistent with the following counsel from President Henry B. Eyring:

---

291. Bruce R. McConkie, "All Are Alike unto God" (Brigham Young University devotional, Aug. 18, 1978), 2–3, speeches.byu.edu; emphasis added.

292. "Interview Jeffrey Holland | The Mormons," PBS, Mar. 4, 2006, https://www.pbs.org/mormons/interviews/holland.html.

President George Q. Cannon gave a warning that I pass on to you as my own. I believe he spoke the truth: "God has chosen His servants. He claims it as His prerogative to condemn them, if they need condemnation. He has not given it to us individually to censure and condemn them. No man, however strong he may be in the faith, however high in the Priesthood, can speak evil of the Lord's anointed and find fault with God's authority on the earth without incurring His displeasure. The Holy Spirit will withdraw himself from such a man, and he will go into darkness. This being the case, do you not see how important it is that we should be careful?"[293]

Brother Mauli Bonner is a Latter-day Saint of Black African descent who wrote, directed, and produced the film *His Name Is Green Flake*. This film is based on the true story of an enslaved Black man who became a Latter-day Saint pioneer in the days of Brigham Young. Brother Bonner was interviewed about the film and was asked his views on following imperfect leaders. He responded:

> When the prophets and apostles say in conference, "We're not perfect," I believe them. And I think we, as members of the Church, need to believe that as well, so that we can acknowledge that things were wrong, and that it's okay. It's okay to acknowledge that these men were flawed and made the wrong decision. We all know slavery was wrong. And I think Brigham was wrong. We all wish that didn't happen, and . . . it's okay to say that. . . . And I think he's on the other side [of the veil], hoping that we say that [and] not find ways around validating his imperfections. He's moved so far past that. And I feel like we do him a disservice—and those men and women who were enslaved a disservice—when we try to minimize what is wrong and what is right. The beauty of it all is that we are here now and have an opportunity to learn and do something good. That's what we have control over. We can't change what was. We were not there. But we are here now.[294]

---

293. Henry B. Eyring, "The Power of Sustaining Faith," *Ensign* or *Liahona*, May 2019, 59.

294. Morgan Jones, Mauli Bonner, and Paul Reeve, "Mauli Bonner and Paul Reeve: Understanding the History of Blacks in the Church," *All In—An LDS Living Podcast* (podcast), May 19, 2021, 27:48–29:13, https://www.ldsliving.com/all-in/mauli-bonner-and-paul-reeve-understanding-the-history-of-blacks-in-the-church; minor edits made.

Some people might question how a Black person can honorably remain a member of the Church knowing its racial past. This must be one of the most difficult issues any member could face. Yet Brother Bonner not only remains faithful, but he has also created a movie to encourage others to take inspiration from the story of Green Flake and stay faithful as well.

Many current members of the Church do not hesitate to characterize the race restrictions initiated by Brigham Young as a terrible mistake. However, others withhold judgment, wondering if there might have been some purpose for it known only to God. That is unknown, but we do know that President David O. McKay prayed for guidance on the matter, and he "did not feel impressed to lift the ban"[295] during his presidency.

While serving in a general Church calling as president of the Genesis Group, an auxiliary organization of the Church established for African American members, Brother Darius Gray taught the following, which he received by personal revelation and was told by President Gordon B. Hinckley that he could teach:

> The issue of race is a test for all Christians, Latter-day Saints included. The priesthood restriction was not imposed by God but was allowed by Him. Race was an assignment agreed to by primordial covenant. A host of statements attempt to justify the apparent inequity of mortal conditions by citing premortal disobedience. The scriptures, however, teach that many of life's most difficult circumstances are not punishments but may entail sacred callings, as in the story of Joseph who was sold into slavery by his brothers. What mortals mean as harm, God meant for good. The priesthood restriction along with other race-related challenges have been as a refiner's fire for both blacks and whites. Would blacks and whites allow pride and/or hatred to displace love?[296]

We can acknowledge the pain and suffering brought on by past race restrictions, and at the same time we can rejoice that Christ's

---

295. Gospel Topics Essays, "Race and the Priesthood," Gospel Library.
296. AffirmationLDS, "Affirmation Conference 2014 - Darius Gray (Keynote)," YouTube, Nov. 22, 2014, 10:35–11:41, https://www.youtube.com/watch?v=M0T7JHaNDmw&t=1s.

Atonement and His eternal gospel plan have the power to correct these and all other injustices that have occurred throughout the millennia of the earth's existence. The scope and influence of Christ's Atonement is infinite.

As we consider the questionable approaches taken by past leaders of the Church, it would be wise to adopt the attitude advocated by the apostle Paul: "Therefore judge nothing before the time, until the Lord come, who both will bring to light the hidden things of darkness, and will make manifest the counsels of the hearts: and then shall every man have praise of God" (1 Corinthians 4:5). Similarly, President J. Reuben Clark said, "We do not tell the Lord how to do things. He frames his own plans, draws his own blueprints, shapes his own course, conceives his own strategy, moves and acts as in his infinite knowledge and wisdom he determines. When lack-faiths and doubters and skeptics begin to map out the plans, methods, and procedures they would demand that God follow, they would do well to remember God's power, wisdom, knowledge, and authority."[297]

Regardless of how we think about these historical issues, we are blessed to live in a day when our current Church leaders do not carry any cultural baggage of racism in their hearts. President Holland told of the highly emotional feeling of joy he experienced when he first heard that the ban had been lifted:

> I started to cry, and I was absolutely uncontrollable. I felt my way to a chair . . . and I sort of slumped from the doorway into the chair and held my head, my face in my hands and sobbed. . . . There's no issue in all my life that I had prayed more regarding—praying that it would change, praying that it would come in due time. I was willing to have the Lord speak, and I was loyal to the position and the brethren and the whole concept, but there was nothing about which I had anguished more or about which I had prayed more. And for that to be said in my lifetime, when I wasn't sure it would

---

[297]. J. Reuben Clark Jr., "When Are Church Leaders' Words Entitled to the Claim of Scripture?," *Church News*, July 31, 1954, 9–10, https://prophetsseersandrevelators.wordpress.com/2013/09/06/when-are-church-leaders-words-entitled-to-the-claim-of-scripture-by-j-reuben-clark-jr/.

happen in my lifetime, . . . it was one of the absolute happiest days of my life.[298]

President Dallin H. Oaks had a similar emotional reaction when he first heard the news of the change in policy. He reminisced:

> My two sons and I were working in the yard . . . when the phone rang inside the house. . . . The caller was Elder Boyd K. Packer. He told me about the revelation on the priesthood, which was just being announced. We exchanged expressions of joy, and I walked back to the hillside. I sat down on the pile of dirt we had been moving and beckoned to my sons. As I told them that all worthy male members of the Church could now be ordained to the priesthood, I wept for joy. That is the scene etched in my memory of this unforgettable announcement 40 years ago—sitting on a pile of dirt and weeping as I told my sons of this divine revelation.[299]

The reactions of overpowering joy felt by these two future Apostles of God were similar to what I felt and what every Church member I knew felt when we first heard of the lifting of the priesthood ban in June of 1978. It was a time of rejoicing, for we all wanted God's children of every race to have full access to the blessing of the restored gospel, including priesthood and temple blessings.

President Russell M. Nelson has been clear on where the Church now stands on racism and prejudice. In the November 2020 general conference, he said:

> Each of us has a divine potential because each is a child of God. Each is equal in His eyes. The implications of this truth are profound. Brothers and sisters, please listen carefully to what I am about to say. God does not love one race more than another. His doctrine on this matter is clear. He invites all to come unto Him, "black and white, bond and free, male and female" (2 Nephi 26:33).
>
> I assure you that your standing before God is not determined by the color of your skin. Favor or disfavor with God is dependent

---

298. "Interview Jeffrey Holland."
299. Dallin H. Oaks, "President Oaks' Full Remarks from the LDS Church's 'Be One' Celebration," *Church News*, June 2, 2018.

upon your devotion to God and His commandments and not the color of your skin.

I grieve that our Black brothers and sisters the world over are enduring the pains of racism and prejudice. Today I call upon our members everywhere to lead out in abandoning attitudes and actions of prejudice. I plead with you to promote respect for all of God's children.[300]

Such prophetic declarations fill me with pride for the position of the Church today. Clearly we, as a Church, have progressed along with society in general. The Restoration of the fulness of the gospel continues to unfold. The following words from Brother Mauli Bonner exemplify the kind of positive attitude of support for our leaders that will continue to propel us forward as we prepare for the Second Coming of Jesus Christ. This quote is taken from the end of the interview about his film, in response to the question "What does it mean to you to be all in the gospel of Jesus Christ?"

> I think of all the early Saints [in] Jesus's time. . . . those Saints that stayed Christian after watching [Peter] deny Christ—that's as "all in" as you get. "All in" through someone's imperfections. How easy would it have been to say, "Okay, I'm not Christian anymore. If he's going to do that, and he walked with Christ, how can I stay?" But they did [stay]. And thank God they did because Christ lived and was real!
>
> I think of Green Flake and other enslaved pioneers and free early Black pioneers . . . giving their tithing and giving their labor to build the temple, knowing that they would not be able to seal their family together. . . . [For] an enslaved person who has only known their family to be torn apart, [the temple] was the place to heal that. And for that to not be [granted], but to stay faithful to the end, how then can I say "I'm out" when I don't agree with something? I'm not out. I'm all in. I'm all in because we are a growing, evolving, restoring Church.
>
> All I can do is pray for our leadership. Pray for them. They are men doing the best that they can, day in and day out. And if there's something I disagree with, Lord help me. Help me stay through it, because look at us now. There were enslaved pioneers and look at us

---

300. Russell M. Nelson, "Let God Prevail," *Ensign*, Nov. 2020, 94.

now. We are leading out [in the] Church. And I hope we continue to do that. So "all in" means if things aren't going well, don't chuck deuces. Stick your ground and stay for Christ. That's what you're in for.[301]

Those who leave the Church because of the mistakes of its leaders leave behind the fulness of the gospel of Jesus Christ. They leave behind the richness of the blessing of the Restoration and the possibility for exaltation with their families in the eternities. These blessings only come by sustaining the imperfect men who carry the priesthood keys of the work of salvation and exaltation—they who are wearing out their lives in service to Jesus Christ.

Does God Change?

Sometimes the changes our leaders make to Church policies and procedures may be influenced by their own personal biases or cultural influences, but I trust that the genesis of the vast majority of these changes is inspiration from heaven. The reality is that God sometimes directs the leaders of His church to change things. This is true in spite of the many scriptures stating that God does not change, such as the following.

- "For I am the Lord, I change not" (Malachi 3:6).
- "And behold, I say unto you he changeth not; if so he would cease to be God" (Mormon 9:19).
- "For I know that God is not . . . a changeable being; but he is unchangeable from all eternity to all eternity" (Moroni 8:18).
- "We know that there is a God in heaven, who is infinite and eternal, from everlasting to everlasting the same unchangeable God, the framer of heaven and earth, and all things which are in them" (D&C 20:17).

---

301. Jones, Bonner, and Reeve, "Mauli Bonner and Paul Reeve," 52:40–55:43; minor edits made.

In addition, there are at least ten verses that say that God or Jesus is the same yesterday, today, and forever.[302] The scriptures are clear: God does not change. And yet we find many examples in scripture where God has changed His approach toward mankind, including some shifts in what He commands us to do.

One notable example of a change in God's approach occurred with Moses. Joseph Smith's translation of Exodus 34 teaches us that when Moses came down from Mount Sinai the first time, he was prepared to give the fulness of the Melchizedek Priesthood to the father of each household, much like we see in the Church today. However, when Moses found the children of Israel reveling in sin and worshipping a golden calf, he reprimanded and punished them and then returned to Mount Sinai. When Moses came down the second time, he was authorized to share only a lesser, preparatory form of the priesthood—the Aaronic Priesthood—and only with the tribe of Levi. He also brought a strict law governing many details of life.

In the Book of Mormon, Abinadi commented on the law Moses instituted, saying, "It was expedient that there should be a law given to the children of Israel, yea, even a very strict law; for they were a stiffnecked people, quick to do iniquity, and slow to remember the Lord their God; Therefore there was a law given them, yea, a law of performances and of ordinances, a law which they were to observe strictly from day to day, to keep them in remembrance of God and their duty towards him" (Mosiah 13:29–30).

This affirms that God shifted His approach and created specific commandments around this new approach. This change was made in response to the nature of the people God was dealing with at the time.

An even bigger change in required rituals and ordinances came after the Atonement of Jesus Christ. Speaking from heaven before His appearance in ancient America, Jesus declared that the law of Moses was fulfilled, and He outlined a different law that must be followed in order to be saved: "Behold, I am Jesus Christ the Son of God. . . . behold, by me redemption cometh, and in me is the law of Moses

---

302. Scriptures that declare the constancy of God or Jesus include Hebrews 13:8; 1 Nephi 10:18; 2 Nephi 2:4; 27:23; 29:9; Alma 31:17; Mormon 9:9; Moroni 10:19; D&C 20:12; 35:1.

fulfilled. . . . And ye shall offer up unto me no more the shedding of blood; yea, your sacrifices and your burnt offerings shall be done away, for I will accept none of your sacrifices and your burnt offerings. And ye shall offer for a sacrifice unto me a broken heart and a contrite spirit. And whoso cometh unto me with a broken heart and a contrite spirit, him will I baptize with fire and with the Holy Ghost" (3 Nephi 9:15–20).

This change was a seismic shift in God's approach toward His children. To us, it was a beautiful change that makes the power of the Atonement of Jesus Christ clearer and more meaningful in our worship. However, for many Jews in the days of the early Apostles, this change was a stumbling block. Most Jews today still do not accept this change.

Another significant change was the shift from Saturday to Sunday as the day for observing the Sabbath. The early Christians met regularly on Sunday as a way of celebrating Christ's Resurrection (see Acts 20:7). They called Sunday "the Lord's Day," and in 1831 the Lord revealed that we should continue to observe our day of rest on the Lord's day (see D&C 59:10–12).

There have also been changes in God's instructions on what we should eat and drink. It used to be that pork was out and wine was in, but now wine is out and pork is in! There might have been practical reasons for these changes. In an era when clean water was not always available, it was probably often healthier to drink wine because the low levels of alcohol killed germs. And pork has long been known to be more likely to carry pathogens than most other meats if not properly cooked.[303] The prohibition on eating pork also provided a symbolic reminder to stay clean, both morally and physically, since swine were known for living in squalor and eating almost anything.

Regardless of the reasons, God has clearly changed His requirements and commandments many times. In both ancient and modern times, He has sometimes directed His prophets to change the

---

303. See Denise Minger, "4 Hidden Dangers of Pork," Healthline, June 22, 2017, https://www.healthline.com/nutrition/is-pork-bad; see also https://science.naturalnews.com/pork.html.

institutional policies and practices of His church and kingdom. God's Church is a "true and living church" (D&C 1:30).

Why then do so many scriptures state that God does not change? It appears that God occasionally makes some changes in order to support other things about Him that will never change. God's unchangeable anchors include His nature, His purpose, and His covenants. These three are constants with God and Jesus Christ.

1. God's nature does not change. His nature includes those principles that guide Him. Chief among these is His love, which is fixed and eternal. In fact, as John declared, "God is love" (1 John 4:16). If God initiates a change in a policy or procedure, it is probably out of love, and we should try to understand it that way.
2. God's purpose does not change. His purpose has been declared succinctly in this revealed truth: "For behold, this is my work and my glory—to bring to pass the immortality and eternal life of man" (Moses 1:39). If God needs to modify His instructions or commandments in a particular time and place in order to achieve this purpose, He will. An example of this was when God told Nephi to kill Laban (see 1 Nephi 4:5–19).
3. God's covenants do not change. His covenants are His word—His sure promises. He said, "My words cannot return void, for as they go forth out of my mouth they must be fulfilled" (Moses 4:30; see also D&C 1:38). Knowing the end from the beginning, God has not made any covenants that will not be fulfilled, and the scriptures repeatedly assure us that all His covenants and promises shall be fulfilled. The book of Psalms says, "He hath remembered his covenant for ever, the word which he commanded to a thousand generations" (Psalm 105:8).

The constancy of God's covenants is of particular interest to those of us who love temple worship. Elder Gerrit W. Gong has said, "Our God is a God of covenant. By His nature, He 'keepest covenant and showest mercy' (D&C 109:1). His covenants endure 'so long as time shall last, or the earth shall stand, or there shall be one man upon the face thereof to be saved' (Moroni 7:36; see also Moroni 7:32)."[304]

The constancy of God's nature, purposes, and covenants provides a mooring when other things change in the way God deals with His people. When something changes in the Lord's Church, we can look to these three anchors to find possible reasons for the change. This can help us find peace amidst change. "For the eternal purposes of the Lord shall roll on, until all his promises shall be fulfilled" (Mormon 8:22).

My Grandmother's Choice

One area where God has sometimes directed His prophets to make changes has been regarding how many women a man may be married to. God began humanity with one man, Adam, married to one woman, Eve, and their monogamous marriage has been the standard for all humankind ever since. However, during some eras, God has commanded or allowed His people to practice plural marriage, including during the early part of the current dispensation.

My grandmother, Mary Hill Musser Wright, grew up in a polygamous family in the early 1900s. For many people who had joined the Church decades earlier, polygamy was a challenge to accept. When Brigham Young was first told about it by Joseph Smith, he said, "It was the first time in my life that I had desired the grave, and I could hardly get over it for a long time. And when I saw a funeral, I felt to envy the corpse its situation, and to regret that I was not in the coffin."[305] It required a lot of scripture study, prayer, and fasting before most of the early Saints could accept polygamy in the mid-1800s. However, once they did accept it, they became fully committed, and most of them taught their children of the personal witnesses they had received, and they encouraged their children to practice it. Many of these children grew up very devout in the belief that plural marriage was ordained of God, so at the end of the nineteenth century, when

---

304. Gerrit W. Gong, "Covenant Belonging," *Ensign* or *Liahona*, Nov. 2019, 80.
305. Brigham Young, in *Journal of Discourses*, 3:266.

God said through His living prophet that the practice should end, many struggled to let it go.

My grandmother's father, Joseph White Musser, was one who had this struggle. He had grown up watching the persecution of his own father, Amos M. Musser, for practicing polygamy in the 1880s. He wrote, "At the tender age of seven or eight I found myself defending my father in his plural life. Two of my older brothers . . . were making light of his life when I, a mere stripling, took his part and shamed the older boys. . . . At the age of twelve, I was frequently called upon to take plural wives with their babies from one place to another, to hide them from the law."[306] At age thirteen, he saw his father carried off to the Utah State Penitentiary where he was incarcerated for six months for refusing to renounce his plural wives.

After the 1890 Manifesto, some Church leaders continued to perform polygamous marriages, although the majority were for couples living outside of the United States. A Gospel Topics essay on plural marriage states, "Like the beginning of plural marriage in the Church, the end of the practice was gradual and incremental, a process filled with difficulties and uncertainties. . . . On an exceptional basis, a smaller number of plural marriages were performed within the United States between the years 1890 and 1904."[307]

Joseph White Musser was among those who entered into one of these late plural marriages. He married his second wife, "Mamie" Mary Caroline Hill, on March 13, 1902. Mamie and her father only agreed to Joseph's marriage proposal after consultation with Apostles John Henry Smith and Matthias F. Cowley. Elder Cowley performed the ceremony. My grandmother, Mary Hill Musser, born a year and a half later, was the first of six children born to this polygamous couple.

My great-grandfather Musser later took additional wives. In spite of repeated attempts by Church leaders to rein him in, he felt called to keep the principle of plural marriage alive. Memories of his own father

---

306. Joseph White Musser, *The Journal of Joseph White Musser*, 12, accessed Sept. 20, 2023, https://www.scribd.com/doc/94929098/The-Journal-of-Joseph-White-Musser.

307. Gospel Topics Essays, "Plural Marriage in The Church of Jesus Christ of Latter-day Saints," Gospel Library.

and counsel he had received from past Church leaders fueled his passion. He clung to those former leaders and could not accept it when the living prophet said that the practice should stop. Joseph Musser ended up being excommunicated from the Church, and he became a prominent leader in the fundamentalist groups that continued the practice.

Mary loved her father. She had grown up so proud of him and his early service in the Church. She thought he was so intelligent and spiritual. However, when her father became separated from the Church, she had to make a choice. Would she follow her father, or would she follow the prophet? When she was married with a family of her own, her father visited her on many occasions and tried to convince her that the Church was wrong and that he was right.

It is a difficult thing to feel like you must choose between loyalty to a family member you love and loyalty to the Church. I am sure my grandmother considered her father's arguments prayerfully because that was her nature. I expect that her decision came with deep struggles and anguish of heart. Many of her father's arguments sounded reasonable. Both she and her father were the offspring of polygamous second marriages, so their very existence sprang from the principle. Surely it was not all bad. Nevertheless, she knew where the keys of the priesthood lay, and she chose to follow the living prophet.

The multitude of blessings that came into the life of my grandmother and her posterity because of her choice to follow the living prophet have been legion. She and her husband, Cleo D. Wright, had fifteen children who gave them 130 grandchildren, all raised in the gospel. The third and fourth generations of their posterity have continued to grow in faith and in numbers. The spiritual blessings this vast family has received have been innumerable because Mary chose to follow the living prophet and president of The Church of Jesus Christ of Latter-day Saints. I am honored to be her grandson.

Mary's story not only highlights the blessing of following the prophet of God who actively holds all the keys of the priesthood; it also includes examples of fallacy and error among some Church leaders. Elder Matthias F. Cowley, the Apostle who performed the sealing of Mary's parents, was later removed from the Quorum of the Twelve and was restricted from using his priesthood because of his continued involvement in polygamous marriages. Another Apostle, John W. Taylor, was excommunicated. This came at a time when the members of the Quorum of the Twelve Apostles were not all united, yet the passage of time has vindicated the decision of the First Presidency and the majority of the Twelve to halt the practice of plural marriage throughout the entire Church. Matthias Cowley himself "later admitted that he had been 'wholly in error.'"[308]

This historical example highlights the complexities of a doctrine that says we should follow the counsel of fallible Church leaders. In this case, it was important to follow the First Presidency and the majority of the Twelve and not to follow some of the individual members of the Twelve. The path ahead is not always clear and obvious to all fifteen of the men called to lead the Lord's Church. When humans are involved, things sometimes get messy. Fortunately, since that era, our Church leaders have consistently made official declarations and policy changes with one united voice. There is strength in following that united voice of the First Presidency and the Quorum of the Twelve Apostles, and there is value in giving things some time to play out if their decisions do not feel right to us at first.

The choice to follow the Lord's anointed servants will always require faith. I am grateful for my grandmother who showed me an example of that kind of faith—faith to follow the prophet even when policies were changed in ways she didn't fully understand. She experienced firsthand the declaration, "I, the Lord, command and revoke, as it seemeth me good" (D&C 56:4). Her faith during a significant policy change strengthens me. She stayed true to her temple covenants and her commitment to follow the Lord's anointed.

Common Sticks That Mark a Safe Path

When I was a young missionary and a newly called trainer, my companion and I found a family who listened to our message. As we taught them, they affirmed their belief in the restored gospel and

---

308. See Gospel Topics Essays, "The Manifesto and the End of Plural Marriage," Gospel Library.

agreed to all the requirements for baptism. However, something didn't feel right to me. I shared my concerns with my district leader, and he said, "Let's move ahead with the interviews, and we'll see if they are ready." So we did. The district leader interviewed them and felt they were ready for baptism. However, I still felt uneasy, so I prayed and told the Lord that even though this family had finished all the discussions and answered all the questions properly, I felt like they were not ready. In response, these words came distinctly into my mind: "You're right. They are not ready. *Follow your leader.*" So I made no further objections, and we moved ahead with their baptisms.

About a month later, the local bishop learned that the father of this family was being physically abusive to his wife and their young son. It had been going on before we met them, and although the frequency had decreased while we taught them, it had never really stopped. The father had truly not been ready for baptism, but the Lord had told me to follow the direction of my priesthood leader anyway. I believe God wanted to bless this woman and her son with some degree of shelter within His Church in spite of the father's sins, but I also believe that God wanted me to learn the importance of following my priesthood leader and allowing the power of the Atonement of Jesus Christ to fill in the gaps.

Our willingness to follow the direction and counsel of our Church leaders can be a test of our faithfulness to Jesus Christ, who is their focus and guide. The first principle of the gospel is faith in the Lord Jesus Christ, not faith in His prophets and apostles, so we should likewise focus on Him. Jesus is our Exemplar, not other humans.[309] Our prophets and apostles are called as witnesses of Jesus Christ, and that is their first and foremost responsibility as leaders of His Church. In other responsibilities, they sometimes make mistakes. As President Jeffrey R. Holland said, "Except in the case of His only perfect Begotten Son, imperfect people are all God has ever had to work with. That must be terribly frustrating to Him, but He deals with it. So should we. And

---

309. I am indebted to Don Bradley for this concept. See Let's Get Real with Stephen Real, "Why LDS Polygamy and Joseph Smith Historian Left and Came Back to the LDS Church (Pt One) | E0012," YouTube, Sept. 14, 2023, 32:09–41:14, https://www.youtube.com/watch?v=SNIOmH7RV2I.

when you see imperfection, remember that the limitation is *not* in the divinity of the work."[310]

It can sometimes be frustrating to follow God's imperfect leaders, especially when we cannot see the endgame that God has in store. The Lord revealed, "For [God] will give unto the faithful line upon line, precept upon precept; and I will try you and prove you herewith" (D&C 98:12). However, He also promised, "If my people will hearken unto my voice, and unto the voice of my servants whom I have appointed to lead my people, behold, verily I say unto you, they shall not be moved out of their place. But if they will not hearken to my voice, nor unto the voice of these men whom I have appointed, they shall not be blest" (D&C 124:45–46). God's appointed leaders are good men and women who are doing their best to build the kingdom of God in a fallen world. They are not perfect, but they are worthy of God's guidance and inspiration.

We can all know, through personal revelation from God, whether the men and women called to lead our Church are indeed worthy disciples of Christ and whether their teachings are inspired by Him. President Russell M. Nelson once invited a group of young adults, "Ask your Heavenly Father if we truly are the Lord's apostles and prophets. Ask if we have received revelation on [any] matters."[311] On another occasion, he said, "You may not always understand every declaration of a living prophet. But when you know a prophet is a prophet, you can approach the Lord in humility and faith and ask for your own witness about whatever His prophet has proclaimed."[312]

When Karl G. Maeser was president of the Swiss and German Mission in the late 1860s, he led a group of young missionaries across the Alps. During part of this trek, they had to follow sticks that others had placed in the deep snow to mark a safe path. A biographer of Brother Maeser wrote, "As they slowly ascended the steep slope, he looked back and saw this row of sticks marking the way and said, 'Brethren, there stands the Priesthood. They are just common sticks

---

310. Jeffrey R. Holland, "Lord, I Believe," *Ensign* or *Liahona*, May 2013, 94.
311. Russell M. Nelson , "The Love and Laws of God" (Brigham Young University devotional, Sept. 17, 2019), 5, speeches.byu.edu.
312. Russell M. Nelson, "Stand as True Millennials," *Ensign*, Oct. 2016, 31.

like the rest of us—some of them are even crooked, but the position they hold makes them what they are to us. If we step aside from the path they mark, we are lost.'"[313]

Brother Maeser's warning remains true for us today. In spite of the imperfections of these common men who are called to be our leaders, the safest path is to follow the guideposts they present as a unified body. President M. Russell Ballard affirmed this, saying, "Though mortal and subject to human imperfection, the Lord's servants are inspired to help us avoid obstacles that are spiritually life threatening and to help us pass safely through mortality to our final, ultimate, heavenly destination."[314]

The safety inherent in following the guidance of the Lord's anointed leaders does not come solely from the wisdom of their specific counsel. Of even greater value is the presence of the Holy Ghost that comes to us when we follow those leaders. As noted earlier, the reason we are counseled in the temple to not speak evil of the Lord's anointed is so that we can have the influence of the Holy Ghost in our lives.

Nephi saw in vision how the original Apostles of Jesus Christ would be rejected at the beginning of the Great Apostasy:

> I saw the multitudes of the earth, that they were gathered together to fight against the apostles of the Lamb. . . .
>
> And I beheld that they were in a large and spacious building. . . . And the angel of the Lord spake unto me again, saying: Behold the world and the wisdom thereof; yea, *behold the house of Israel hath gathered together to fight against the twelve apostles of the Lamb.*
>
> And . . . the great and spacious building was the pride of the world; and it fell, and the fall thereof was exceedingly great. And the angel of the Lord spake unto me again, saying: Thus shall be the destruction of all nations, kindreds, tongues, and people, that shall fight against the twelve apostles of the Lamb. (1 Nephi 11:34–36; emphasis added)

---

313. Alma Burton, "Karl G. Maeser: Mormon Educator," *Theses and Dissertations* (BYU ScholarsArchive, 1950), 33–34, https://scholarsarchive.byu.edu/etd/4572/.

314. M. Russell Ballard, "God Is at the Helm," *Ensign* or *Liahona*, Nov. 2015, 24.

It is sad to read that some of the house of Israel would fight against Christ's first Apostles. However, in the same way that many of the prophecies of Isaiah have a dual fulfillment, this vision of Nephi appears to have a second fulfillment in our own day as people who were once faithful members of the Church and counted themselves as part of the house of Israel do once again "fight against the twelve apostles of the Lamb." It is the pride of the world that motivates these enemies of righteousness, but in the end, they will fall, "and the fall thereof [will be] exceedingly great."

Jesus said to His original Apostles, "If the world hate you, ye know that it hated me before it hated you. If ye were of the world, the world would love his own: but because ye are not of the world, but I have chosen you out of the world, therefore the world hateth you. Remember the word that I said unto you, The servant is not greater than his lord. If they have persecuted me, they will also persecute you; if they have kept my saying, they will keep yours also" (John 15:18–20).

Those who follow Jesus Christ will follow His prophets and apostles. We should make Jesus Christ our only exemplar, and at the same time, we should adhere to the model presented in the temple of following His chosen prophets and apostles as well as our covenant promise to not speak evil of the Lord's anointed. When we do so, we benefit from blessings inherent in following their specific counsel, we qualify for the guidance of the Holy Ghost, and we are promised divine protection when the Lord returns. There is safety in following and sustaining the Lord's anointed as we progress along the covenant path.

6

Armed with Power: The Many Powers of Christ's Atonement

At the center of our temple worship is the atoning sacrifice of our Savior, Jesus Christ. This is because Jesus Christ is at the center of God's plan for our exaltation. In that grand premortal council, when our Heavenly Father presented this plan, He explained that a supreme sacrifice would be needed to redeem all mankind from the inevitable mistakes all would make in our mortal school-ground. Prideful Satan offered to be that redeemer if he could retain all the glory for himself. He also claimed that none would be lost. If everyone could be saved, then Satan's plan probably meant that nothing would be considered sin and therefore nothing would need to be atoned for. Satan wanted all the glory with no suffering on his part.

Jesus, who was the firstborn spirit Son of God and His Chosen from the beginning, also stepped forward and offered to be the Redeemer. He agreed to carry out God's plan in the way our Father originally proposed, which meant He would have to suffer for the sins and struggles of all mankind. Jesus humbly said, "Father, thy will be done, and the glory be thine forever" (Moses 4:2). God said he would send Jesus (see Abraham 3:27).

Jesus Christ was also at the center of the Creation of the world, carrying out God's plan to create an earth where we could all have the opportunity to become like our heavenly parents. Christ's roles as both Redeemer and Creator are taught in the temple.

President Russell M. Nelson said, "Jesus Christ is at the center of everything we do in the temple."[315] He also explained, "Each person who makes covenants in baptismal fonts and in temples—and keeps them—has increased access to the power of Jesus Christ. . . . The reward for keeping covenants with God is heavenly power—power that strengthens us to withstand our trials, temptations, and heartaches better. This power eases our way."[316] In the temple we are "endowed with power" (D&C 38:32) from Jesus Christ so that we "may go forth from [His] house armed with [His] power" (D&C 109:22).

This chapter will explore Christ's role as our Redeemer and the many powers He extends to us through His Atonement. The Atonement of Jesus Christ redeems us from sin; it enables us to deal with trials and suffering; it heals us spiritually, emotionally, and physically; and it has the power to transform us, making us like our heavenly parents and Jesus Christ. Each of these four powers is taught or experienced in the temple, the place where the Lord declared, "I will manifest myself to my people in mercy in this house" (D&C 110:7).

Christ in Gethsemane

Occasionally, I enjoy listening to the different perspectives I hear on my local Christian radio station. One day, while working in my basement, I tuned in to that station and heard a popular evangelist talk about Christ's experience in the Garden of Gethsemane, which Luke described as follows: "[Jesus] kneeled down, and prayed, Saying, Father, if thou be willing, remove this cup from me: nevertheless not my will, but thine, be done. And there appeared an angel unto him from heaven, strengthening him. And being in an agony he prayed

---

315. Russell M, Nelson, "Go Forward in Faith," *Liahona*, May 2020, 115.
316. Russell M, Nelson, "Overcome the World and Find Rest," *Liahona*, Nov. 2022, 96.

more earnestly: and his sweat was as it were great drops of blood falling down to the ground" (Luke 22:42–44).

The radio preacher related a personal experience with a serious illness he once had that reminded him of his own mortality. He said, "No one who has not come close to death can understand the fear that comes to one who knows he is approaching the end of his life." This was the context in which the radio teacher sought to explain the experience of Jesus in the Garden of Gethsemane: that the anguish Jesus felt was merely a fear of his own impending death.

What a diminishment of the character of Jesus Christ! There have been many people who have bravely faced death. Certainly, the Son of God, who knew that He would be resurrected, did not fear death itself. He knew that death would bring His victory over it. He had already prophesied of His Resurrection, saying, "Destroy this temple, and in three days I will raise it up" (John 2:19). Explaining this statement, John clarified, "But he spake of the temple of his body" (John 2:21).

Christ was not fearing his impending crucifixion, as terrible as that tortuous mode of death was. Rather, it was a struggle over sin that occurred right there in the Garden of Gethsemane that brought about His suffering. Elder James E. Talmage wrote of this event:

> Christ's agony in the garden is unfathomable by the finite mind, both as to intensity and cause. The thought that He suffered through fear of death is untenable. Death to Him was preliminary to resurrection and triumphal return to the Father from whom He had come, and to a state of glory even beyond what He had before possessed; and, moreover, it was within His power to lay down His life voluntarily.
>
> He struggled and groaned under a burden such as no other being who has lived on earth might even conceive as possible. It was not physical pain, nor mental anguish alone, that caused Him to suffer such torture as to produce an extrusion of blood from every pore; but a spiritual agony of soul such as only God was capable of experiencing. No other man, however great his powers of physical or mental endurance, could have suffered so; for his human organism would have succumbed, and [a drop in blood pressure] would have produced unconsciousness and welcome oblivion. In

that hour of anguish Christ met and overcame all the horrors that Satan, 'the prince of this world' could inflict. . . .

In some manner, actual and terribly real though to man incomprehensible, the Savior took upon Himself the burden of the sins of mankind from Adam to the end of the world.[317]

This terrible suffering that Jesus Christ endured occurred in the Garden of Gethsemane. It was added upon by His subsequent crucifixion, but it was in Gethsemane where He first took upon Himself our sins and suffered the pains of the whole world.

One of the first truths restored through the Prophet Joseph Smith was a revelation recorded in Doctrine and Covenants 19 that teaches us more about what happened in the Garden of Gethsemane. Note these words spoken to the Prophet by Christ Himself as He described His excruciating experience:

> How sore you know not, how exquisite you know not, yea, how hard to bear you know not.
>
> For behold, I, God, have suffered these things for all, that they might not suffer if they would repent. . . .
>
> Which suffering caused myself, even God, the greatest of all, to tremble because of pain, and to bleed at every pore, and to suffer both body and spirit—and would that I might not drink the bitter cup, and shrink—
>
> Nevertheless, glory be to the Father, and I partook and finished my preparations unto the children of men. (D&C 19:15–16, 18–19)

Can you hear the emotion in that first-person retelling of such a painful experience? Can you sense the anguish in the memory? It was recounted 1800 years after the event occurred, yet it seems Jesus remembered the pain like it had just happened. And notice that Jesus did not speak of the scourging He had endured nor of the pain of having nails pounded through His hands and feet. He did not refer to the agonizing hours He spent hanging from those spikes on the cross with only His exposed bones and tendons holding up the weight of His body. He did not tell of the humiliation of hanging there exposed

---

317. James E. Talmage, "Chapter 33: The Last Supper and the Betrayal," *Jesus the Christ* (2006), https://www.churchofjesuschrist.org/study/manual/jesus-the-christ/chapter-33.

to the elements, with arms outstretched and likely naked, as infection and exhaustion set in. No, Jesus recounted nothing about His Crucifixion in this 1829 retelling of the pains He suffered; rather, He spoke of trembling from pain as he bled from every pore while suffering for all the sins of the world—which suffering occurred in the Garden of Gethsemane.

Modern medical experts would say that Christ suffered a malady that they call hematidrosis or hematohidrosis.[318] It is a rare and extremely difficult condition where a person's pain and anxiety are so great that the capillary blood vessels near the surface of the skin burst and blood oozes from the pores. There are modern documented cases of this occurring in some people on small areas of their bodies. However, a mere human could not survive if hematidrosis bleeding occurred from every pore, like Jesus Christ endured.

Why? Why did Christ have to suffer so terribly? This chapter will discuss four reasons Jesus Christ carried out His infinite Atonement—reasons that bless us all.

The Redeeming Power of Christ's Atonement

Paul wrote to the Romans, "For the wages of sin is death; but the gift of God is eternal life through Jesus Christ our Lord" (Romans 6:23). We all sin. We all make mistakes. And a price must be paid for each of these sins and mistakes. However, we don't have to pay that price ourselves because Jesus already did so on our behalf in the Garden of Gethsemane and on the cross of Calvary.

I am humbled as I reflect on the fact that Jesus suffered not only *for* me but *because* of me. Some of that pain and some of those drops of blood were caused by me and my choices to sin. And what does He want from me in return? He answered this in the same revelation in which He described his suffering:

> Therefore I command you to repent. . . .
>
> For behold, I, God, have suffered these things for all, that they might not suffer if they would repent;

---

318. Hematidrosis, or hematohidrosis, is described at https://www.webmd.com/a-to-z-guides/hematidrosis-hematohidrosis.

But if they would not repent they must suffer even as I. (D&C 19:15–17)

Jesus Christ just wants us to repent. And if we do, then on Judgment Day, He will intercede on our behalf and tell the Father that He already paid the price for our sins. He will plead our cause, and we will not have to suffer ourselves (see D&C 45:3–5). What is more, we do not have to wait until the Day of Judgment to know we are forgiven. It can happen now. This is the redeeming power of the Atonement of Jesus Christ.

However, if we do not repent, Christ will remain silent in that Judgment hearing, and we too will have to suffer for our own sins. In that case, our suffering will be a duplication of what Christ already did for us, making His suffering for us at least partially in vain. No wonder Christ sounds so anxious that we all repent. We must not let His suffering for us be for naught. We need to show Jesus that we are eternally grateful for what He has done by repenting. This is what He wants most from us.

In the temple, we learn that the redeeming power of Christ's Atonement was first taught to Adam and Eve when an angel explained the reason that they had been commanded to offer animal sacrifices. The angel declared:

> This thing is a similitude of the sacrifice of the Only Begotten of the Father, which is full of grace and truth.
>
> Wherefore, thou shalt do all that thou doest in the name of the Son, and thou shalt repent and call upon God in the name of the Son forevermore.
>
> And in that day the Holy Ghost fell upon Adam, which beareth record of the Father and the Son, saying: I am the Only Begotten of the Father from the beginning, henceforth and forever, that as thou hast fallen thou mayest be redeemed, and all mankind, even as many as will. (Moses 5:7–9)

As the offspring of Adam and Eve, we all need this redeeming power that emanates from the Atonement of Jesus. Alma the Younger experienced that power. Alma was living a life of rebelling against his prophet father and trying to destroy the church. However, once he realized he was wrong and that God might destroy him, he felt deep remorse and guilt in the depths of his soul. Then he remembered that his father had taught about Jesus Christ, the Son of God, who would atone for the sins of the world. He recounted:

> Now, as my mind caught hold upon this thought, I cried within my heart: O Jesus, thou Son of God, have mercy on me, who am in the gall of bitterness, and am encircled about by the everlasting chains of death.
>
> And now, behold, when I thought this, I could remember my pains no more; yea, I was harrowed up by the memory of my sins no more.
>
> And oh, what joy, and what marvelous light I did behold; yea, my soul was filled with joy as exceeding as was my pain!
>
> Yea, . . . there could be nothing so exquisite and so bitter as were my pains. Yea, and . . . there can be nothing so exquisite and sweet as was my joy. (Alma 36:18–21)

This is what can happen with us when we repent and show faith in the redeeming power of the Atonement of Jesus Christ. His Atonement resolves remorse of conscience and lifts us from the pain of our sins. It can replace deep emotional and spiritual burdens with love, peace, and confidence. This redeeming power is accessible through faith in Jesus Christ and repentance, and it is further strengthened through the making or renewing of baptismal covenants. The outcome is purification and joy from the Holy Ghost.

This outcome was experienced by the people of King Benjamin. After he delivered his powerful farewell sermon, covering such topics as humility, service, and redemption through Christ, his people were humbled and unitedly declared:

> O have mercy, and apply the atoning blood of Christ that we may receive forgiveness of our sins, and our hearts may be purified; for we believe in Jesus Christ, the Son of God, who created heaven and earth, and all things; who shall come down among the children of men.
>
> And it came to pass that after they had spoken these words the Spirit of the Lord came upon them, and they were filled with joy, having received a remission of their sins, and having peace of

conscience, because of the exceeding faith which they had in Jesus Christ. (Mosiah 4:2–3)

This joy and peace can come not only when we repent from serious sins or willful rebellions but also when we need mercy for the common, everyday mistakes we make through misguided actions, accidents, or other unintentional behaviors: "For behold, and also his blood atoneth for the sins of those . . . who have ignorantly sinned" (Mosiah 3:7).

My wife experienced this grace. One Saturday, she was listening to a program about how leaders should deal lovingly with others. It brought back a memory of when, as a BYU instructor for freshman English, she had come down pretty hard on a student for plagiarizing his research paper. She had felt that her reaction to the student's dishonesty was justified, but the student complained to my wife's adviser who later talked with her, pointing out the need to prioritize helping her students learn and improve. My wife also remembered a couple of times at Young Women camp when she had to discipline youth camp leaders who were setting bad examples for the younger campers, and she worried that she hadn't handled those situations in the best way. As she contemplated these unpleasant memories, she felt deep regret and shame. She didn't know if she would ever be able to shake off those feelings. However, the next morning as she was preparing to take the sacrament, she realized she could turn those feelings over to the Savior once and for all. Miraculously, the guilt completely lifted from her. She felt she was given a fresh start and could move on. Christ removed from her all feelings of guilt and remorse for these mistakes. His redeeming power covers all repented errors, great and small.

President Russell M. Nelson admonished us to take advantage of the redeeming power of Christ's Atonement when he said:

> There is no limit to the Savior's capacity to help you. His incomprehensible suffering in Gethsemane and on Calvary was for you! His infinite Atonement is for you! . . . My heart aches for those who are mired in sin and don't know how to get out. I weep for those who struggle spiritually or who carry heavy burdens alone because they do not understand what Jesus Christ did for them.

Jesus Christ took upon Himself your sins, your pains, your heartaches, and your infirmities. You do not have to bear them alone! He will forgive you as you repent. He will bless you with what you need. He will heal your wounded soul. As you yoke yourself to Him, your burdens will feel lighter. If you will make and keep covenants to follow Jesus Christ, you will find that the painful moments of your life are temporary. Your afflictions will be "swallowed up in the joy of Christ."[319]

The hymn "I Stand All Amazed" describes with emotional depth the way most Christians feel about the redeeming power of the Atonement of Jesus Christ:

> I stand all amazed at the love Jesus offers me,
> Confused at the grace that so fully he proffers me.
> I tremble to know that for me he was crucified,
> That for me, a sinner, he suffered, he bled and died.
>
> I marvel that he would descend from his throne divine
> To rescue a soul so rebellious and proud as mine,
> That he should extend his great love unto such as I,
> Sufficient to own, to redeem, and to justify.
>
> I think of his hands pierced and bleeding to pay the debt!
> Such mercy, such love and devotion can I forget?
> No, no, I will praise and adore at the mercy seat,
> Until at the glorified throne I kneel at his feet.[320]

The fact that Jesus redeems us from our sins is indeed amazing. His Atonement makes us worthy to enter into His holy house. All who worthily enter therein can rest assured that they qualify for the redeeming power of the Atonement of Jesus Christ. We can feel the weight of our sins and mistakes lifted, knowing that Jesus willingly accepted the burden of those sins and that all He has ever asked in return is that we repent and come unto Him.

---

319. Russell M. Nelson, "The Lord Jesus Christ Will Come Again," *Liahona*, Nov. 2024, 122.
320. "I Stand All Amazed," *Hymns*, no. 173.

My Experience with Christ's Redeeming Power

As a teenager in Indiana in the early 1970s, I participated in home-study seminary, which was supplemented by a monthly seminary meeting at our stake center. On these "Super Saturdays," we had lessons presented by a Church Educational System (CES) teacher, scripture chases, and instructional movies. I remember watching the *Tom Trails* video series in a darkened room, shown from a noisy reel-to-reel projector before the advent of video tapes or DVDs. From those stories, I learned about the steps of repentance for the first time in my life. I learned that repentance involves a series of steps: recognition, remorse, confession, restitution, forsaking, and forgiving others. I came to believe that if a person had not gone through each of these steps for every sin, he or she had not fully repented.

Like many teenagers, I carried some sins that needed to be confessed as part of my repentance. These sins had occurred in my early teens, during that transitional period of life when many young people struggle with a mixture of curiosity, confusion, and naivety. I had forsaken them but had never mustered the courage to confess them. Later, as I was preparing to receive the Melchizedek Priesthood after graduating from high school, I remembered these sins and knew I needed to resolve them with a priesthood leader. However, I honestly feared that I would be excommunicated or at least disfellowshipped if they were known. Yet I felt such a sense of reverence for the higher priesthood and such a deep sense of duty to follow the steps of repentance I had learned in seminary that I felt obligated to confess my sins and accept whatever consequences might follow.

I could not bring myself to admit these serious sins to my bishop, so I held back until my interview with the stake president. His office was in a side wing of the stake center, and when the time came for my interview, rather than going into that wing, I waited in an adjoining empty foyer, reading my scriptures. I dreaded the interview and could not bring myself to move any closer to his office. At one point, the stake executive secretary came out to the foyer looking for me, but since he did not know me personally and I did not look up from my scripture reading, he said nothing and went back. I felt sick inside at the thought of what I had to face and could not bring myself to volunteer my identity. I had come this far, and God was going to have to push me the rest of the way. A few minutes later, the executive secretary came out again and approached me, asking my name. When I told him, he ushered me into the interview.

In tears, I humbly confessed my sins and committed never to repeat my mistakes, which was not hard because they had occurred when I was younger and because I felt so bad that I never wanted to repeat them. However, I knew they were serious, so at the end of the interview, I was surprised to learn that not only was my membership status not going to change, but the stake president deemed me worthy to be ordained to the higher priesthood. I could hardly believe it. What a relief! I learned that God and His Church were both truly merciful. They just wanted to make sure I had repented and was on the right path.

During the following year, as I prepared for a full-time mission, I continued to review my life, looking for sins, past and present, that I needed to apply the steps of repentance to. With each sin I needed to discard, I checked the boxes of each step in my mind: recognition, remorse, confession, restitution, forsaking, and forgiving others. I was following a checklist, but I found that the process was having a positive effect. It caused me to be truly humble, and it brought me nearer to the Lord as I corrected my behaviors. I could tell I was changing by following the repentance steps, for "faith and repentance bringeth a change of heart" (Helaman 15:7).

Noticing the changes that had come into my life by following this process only served to validate it as the one and only way to repent and receive forgiveness from God. I thought that everyone needed to complete this checklist of requirements in order to qualify for forgiveness. I focused more and more on the process rather than the objective: a change of heart. The Bible Dictionary says of repentance, "The Greek word of which this is the translation denotes a change of mind, a fresh view about God, about oneself, and about the world. Since we are born into conditions of mortality, repentance comes to mean a turning of the heart and will to God, and a renunciation of sin to which we are naturally inclined."[321]

When my mission began and I was learning Spanish in the Language Training Mission (a precursor to the Mission Training Center), I had a very special "born again" spiritual experience. It happened one night when lights were out and the other missionaries in my room were finishing their prayers or already sleeping. I was saying my own personal prayer and was overcome with a powerful spiritual experience wherein God told me that I was pure and clean before Him. I felt like Enos who wrote, "I kneeled down before my Maker, and I cried unto him in mighty prayer and supplication for mine own soul. . . . And there came a voice unto me, saying: Enos, thy sins are forgiven thee, and thou shalt be blessed. And I, Enos, knew that God could not lie; wherefore, my guilt was swept away. And I said: Lord, how is it done? And he said unto me: Because of thy faith in Christ" (Enos 1:4–8).

I had already repented of as many of my sins as I could think of before starting my mission; however, during this purifying prayer experience, the Lord brought to my mind some sins I had long forgotten. It was like He was saying to me, "You are cleansed not only from the sins you formally repented of but also from these other sins you had forgotten about."

I marveled at the experience. I floated on a high spiritual cloud for days. I became emotional easily, and I was filled with love for everyone. I was not bothered by any inconvenience or nuisance done by anyone else. It was a powerfully spiritual time. However, I became concerned with the fact that I had not completed all the repentance steps for the newly remembered sins that God had told me I had also been forgiven of. How could that be? These were not sins that necessarily needed to be confessed to a priesthood leader, but I had not confessed them to the people I had offended, nor had I tried to make restitution. I had stopped the behaviors but had not completed the full repentance checklist for these additional sins. So in my next interview with my branch president, I told him about my experience, and I

---

321. Bible Dictionary, "Repentance."

asked him how I could possibly be forgiven of sins that I had not gone through all the steps of repentance for.

My branch president reminded me of the Book of Mormon story of Nephi and Lehi, the sons of Helaman, who were put into prison after preaching to the Lamanites. These two prophets were encircled with fire, the earth shook, and a voice from above called the Lamanites around them to repentance. However, the people were frozen in fear. A former Nephite who was there told everyone that they needed to repent and have faith in Christ. The Lamanites then cried out to the Lord until they too were encircled about by fire. They were purified by the Spirit because of their faith in Christ (see Helaman 5:20–52). My branch president explained that these Lamanites had been forgiven of their sins even though they had not been able to confess to those they had wronged nor make restitution for their sins. They were forgiven through the Atonement of Jesus Christ because their hearts had been changed. They had achieved the objective of the forgiveness process without completing each step in the way I had been taught. They were accepted by God, and so was I.

Since then, I have thought about other people in the scriptures who received the forgiveness of Jesus Christ even though they had clearly not checked off the boxes for each step of forgiveness. Alma the Younger, a rebellious sinner who had tried to destroy the Church of God, fell to the earth in a stupor for three days before he was awakened with the knowledge that his sins were forgiven (see Mosiah 27; Alma 36). He made no recompense for his sins before he was forgiven by Christ. It is true that for the rest of his life he tried to build up the Church and undo the harm he had previously done, but he did not do this as a condition of his forgiveness. He did it because his heart had been changed and he wanted others "to taste of the exceeding joy of which I did taste" (Alma 36:24).

The people of King Benjamin received remission of their sins during the time that they were gathered at the temple, listening to their righteous king. They did not line up outside their local bishops' tents to confess their sins, nor did they make restitution for all their mistakes before forgiveness was granted. However, they did experience a mighty change in their hearts (see Mosiah 5:2). They achieved the objective of the repentance process without ticking all the boxes in between, and this was sufficient.

The objective of the repentance process is a change of heart, and if God sees that we have achieved this even though we may not have completed every step in the outlined process, then He will be satisfied. It is Christ who takes upon Himself our sins, and what He wants to see in each of us is a mighty change of heart.

In telling this, I do not want to diminish the value of confession and restitution. They are important actions that help us achieve the state of humility we need to reach before a spiritual heart transplant can occur. I don't think I could have experienced my own change of heart without them. Confession is particularly important because when we admit, verbally, our mistakes and sins, something happens in our mind and in our spirit so that healing can progress more easily. In addition, restitution, when possible, helps restore the trust that others need to have in the reality of our repentance. So I am not suggesting that people should use the examples I have cited to justify omitting confession or restitution in their own personal repentance journeys. However, we need to remember that it is the change of heart that matters to God. My personal change of heart occurred when I humbly engaged with the redeeming power of the Atonement of Jesus Christ and surrendered my heart and my will to Him.

My experience with repentance and feeling the redeeming and purifying grace of Jesus Christ set me on a firm foundation that made my mission a season of joyous service and devotion to my Redeemer. Because I had felt the joy that comes from being cleansed, I wanted everyone I contacted to know the truths I knew and to feel Christ's redeeming power in the way I felt it. Tasting of that redemption instilled in me a passion to follow Jesus Christ for the rest of my life. It also drew me to His holy house where I frequently felt that same cleansing power.

The Enabling Power of Christ's Atonement

Is that all there is to Christ's Atonement—redemption from sin? No, there is more. There is another power—the strengthening or enabling power of the Atonement of Jesus Christ. Elder David A.

Bednar has taught that this enabling power strengthens us to deal with difficult circumstances and challenges in life.[322] Elder Gerrit W. Gong taught, "Jesus Christ's Atonement can deliver and redeem us from sin. But Jesus Christ also intimately understands our every pain, affliction, sickness, sorrow, separation. . . . He helps heal the broken and disparaged, reconcile the angry and divided, comfort the lonely and isolated, encourage the uncertain and imperfect, and bring forth miracles possible only with God."[323]

The scriptural basis for this sometimes-overlooked Atonement power is found in Isaiah 61 and Alma 7:

> The Lord hath anointed me to preach good tidings unto the meek; he hath sent me to bind up the brokenhearted, to proclaim liberty to the captives, and the opening of the prison to them that are bound;
> To proclaim the acceptable year of the Lord . . . ; to comfort all that mourn;
> To appoint unto them that mourn in Zion, to give unto them beauty for ashes, the oil of joy for mourning, the garment of praise for the spirit of heaviness. (Isaiah 61:1–3)

> And he shall go forth, suffering pains and afflictions and temptations of every kind; and this that the word might be fulfilled which saith he will take upon him the pains and the sicknesses of his people.
> And . . . he will take upon him their infirmities, that his bowels may be filled with mercy, according to the flesh, that he may know according to the flesh how to succor his people according to their infirmities. (Alma 7:11–12)

BYU Professor Robert L. Millet taught, "The grace of God is a precious gift, an enabling power to face life with quiet courage, to do things we could never do on our own. The Great Physician does more than forgive sins. He ministers relief to the disconsolate, comfort to the bereaved, confidence to those who wrestle with infirmities and

---

322. See David A. Bednar, "In the Strength of the Lord" (Brigham Young University devotional, Oct. 23, 2001), speeches.byu.edu.

323. Gerrit W. Gong, "All Things for Our Good," *Liahona*, May 2024, 41.

feelings of inadequacy, and strength and peace to those who have been battered and scarred by the ironies of this life."[324]

This enabling power is Christ's capacity to succor, which means to give aid or relief. President Dallin H. Oaks explained:

> Our Savior experienced and suffered the fulness of all mortal challenges "according to the flesh" so He could know "according to the flesh" how to "succor his people according to their infirmities." He therefore knows our struggles, our heartaches, our temptations, and our suffering, for He willingly experienced them all as an essential part of His Atonement. And because of this, His Atonement empowers Him to succor us—to give us the strength to bear it all.[325]

Our first mother, Eve, seems to have understood the nuance of choice and agency that came when she and Adam were given two commandments, the first of which (multiply and replenish the earth) they could not fulfill without transgressing the second (don't eat a specific fruit). Eve declared her insight: "Were it not for our transgression we never should have had seed, and never should have known good and evil, and the joy of our redemption, and the eternal life which God giveth unto all the obedient" (Moses 5:11). Earlier they had been told the consequences of their choice: Eve would have to bear their children in sorrow, and Adam would have to fight thorns and thistles to raise food by the sweat of his brow (see Moses 4:22–25). However, knowing that the enabling power of the Lord would strengthen them, Adam and Eve faced the burden of these mortal trials and challenges with courage. Their insight is taught both in the scriptures and in the temple.

This strengthening power of Christ's Atonement brings us comfort when we struggle with illness. It brings us consolation when we suffer loss, sorrow, or grief. It brings us peace when we encounter questions for which we find no answers. This expansive power is the source of revealed insights that help us overcome many challenges in this life,

---

324. Robert L. Millet, "What We Believe" (Brigham Young University devotional, Feb. 3, 1998), 6, speeches.byu.edu.

325. Dallin H. Oaks, "Strengthened by the Atonement of Jesus Christ," *Ensign* or *Liahona*, Nov. 2015, 61–62.

and it brings us calm when we are given other challenges that we sense will not be fully resolved in mortality. It brings us hope, peace, and serenity in this fallen world. This is the strengthening or enabling power of the Atonement of Jesus Christ.

Sister Carolyn Rasmus taught:

> Christ stands ready with outstretched arms as He waits for us to come unto Him and be encircled in the arms of His love (see D&C 6:20). It is here that we can be healed, nourished, loved, enabled, strengthened, and made whole. Although the trial may be hard and the relief may not be immediate, we need to learn to allow God to help carry our burdens. We can do this by turning to Him regularly to seek His enabling power. . . .
>
> When we understand the enabling power of the Atonement, we will be changed; we will have access to strength beyond our natural abilities, our weakness can be turned to strength, and we can know that "in the strength of the Lord" we can "do all things" (Alma 20:4).[326]

Sometimes this strengthening power is bestowed through compensatory blessings that fill spiritual and emotional voids that cannot be directly satisfied in ways we might prefer. Sister Kristin M. Yee shared, "I grew up in a home where I didn't always feel safe because of emotional and verbal mistreatment. . . . [However,] the Lord has sent me compensatory blessings. . . . He has sent mentors into my life. And sweetest and most transformative of all has been my relationship with my Heavenly Father. Through Him, I've gratefully known the gentle, protective, and guiding love of a perfect Father."[327] Elder Neil L. Anderson similarly taught, "There is a compensatory spiritual power for the righteous . . . [including] greater assurance, greater confirmation, and greater confidence in the spiritual direction they are

---

326. Carolyn J. Rasmus, "The Enabling Power of the Atonement," *Ensign*, Mar. 2013, 20–21.
327. Kristin M. Yee, "Beauty for Ashes: The Healing Path of Forgiveness," *Liahona*, Nov. 2022, 37.

traveling. The gift of the Holy Ghost becomes a brighter light in the emerging twilight."[328]

In the hymn "How Firm a Foundation," the following verses describe the strengthening and enabling power of the Atonement of Jesus Christ in first-person language spoken directly by Him:

> Fear not, I am with thee; oh, be not dismayed,
> For I am thy God and will still give thee aid.
> I'll strengthen thee, help thee, and cause thee to stand,
> Upheld by my righteous, omnipotent hand.
>
> When through the deep waters I call thee to go,
> The rivers of sorrow shall not thee o'erflow,
> For I will be with thee, thy troubles to bless,
> And sanctify to thee thy deepest distress.
>
> When through fiery trials thy pathway shall lie,
> My grace, all sufficient, shall be thy supply.
> The flame shall not hurt thee; I only design
> Thy dross to consume and thy gold to refine.[329]

Whereas the redeeming power of Christ's Atonement purifies us, the enabling power of His Atonement magnifies and strengthens us. Many Saints go to the temple when they need to feel this strengthening power in greater measure. The reverent and peaceful spirit there makes it easier to sense this strength. The temple is the place where the powers of heaven can overcome the pains of this world and we can be blessed like Alma and his missionary companion, of whom it was said, "The Lord . . . gave them strength, that they should suffer no manner of afflictions, save it were swallowed up in the joy of Christ" (Alma 31:38).

Strengthened When Polio Struck Our Family

My parents were sustained by the strengthening and enabling power of Christ's Atonement when my sister contracted polio at the

---

328. Neil L. Andersen, "A Compensatory Spiritual Power for the Righteous" (Brigham Young University devotional, Aug. 18, 2015), 3, speeches.byu.edu.
329. "How Firm a Foundation," *Hymns*, no. 85.

tender age of five. As the eldest child with three little brothers at the time, Sandra held a special place in her parents' hearts, so they were devastated at the thought of her possible paralysis or even death. This was the mid-1950s, and even though the Salk vaccine had been recently developed, it had not yet been widely dispensed.

After two days of fever and aching legs, my mother took little Sandra to our family doctor, leaving my brothers and me with our grandmother while our father was at work. The doctor examined Sandra but was not sure what was causing her illness, so he told my mother to take her to the county hospital for some tests and a spinal tap. My mother started heading to the hospital, but while waiting at a stoplight, she thought that maybe she should wait and talk to our father after he got home from work that night.

My mother wrote, "When the traffic again moved, I drove on but pulled to the side of the road, said a prayer, and asked my Father in Heaven to help me to know what to do. I turned the car around and headed back to my mother's home. Momma didn't question my hesitation. I took all of the children to our home and put Sandra back in bed." My mother's prayer engaged her with the strengthening power of Christ's Atonement, and that power guided her from that moment forward.

When our father got home that evening, he said that a friend he had been working with that day had a son who had experienced symptoms like Sandra's, and he had been diagnosed with polio. The boy had been treated by a Dr. Maurice Taylor. My parents telephoned Dr. Taylor at his home, and he asked them to bring Sandra to his office early the next morning.

My mother wrote, "Dr. Maurice Taylor worked with the 'Sister Kenny' polio treatment method, and with only a few minutes of examination of Sandra Lyn, he told us that she had poliomyelitis. Dr. Taylor immediately ordered gamma globulin serum. While waiting for the serum to arrive, he talked with us. He was serving as a stake president at the time, and as he looked at me, I thought he could see into my very soul. He asked me if I could follow his instructions exactly. Before I even had time to answer, he said, 'Yes, I know you can and will do it.'"[330]

My mother then began a regimen that included heating in a pressure cooker some strips of wool that had been cut from a blanket and then wrapping Sandra in these strips from toe to neck. This was repeated every two hours, day and night. In addition, during the nighttime, my mother and father took turns sitting in a chair next to the bed with their arms stretched across Sandra's legs to keep her leg muscles straight while she slept. The regimen was exhausting. After eight days of this continuous effort, Sandra's fever broke. They were then able to gradually decrease the frequency of the heat treatments over several weeks as the muscle spasms came under control.

Two years of clinical physical therapy followed. During that period, my mother went through another pregnancy and birth. My father was working two jobs while also overseeing the construction of a new home, so Mom usually took Sandra to physical therapy on her own with three or four other small children in tow. I don't know how my parents could have done all they did without the enabling power of the Atonement of Jesus Christ to strengthen them.

My mother described one special visit with Doctor Taylor that occurred after many months of physical therapy:

> Every month as we visited Dr. Taylor's office, he would make a fuss over muscles that were responding to therapy, always encouraging. During one visit, after examining Sandra's arms, back, and stomach muscles, he said, "My Sweet Little Potato, the nurse tells me that you can walk. Let me see if you really can." He stood Sandra Lyn up next to the examination table, and he sat on a stool about four feet away, holding out his hands. Sandra's thin little body really worked, the left side stronger than the right, as she slowly kind of limped to his waiting arms.
>
> This huge man, with tears streaming down his cheeks, enveloped Sandra Lyn close to his own body. After a few moments, he placed her on his knee. Looking her directly in the eyes, he said, "I want you to remember something all of your life. Dr. Taylor didn't

---

330. Rosemary Wright Jones, "Sandra Lyn's Bout with Polio, June 1956," written in 1989, personal family records in possession of the author.

make you well. Your mother didn't make you well. Your Heavenly Father made you well, and don't you ever forget it." We all wept together.[331]

It was the strengthening and enabling power of the Atonement of Jesus Christ that carried my parents and sister through this lengthy struggle to the light and joy that emerged on the other side. Although one side of her body has always been weaker than the other, Sandra eventually grew healthy and strong and was blessed with six children of her own. By tapping into the strengthening and enabling power of the Atonement of Jesus Christ, we can likewise be carried through the daily trials of our lives. And as we worship in the temple, we will often feel the comfort of that power in greater measure.

The Healing Power of Christ's Atonement

Now that we understand that the Atonement of Jesus Christ includes both redeeming and enabling powers, are these the end of the powers of His Atonement? No, there is still more! The Atonement of Jesus Christ also brings a healing power.

One of the purposes of both the redeeming and enabling powers of the Atonement of Jesus Christ is to heal us. Christ not only wants to redeem us from our sins, but He also wants to heal us from the effects of those sins. And Christ not only wants to strengthen us in our sorrows, struggles, and griefs; He wants to heal our hearts and our spirits amid those challenges. Thus, the healing power of Christ's Atonement is a natural extension of those two primary powers.

A review of the ministry of the Savior in both the old world and the new shows that He was always healing. In fact, nearly everything He did can be categorized as teaching, healing, or both. Before He appeared in ancient America, He spoke from heaven: "Will ye not now return unto me, and repent of your sins, and be converted, that I may heal you?" (3 Nephi 9:13). Later He appeared at the temple in Bountiful and healed all who came to Him. The ancient record states:

> And he said unto them: Behold, my bowels are filled with compassion towards you.

---

331. Rosemary Wright Jones, "Sandra Lyn's Bout with Polio."

Have ye any that are sick among you? Bring them hither. Have ye any that are lame, or blind, or halt, or maimed, or leprous, or that are withered, or that are deaf, *or that are afflicted in any manner?* Bring them hither and *I will heal them, for I have compassion upon you; my bowels are filled with mercy.*

For I perceive that ye desire that I should show unto you what I have done unto your brethren at Jerusalem, for I see that your faith is sufficient that *I should heal you.*

And it came to pass that when he had thus spoken, all the multitude, with one accord, did go forth with their sick and their afflicted, and their lame, and with their blind, and with their dumb, *and with all them that were afflicted in any manner; and he did heal them* every one as they were brought forth unto him. (3 Nephi 17:6–9; emphasis added)

Today, faithful Saints who are "afflicted in any manner," be it physical, emotional, or spiritual, continue to go to temples seeking healing from Jesus Christ. We put the names of loved ones on the temple prayer rolls, and we meditate on our desires for healing while we are in the temple. We exercise our faith through temple service for others, and we pray in the house of the Lord for insights into how to achieve the healing we desire. As Sister Reyna I. Aburto has said, "We all come to the temple to be spiritually healed and to give those on the other side of the veil the opportunity to be healed as well. When it comes to healing, we all need the Savior desperately."[332]

Jesus Christ sometimes chooses to test our faith by requiring that those who are afflicted continue to live with some elements of their challenges. Rarely do we see immediate, miraculous physical healings nowadays like those performed by Jesus while He was on the earth. Perhaps those were more prevalent at that time to provide witnesses of His divinity. Nevertheless, I have observed that Christ eventually offers some degree of healing in this life for all who faithfully seek it. Often those healings are more spiritual than physical in nature. President Dallin H. Oaks taught, "Sometimes [Christ's] power heals an infirmity, but the scriptures and our experiences teach that

---

332. Reyna I. Aburto, "Miracles of Healing Through Temple Ordinances," *Ensign*, Sept. 2020, 44.

sometimes He succors or helps by giving us the strength or patience to endure our infirmities."[333]

Regarding the healing of emotional and spiritual wounds, Elder Bruce C. Hafen, later a member of the Seventy, wrote:

> Life is a school, a place for us to learn and grow. Our Teacher and Headmaster has placed us on the earth in a risk-filled environment called mortality. Here we may learn what we must know and become what we must be, not only to live with Him someday, but to be like Him.
>
> To learn these profound lessons of life, we must undergo many experiences that subject us to the sorrow and contamination of a lone and dreary world. These experiences may include sin, but they also include undeserved pain, disappointment, and adversity.
>
> But how, then, can we overcome the ill effects and consequences of this necessary contamination? The blessed news of the gospel is that the Atonement of Jesus Christ can purify us from all uncleanness and sweeten all the bitterness we taste. The Atonement not only pays for our sins, *it heals our wounds*—the self-inflicted ones and those inflicted from sources beyond our control.[334]

It can be disappointing to become contaminated or wounded by our own sins, but it can be devastating to be the victim of the sins of others. Many people today are wounded because of abuse or neglect they suffered as a child. Christ has the power to heal all such wounds; however, He usually does so over long periods of time and with a lot of effort on our part. I have found that God would rather develop our souls by guiding us through a lengthy process of healing than provide a swift and easy cure. Quick, miraculous changes do not develop us in the same way that prolonged struggling and suffering do. Professional and spiritual counselors can often help in these healing processes.

President Russell M. Nelson said, "I plead with you to come unto [Christ] so that He can heal you! He will heal you from sin as you repent. He will heal you from sadness and fear. He will heal you from the wounds of this world. Whatever questions or problems you have,

---

333. Dallin H. Oaks, "Strengthened by the Atonement of Jesus Christ," 62.
334. Bruce C. Hafen, *The Broken Heart: Applying the Atonement to Life's Experiences* (Deseret Book, 2004), 29; emphasis added.

the answer is always found in the life and teachings of Jesus Christ. Learn more about His Atonement, His love, His mercy, His doctrine, and His restored gospel of healing and progression. Turn to Him! Follow Him!"[335]

The beautiful hymn "Come Ye Disconsolate" encourages all who suffer from wounded hearts to come to Christ and look to heaven for healing consolation.

> Come, ye disconsolate, where'er ye languish;
> Come to the mercy seat, fervently kneel.
> Here bring your wounded hearts; here tell your anguish.
> Earth has no sorrow that heav'n cannot heal.
>
> Joy of the desolate, Light of the straying,
> Hope of the penitent, fadeless and pure!
> Here speaks the Comforter, tenderly saying,
> "Earth has no sorrow that heav'n cannot cure."
>
> Here see the Bread of Life; see waters flowing
> Forth from the throne of God, pure from above.
> Come to the feast of love; come, ever knowing
> Earth has no sorrow but heav'n can remove.[336]

The healing that is shepherded by Christ is one of the ways that the Atonement of Jesus Christ can bless us. Worshipping at the temple can facilitate this type of healing. President James E Faust said, "The Lord has provided many avenues by which we may receive [His] healing influence. . . . Our temples provide a sanctuary where we may go to lay aside many of the anxieties of the world. Our temples are places of peace and tranquility. In these hallowed sanctuaries God 'healeth the broken in heart, and bindeth up their wounds.' (Psalms 147:3.)"[337]

The celestial room of each temple is intended to mimic the beauty and peace that will be present in the celestial kingdom. John the Revelator described that kingdom as a place where "God shall wipe

---

335. Russell M. Nelson, "The Answer Is Always Jesus Christ," *Liahona*, May 2023, 127.

336. "Come, Ye Disconsolate," *Hymns*, no. 115.

337. James E. Faust, "Spiritual Healing," *Ensign*, May 1992, 7.

away all tears from their eyes; and there shall be no more death, neither sorrow, nor crying, neither shall there be any more pain" (Revelation 21:4). I have sat in celestial rooms and felt that healing wholeness there. Those feelings were always greatest in the temple, but a portion of that spirit has always accompanied me as I left those hallowed walls and returned to my challenges in the world. Christ heals.

My Sister's Healing through Christ

My youngest sister experienced the healing power of the Atonement of Jesus Christ as she faced the effects of some childhood emotional wounds later in life. Our father raised us under some misguided parenting philosophies that he had learned from his own father. Dad often ruled my brothers and me with a heavy hand and other harsh physical punishments, and while my sisters were never struck, they were subjected to the same verbal criticism and bursts of outrage that frequently frightened us all. Our father, with his red hair and red face that would brighten with his anger, would use his powerful voice and assertive manner to magnify the intensity of his discipline. However, despite his harsh approach, he also had a spiritual side with a deep love of the gospel, which he lived imperfectly but without hypocrisy: He was usually as outspoken and bombastic at church as he was at home. My siblings and I dealt with his manner in different ways, but my little sister protected herself by bottling up all her fears inside.

When this sister was in her early forties, raising a family of her own, she started having severe muscle pain in her back and neck that led to tingling and numbness in her extremities. After months of testing with different doctors, she was eventually referred to a psychologist. With his guidance, supplemented by long talks with our other sisters, my ailing sister realized what was going on. Some months before the onset of her nerve problems, she and her family had moved to a new ward. Their new bishop had red hair and spoke with a commanding voice. At the same time, my sister was given a church calling alongside someone who made her feel like she could not measure up. She realized that the situation in her new ward was stirring up childhood stresses that had been bottled up for decades. This realization started a path of healing.

My sister was grateful for a professional counselor who helped her uncover the source of her afflictions, but she found most of her healing in the scriptures. She wrote to me at that time:

> I found that there is gracious healing power in the scriptures. I started reading them in a new light. For example: "He suffereth the pains of all men, yea, the pains of every living creature, both men, women, and children, who belong to the family of Adam" (2 Nephi 9:21). Christ suffered for the pains that I could not handle as a child and had to deal with as a woman.
>
> I noticed a lot of scriptures that dealt with children, healing, and angels. I noticed scriptures that rejoiced in healing. I noticed scriptures condemning those who injure others. I got a notebook and started copying down all those scriptures. After searching and recording around 200 scriptures, the Spirit whispered to me, "You can stop now." When I asked why, the Spirit answered, "Don't you feel healed? Hasn't my word healed your wounded soul?" And it was true![338]

My sister also found healing strength at the temple. During this season of her life, her youngest child started grade school, making it possible for her to attend the temple more frequently than ever before. She felt that it was no coincidence that her healing journey occurred at a time when she could give more time to both temple attendance and scripture study. They helped her tap into the healing power of the Atonement of Jesus Christ.

The Transforming Power of Christ's Atonement

So now, with all of that, are we finally at the end of the list of what Christ can provide through His Atonement? No, there is still more! His Atonement has the power to transform our nature; it can sanctify us.

The word is literally *at-one-ment*. The Atonement of Jesus Christ is the process by which He takes us under His wings and, through the constant companionship of the Holy Ghost, makes us one with Him so that we become like Him. Elder Bruce C. Hafen wrote, "The

---

338. Personal letter in possession of the author, June 5, 2002; edited.

Atonement . . . completes the process of our learning by perfecting our nature and making us whole. In this way, Christ's Atonement makes us as He is."[339]

As we consistently strive to follow Jesus Christ with a desire to become like Him, He will gradually change our nature. He will transform us so that we are ready to enter into God's presence. "No man cometh unto the Father, but by me" (John 14:6), Jesus said. Our covenants help in that process. This is the whole objective of the endowment ceremony: We enter into covenants that will make us more like Jesus Christ as we live them, preparing us to enter into the presence of God and partake of eternal life.

Christ helps us change our nature so that we don't keep making the same mistakes over and over again; however, we must be humble and constantly repent in order for this sanctification—this *at-one-ment*—to take anchor in our lives. And the Lord has established an improvement process to facilitate this. It is a process that integrates the Atonement of Jesus Christ into our weekly worship services through the sacrament.

As we approach the sacrament each week, we show our faith by reflecting on the Savior and His Atonement, we lay our weaknesses before the Lord and repent as needed, we recommit to keep our covenants with Him, and we receive a fresh infusion of the Holy Ghost to guide us through the coming week and to help us see the next level of improvement we need to take. In simple terms, the steps are:

Faith → Repentance → Covenant → Holy Ghost

Wash. Rinse. Repeat. Every week. This is the improvement process by which we are supposed to incorporate the transforming power of Christ's Atonement into our lives. This is how we endure to the end.[340] If we approach the sacrament each week with humility, sincerity, and

---

339. Bruce C. Hafen, *The Broken Heart*, 29.

340. For a full discussion of this improvement process, see Valiant K. Jones, *The Covenant Path: Finding the Temple in the Book of Mormon* (Cedar Fort, 2020), 88–91; see also Dale G. Renlund, "The Powerful, Virtuous Cycle of the Doctrine of Christ," *Liahona*, May 2024.

real purpose of heart, our hearts will be softened, our natures will be changed, and our souls will be transformed.

This is the power to change our character, to overcome mortal deficits and weaknesses, and to become a new creature in Christ, at one with Him. Brother Bradley R. Wilcox has said, "The miracle of the Atonement is not just that we can be cleansed and consoled but that we can be transformed."[341] This power helps us advance toward perfection.

This transforming power is not independent of the other powers of Christ's Atonement. The desired transformation comes as a result of applying the redeeming, the enabling, and the healing powers of Christ's Atonement in our lives. As we pursue these influences, they will bring about a change in us, and the transforming power of the Atonement of Jesus Christ will sanctify us and make us into a new creature with a new heart.

An example from classic literature of a person who went through this type of transformation is Jean Valjean in Victor Hugo's classic, *Les Misérables*. Most people know this story. Jean, an ex-convict, was shown mercy by a Catholic bishop after trying to steal a pair of silver candlesticks from him. That act of compassion and mercy changed Jean, and the rest of the novel chronicles the many ways he selflessly served and blessed others as a transformed person. His life is contrasted with that of the policeman, Javert, whose own struggle against mercy and refusal to change caused him to end his own life in despair.

Hugo's novel includes a beautiful commentary on Christ's Atonement, spoken by the Catholic bishop who showed mercy to Jean: "Whom man kills, God restores to life; whom the brothers pursue, the Father redeems. Pray and believe and go onward into life. Your Father is there."[342] The grateful Jean Valjean did exactly that. Hugo's novel shows how much a person can change and the great impact that a person filled with love and mercy can have on others.

---

341. Brad Wilcox, "His Grace Is Sufficient" (Brigham Young University devotional, July 12, 2011), 3, speeches.byu.edu.
342. Victor Hugo, *Les Misérables* (Thomas Y. Crowell & Co, 1887), part 1, book 1, chapter 4, line 11.

The beloved hymn "Come, thou Fount of Every Blessing" also reminds us how we can be changed if we turn our hearts over to God, especially this version arranged by Mack Wilberg:

> Come, thou fount of every blessing, tune my heart to sing thy grace.
> Streams of mercy, never ceasing, call for songs of loudest praise.
> Teach me some melodious sonnet sung by flaming tongues above;
> Praise the mount, I'm fixed upon it, mount of thy redeeming love.
>
> Jesus sought me when a stranger wandering from the fold of God.
> He, to rescue me from danger, interposed His precious blood.
> Prone to wander, Lord, I feel it, prone to leave the God I love.
> Here's my heart, O take and seal it, seal it for thy courts above.
>
> O to grace, how great a debtor, daily I'm constrained to be!
> Let thy goodness like a fetter bind my wandering heart to thee.
> Prone to wander, Lord, I feel it, prone to leave the God I love.
> Here's my heart, O take and seal it, seal it for thy courts above.[343]

Our hearts are prone to wander, which is why we need Christ to transform us, sealing our hearts to Him. There is no greater power to change a person's heart than the power of the Atonement of Jesus Christ. Elder Tad R. Callister shared the following experience:

> As a mission president, I met several times with a missionary who was struggling with obedience. One day in frustration he blurted out: "What is it you want me to do?" I replied: "You have missed the point. It is not what I want you to do that matters; it should be what do you want to do." There was a moment of silence and then he made this insightful observation: "You are not just asking me to change my behavior; you are asking me to change my nature." How right he was.[344]

---

343. Robert Robinson, "Mack Wilberg's Arrangement of Come Thou Fount of Every Blessing," The Tabernacle Choir at Temple Square, verses 1, 3, and 4, accessed Oct. 20, 2024, https://www.thetabernaclechoir.org/articles/the-history-of-come-thou-fount-of-every-blessing.html; see also "Come Thou Fount of Every Blessing," *Hymns—For Home and Church*, no. 1001.

344. "Elder Tad R. Callister: Are We Just Changing Our Behavior When We Should Be Changing Our Nature?," *Church News*, Feb. 16, 2020.

President Dallin H. Oaks taught, "It is not even enough for us to be *convinced* of the gospel; we must act and think so that we are *converted* by it. In contrast to the institutions of the world, which teach us to *know* something, the gospel of Jesus Christ challenges us to *become* something."[345] It is through striving to keep our covenants that much of this becoming occurs. Our temple covenants help us access the transformational power of the Atonement of Jesus Christ so that we can become like our heavenly parents and Jesus Christ. This is the objective of the entire design of the temple ordinances.

My Father's Transformation

I earlier told how my father's parenting mistakes caused some emotional wounds in my sister and how she found healing through Jesus Christ. Now let me tell you about my father's transformation. He was born in 1927 and grew up during the Great Depression. His father was a dairy farmer in the Salt Lake Valley, and Dad started milking cows at the age of five. Their family was poor, and they knew nothing but hard work.

At school, my dad was considered a country hick and was taunted and bullied by some of his classmates. He was ridiculed for his red hair, freckles, crooked teeth, and glasses. He only had one bath a week in a steel tub in the kitchen on Saturday nights, so he usually went to school smelling like the manure he was always around. He did poorly in school and felt dumb. He was usually too tired from his chores to do any homework that might have improved his standing at school.

When Dad was in the ninth grade, he had a teacher who stood him in front of the class and shamed him, saying how stupid he was. He managed to hold it together until lunchtime when he went into the gym, where he knew of an access door to the ductwork for the air handling system, and he crawled in there and cried.

At about the same time, his own father became disabled. Years earlier, my grandfather had fallen from a horse onto a surveyor's stake and wrenched his back. Later he slid off a hay wagon and wrenched

---

345. Dallin H. Oaks, "The Challenge to Become," *Ensign*, Nov. 2000, 32; emphasis in original.

his back again. He wore a large leather brace and lived with constant back pain. He carried on as best he could with the farm, but as the years progressed, he started getting spasms on one side, and his pain became so severe that his mind became affected, so Grandma was forced to place him in the state mental hospital in Provo. He died there four months later when my dad was only fifteen years old. I expect that having his father die in a mental hospital didn't help my father's already fragile self-esteem, especially in an era when mental illness was stigmatized.

At the end of high school, as WWII was ending, my dad and some buddies went to California to enlist in the Merchant Marines. Because of his bad eyesight and a hernia, he was turned away as class 4-F, so he again felt rejected and inferior. He worked in California until he got homesick and returned home.

Two things followed that changed my father's life. First, he started reading *Jesus the Christ* by Elder James E. Talmage. He came to know the Savior through that book. He once told me that reading that book was the biggest turning point in his life. The second thing was that he decided to serve a mission for the Church. He was called to the Great Lakes Mission in February of 1947, and he spent most of his two years of service in Michigan. He worked hard to share the gospel and serve people, and he spent whatever free time he had studying the scriptures and every gospel book he could get his hands on.

My father became a voracious reader, mostly of Church books. For decades, he bought and read almost every Latter-day Saint book he could acquire. This man, who, as a boy, had been ridiculed and called stupid, became a solid scholar who was revered for his gospel knowledge and his skills as a speaker and teacher.

My father's intellectual and spiritual abilities grew; however, it's hard to have a childhood like he did and not carry some anger and other emotional baggage into adulthood. After marriage, life brought him new challenges, including my oldest sister's polio, bankruptcy due to a failed business, and an emotional breakdown. Sometimes Dad's anger and need for control were taken out on his children, but over time, the influence of Jesus Christ overpowered the struggles, softening him and turning the anger into compassion. His emotional well-being seemed to grow as his children grew. His outbursts became less frequent, his spirituality increased, and he became more loving. He was healing inside.

When my parents were preparing for the first of what would eventually be four full-time senior missions for the Church, my father wanted to make sure he was clean and pure before the Lord. He knew that he had made many mistakes as he raised his children, so he talked to each one of us personally and apologized for his outbursts and excessive punishments. I lived far away, so his conversation with me was over the phone. I will never forget his humility as he admitted that he had done wrong and had harmed the children he loved. He cried tears of sorrow and remorse as he said to me, "Val, I need your forgiveness."

I wrote in a letter to my father afterward:

> Thank you for the good talk. I was so moved by your humility and love. . . . I know it took a lot of courage to do what you did, and I only love and admire you more for having done it. . . .
>
> I've seen your harshness mellow, and I've seen you be more affectionate and considerate and loving than in those earlier years. I think those [qualities] were always a part of you, but I think that they have increased, and I have also been more perceptive to them. I saw that you were improving yourself, and I realized that we are all on this earth to learn and grow—even parents. As children, we all think our parents are perfect. When we begin to realize they are not, we resent them for not being so. Then as we approach parenthood ourselves, we realize no parent is perfect and that we are all just children of God, learning and growing together. That's when we accept our parents for what they are and have been and appreciate them more. . . .
>
> As I think of all the things you've taught me, both directly and indirectly, I can only be grateful. If I gained any weaknesses from you, I also gained the strength of character to overcome those weaknesses, as well as other weaknesses that I've acquired on my own. That is the greatest thing anyone could gain from [their] parents.[346]

---

346. Valiant K. Jones, personal communication in possession of the author, Oct. 7, 1985.

Years later, when my youngest sister was working through her own emotional healing, she wrote to me the following:

> Boy, was my counselor impressed when I told him that my dad went to every one of his kids before his and Mom's first mission and asked for their forgiveness. You may know that I was living near Mom and Dad at the time. I remember that time very well. The most impressive moment was when I walked into Dad's shop and he was sobbing like a baby. Boy, it will throw you to see something like that! He had just gotten off the phone with one of our brothers. Do you remember the time Dad beat the crap out of him and belittled him so badly? Well, Dad remembered that time too, and he had just been asking our brother if he could ever forgive him. I walked into Dad's shop, and Dad was rehearsing what our brother told him: "He told me, 'Dad, I forgave you for that a long time ago.'" Then Dad sobbed like a baby and said, "Can you imagine? Can you imagine that after what I did to him, that he would forgive me?"[347]

My father's humble admissions of these serious mistakes and his pleas to his children for forgiveness aided not only his children's healing but also his own transformation.

My parents' first mission was to Salt Lake City in 1986 where they served under Brother Arch Madsen, the director of Temple Square and former president of Bonneville International Corporation. My mother served as his secretary, and my father served as one of his associate directors. Temple Square was undergoing some renovations at the time, and Brother Madsen wanted to improve the recording that was used for the Christus statue, which he felt wasn't doing justice to that beautiful stone carving of the Savior. Having become acquainted with my father's extensive knowledge of the scriptures as well as his love for the Savior, Brother Madsen assigned Dad to come up with the text for a new presentation.

My father explained, "After receiving this assignment, I went to my office and began to ponder when the scriptures started to flood my mind. I think it took me less than an hour to put it all together."

---

347. Christine Jones Cole, personal letter in possession of the author, June 5, 2002; edited.

He took his compilation to my mother who typed it up. He reviewed it and then rearranged only two verses. He felt it was a miraculous revelatory experience. Brother Madsen heartily approved but had it shortened, aware that most visitors had a limited attention span. My father's arrangement of first-person scriptural declarations by Jesus Christ continues to be used on Temple Square and in other Church visitor centers around the world.

I am proud of my father and grateful for the revelation he gained through repentance, humility, and immersing himself in the words of Christ. Although he was never perfect, he overcame many of his childhood deficits and was transformed into a better person—a true disciple of Jesus Christ. By engaging the redeeming, enabling, and healing powers of the Atonement of Jesus Christ, these influences changed him over time. I am sure he continues to grow and develop as he now shares his strong testimony of Jesus Christ on the other side of the veil.

We all need to be transformed into new creatures, fully aligned with Christ. This is sanctification. It is a process, not an event, so we must be patient with ourselves and with others. Nephi experienced the highs and lows of this process of transformation. Even though he was ministered to by angels and had seen Christ in a vision, he later pined, "O wretched man that I am! Yea, my heart sorroweth because of my flesh; my soul grieveth because of mine iniquities. I am encompassed about, because of the temptations and the sins which do so easily beset me. And when I desire to rejoice, my heart groaneth because of my sins; nevertheless, I know in whom I have trusted. My God hath been my support" (2 Nephi 4:17–20).

None of us will become perfect in this life, but we can choose a path of continual improvement. If we follow the promptings of the Holy Ghost, Jesus Christ will combine the powers of His Atonement with the life lessons and humility that come with our personal struggles, transforming us into new creatures—creatures designed for God's glory and for our future exaltation and eternal happiness.

When we embrace this covenant path of continual improvement, we are covered by the grace of Jesus Christ and are considered "perfect in Christ." Moroni wrote of this in the final verses of the Book of Mormon where he made this plea:

> I would exhort you that ye would come unto Christ. . . .
>
> Yea, come unto Christ, and be perfected in him, and deny yourselves of all ungodliness; and if ye shall deny yourselves of all ungodliness and love God with all your might, mind and strength, then is his grace sufficient for you, that by his grace ye may be perfect in Christ; . . .
>
> [And] if ye by the grace of God are perfect in Christ, and deny not his power, then are ye sanctified in Christ by the grace of God, through the shedding of the blood of Christ, which is in the covenant of the Father unto the remission of your sins, that ye become holy, without spot. (Moroni 10:30, 32–33)

This process of sanctification is achieved through the transformational power of the Atonement of Jesus Christ. It is the objective of the temple initiatory, endowment, and sealing ordinances. Through our covenants, the Lord guides us on this transformational journey. And when we fall short through sin or weakness, He uses our mistakes to teach us to tap into the power of His grace. He invites us to be part of His *at-one-ment*—to submit our will to His, just as He submitted to the will of the Father in the Garden of Gethsemane. Through His transformational power, we can become "perfect in Christ."

The Holy Ghost and Christ's Atonement

The way in which I have most frequently experienced the power of the Atonement of Jesus Christ in my life is through the inspiration of the Holy Ghost. The Spirit has frequently taught me how to deal with my own weaknesses and challenges. The Holy Ghost has led me to specific scriptures or inspired talks by Church leaders that have helped me. He has whispered insights and guidance to my mind and to my heart. He has warned me in times of spiritual danger. He has encouraged me to be patient in periods filled with questions and confusion. He has given me peace when some answers have been withheld.

In March of 2017 President Henry B. Eyring and President Jeffrey R. Holland held a face-to-face dialogue with many youth of the Church. These two Apostles responded to a question about accessing the power of Christ's Atonement in a person's life. President Eyring taught, "The Atonement was something Jesus Christ did. It's not a thing itself. He atoned for our sins, and He paid the price to allow us to be forgiven and to be resurrected. So it's what He did that qualified Him to give us forgiveness, to change our hearts. *And it's the Holy Ghost doing that, it's not the Atonement as if it's a thing itself.*"[348]

President Holland added to this response by referring to the teachings of Mormon to his son as recorded in Moroni 8:

> When [Mormon] talks about the blessing of the Atonement in our lives—the fruits of it—he says, "The remission of sins bringeth meekness, and lowliness of heart." If we understand the Atonement, we're going to be meek and lowly and very grateful. "And because of meekness and lowliness of heart cometh the visitation of the Holy Ghost." Now you start to tie those together. "Which Comforter filleth with hope and perfect love, which love endureth by diligence unto prayer, until the end shall come, when all the saints shall dwell with God" (Mormon 8:26).
>
> We've just been swept right into the celestial kingdom here on the strength of the Atonement of Jesus Christ because it made us meek, it made us lowly, it made us grateful, it made us know somebody helped us, and that brings the Holy Ghost. I don't know that I had ever quite tied *the gift of the Holy Ghost [to] an extension of the Savior's Atonement.* . . . [We] can access that Atonement by being meek and lowly and grateful and feeling the Spirit in our lives.[349]

Just as Jesus Christ is one with the Father, the Holy Ghost is one with Them both. The three members of the Godhead are unified, so the Holy Ghost is able to communicate what Christ learned through His Atonement, making it available to us at any time and in any place. The key to receiving the power of Christ's Atonement in our lives is to have the Holy Ghost with us and to follow His guidance. This is why

---

348. Strive To Be, "Face to Face with President Eyring and Elder Holland," YouTube, Mar. 4, 2017, 1:04:06–1:04–40, https://www.youtube.com/watch?v=8nmiWnZPzEo; emphasis added.

349. Strive To Be, "Face to Face with President Eyring and Elder Holland," 1:06:02–1:07–32; emphasis added.

we are given an opportunity each week to receive a fortification of the companionship of the Holy Ghost through the sacrament.

In the Church, we sometimes hear that we need to be worthy to receive guidance from the Holy Ghost; however, the root of the word *worthy* is *worth*, and we must remember that our worth is infinite. My experience is that there is very little that will make us unworthy of the Spirit's guidance. We do not have to be without sin. We do not have to be keeping every commandment fully. We only need to have faith in Christ and be humble and sincere in our efforts to try to do better. Brother Bradley R. Wilcox has said, "When a young pianist hits a wrong note, we don't say he is not worthy to keep practicing. We don't expect him to be flawless. We just expect him to keep trying."[350]

If we are humble and approach the Lord with a sincere heart, He will bless us with the Holy Ghost, and that gift will guide us to resolve all our "worthiness" issues, even if it takes a long time. That is the power of the Christ's Atonement in our lives. President Holland has said, "With the gift of the Atonement of Jesus Christ and the strength of heaven to help us, we can improve, and the great thing about the gospel is we get credit for trying, even if we don't always succeed."[351]

The prerequisites of humility and sincerity deserve further discussion. Humility, which the scriptures often describe as being meek and lowly of heart, makes us teachable so the Holy Ghost can guide us. And sincerity means without hypocrisy. The Book of Mormon promises a witness of its truth, through the Holy Ghost, to those who read it and ask God if it is true "with a sincere heart, with real intent, having faith in Christ" (Moroni 10:4). So when we talk about being worthy of the guidance of the Holy Ghost, we should focus less on being free from sin or perfect in our duties, and we should focus more on being humble and sincere. The Spirit will then help us with the rest. Christ's grace is sufficient.

King Benjamin described the need for humility and sincerity in these terms: "For the natural man is an enemy to God, . . . unless he *yields to the enticings of the Holy Spirit*, and putteth off the natural man

---

350. Brad Wilcox, "His Grace Is Sufficient, 4.
351. Jeffrey R. Holland, "Tomorrow the Lord Will Do Wonders Among You," *Ensign*, May 2016, 125–6.

and becometh a saint through the atonement of Christ the Lord, and becometh as a child, submissive, meek, humble, patient, full of love, willing to submit to all things which the Lord seeth fit to inflict upon him, even as a child doth submit to his father" (Mosiah 3:19, emphasis added; see also Mosiah 4:10).

If we are humble and sincere, we will be teachable and receptive to "the enticings of the Holy Spirit." And that member of the Godhead will guide us with inspiration from the wellspring of Christ's Atonement to transform us into new creatures. President Henry B. Eyring confirmed this, saying, "When we feel the influence of the Holy Ghost, we also can feel that our natures are being changed because of the Atonement of Jesus Christ."[352] This is true when we need guidance in dealing with sin or bad habits as well as help in dealing with non-sin-related burdens such as grief and pain and anguish. Through the Holy Ghost, the power of Christ's Atonement will fortify us with all the comfort and guidance we need for joy in this life and exaltation in the life to come.

From Pain to Joy

The beginning of this chapter told of the tremendous pain that Jesus Christ suffered as he carried out His Atonement for all mankind: "Which suffering caused myself, even God, the greatest of all, to tremble because of pain, and to bleed at every pore, and to suffer both body and spirit" (D&C 19:18).

It was not very long after this ordeal that Jesus Christ appeared to the Nephites in His resurrected body. He taught them, healed their sick, and prayed for them. After documenting these things, the Book of Mormon records states:

> And no tongue can speak, neither can there be written by any man, neither can the hearts of men conceive so great and marvelous things as we both saw and heard Jesus speak; and no one can conceive of *the joy which filled our souls* at the time we heard him pray for us unto the Father.

---

352. Henry B. Eyring, "Gifts of the Spirit for Hard Times" (Brigham Young University devotional, Sept. 10, 2006), 2, speeches.byu.edu.

> And it came to pass that when Jesus had made an end of praying unto the Father, he arose; but *so great was the joy of the multitude* that they were overcome.
>
> And it came to pass that Jesus spake unto them, and bade them arise.
>
> And they arose from the earth, and he said unto them: Blessed are ye because of your faith. And now behold, *my joy is full.*
>
> And when he had said these words, *he wept*, and the multitude bare record of it, and he took their little children, one by one, and blessed them, and prayed unto the Father for them.
>
> And when he had done this *he wept again.* (3 Nephi 17:17–22; emphasis added.)

What a contrast this joyous experience was compared to the extreme pain Jesus had so recently suffered. This sweet joy was so full that it made our Lord weep repeatedly. This same joy is the object of our temple worship. This becomes clear as we hear Eve speak of "the joy of our redemption" (Moses 5:11). President Russell M. Nelson taught this about the Lord's transition from pain to joy:

> Jesus Christ is our ultimate exemplar, "who for the joy that was set before him endured the cross." Think of that! In order for Him to endure the most excruciating experience ever endured on earth, our Savior focused on joy! And what was the joy that was set before Him? Surely it included the joy of cleansing, healing, and strengthening us; the joy of paying for the sins of all who would repent; the joy of making it possible for you and me to return home—clean and worthy—to live with our Heavenly Parents and families.[353]

We can personally experience this same transition from pain to joy through the power of the Atonement of Jesus Christ. Past pains can be swallowed up in new joy. There is no sin, no sorrow, no wound, no trouble, no mistake, no anguish that cannot be touched by the Atonement of Jesus Christ and made better. As President Holland has said, "It is not possible for you to sink lower than the infinite light of

---

353. Russell M. Nelson, "Joy and Spiritual Survival," *Ensign* or *Liahona*, Nov. 2016, 83.

Christ's Atonement shines."[354] Jesus Christ redeems, He strengthens, He heals, and He transforms. Together, these form the sanctifying power of the Atonement of Jesus Christ. All these powers are available to us because of what Christ did for us in the Garden of Gethsemane and on the hill of Golgotha.

We might enumerate additional powers of Christ's Atonement. For example, resurrection is usually listed in the scriptures as a separate gift provided by Jesus Christ, but it could also be included as one of the powers arising from His Atonement. In the classic book *The Infinite Atonement,* Elder Tad R. Callister described eight blessings that come from the Atonement of Jesus Christ: Resurrection, Repentance, Peace of Mind, Succor, Motivation, Exaltation, Freedom, and Grace.[355] Also, BYU professor Steven J. Hafen presented a list of five ways in which the Atonement of Jesus Christ blesses us: It purifies, enables, assures, comforts, and exalts.[356] While each of the additional descriptions could be aligned with the four primary powers presented in this chapter, new insights can come from considering the power of Christ's Atonement in different terms. The Atonement of Jesus Christ is truly infinite.

The many powers of the Atonement of Jesus Christ are taught and modeled in the temple. President Russell M. Nelson declared, "The temple lies at the center of strengthening our faith and spiritual fortitude because the Savior and His doctrine are the very heart of the temple. Everything taught in the temple, through instruction and through the Spirit, increases our understanding of Jesus Christ. His essential ordinances bind us to Him through sacred priesthood covenants. Then, as we keep our covenants, He endows us with *His* healing, strengthening power. And oh, how we will need His power in the days ahead."[357]

---

354. Jeffrey R. Holland, "The Laborers in the Vineyard," *Ensign* or *Liahona,* May 2012, 33.

355. See Tad R. Callister, *The Infinite Atonement* (Deseret Book, 2000), 166–277.

356. See Steven J. Hafen, "Our Path to Lasting Personal Peace" (Brigham Young University devotional, Mar. 12, 2024), speeches.byu.edu.

357. Russell M. Nelson, "The Temple and Your Spiritual Foundation," *Liahona,* Nov. 2021, 93–94; emphasis in original.

It is by keeping our covenants that we are given full access to the many powers of Christ's Atonement. That is one of the promises God gives to us when we enter into a covenant relationship with Him. In the revealed dedicatory prayer for the Kirtland Temple, we read, "And we ask thee, Holy Father, that thy servants may go forth from this house *armed with thy power*" (D&C 109:22, emphasis added). Nephi saw in vision that this same power would settle upon the Saints of our day: "And it came to pass that I, Nephi, beheld *the power of the Lamb of God*, that it descended upon the saints of the church of the Lamb, and upon the covenant people of the Lord, who were scattered upon all the face of the earth; and they were armed with righteousness and with the power of God in great glory" (1 Nephi 14:14; emphasis added). The "power of the Lamb of God" includes the powers of His Atonement: His redeeming, strengthening, healing, and transforming powers.

I am personally grateful for the many powers of the Atonement of Jesus Christ, and I am grateful for the ordinances of the temple that continue to teach me about those powers and help me experience them more fully. They are sanctifying me. They are preparing me to feel the embrace of my Savior, Jesus Christ, and enter into the presence of Him and our heavenly parents. The temple fortifies me as I strive to be more like Jesus Christ.

Afterword

Like most active Latter-day Saints, I have had many interviews to renew my temple recommend. During one of these, a good friend who was a counselor in our bishopric asked me, "Val, what does the temple mean to you?" I was not ready for that question. It was not part of the normal routine. However, it only took a moment of reflection before tears started to well up in my eyes, and with emotion in my voice I told him, "For me, the temple is a place of revelation and healing."

My life, like everyone's, has had its unique challenges. I am the fourth of eight children, all born within a ten-and-a-half-year window. You cannot grow up in an environment like that without some natural dysfunction. As a middle child, I felt lost in that tight crowd. Sometimes I felt like I didn't matter. My reaction to those feelings, along with other personal challenges, gave me certain personality quirks that frequently led to accusations of "You're weird." I often felt lonely and insignificant.

Nevertheless, having so many siblings born in such a short time was also a blessing. We developed a close bond between us that remains strong to this day. Our home was also filled with the gospel.

Both of our parents loved the Lord, had strong testimonies of His restored gospel, and served diligently in the Church. I acquired from them a similar love for the gospel and a sensitivity to the Spirit, so in my loneliness I often sought solace in prayer, even as a boy. And when I prayed, I felt something. I felt the love of God, and I felt a warmth with empathy and comfort from my Savior, Jesus Christ. I felt like He knew me and loved me and understood me.

Those early prayers are the roots of my love for the temple, for I felt that same spirit of love and comfort when I began attending the Lord's house. I have attended consistently ever since my mission, even though for many years this meant a six-hour drive each way along with a hotel stay. The temple has always been a priority for me, and as I matured spiritually, I found in that holy house a place where I could face the deficits of my own personality and come to terms with certain challenges within myself that I would have preferred to bury. As I opened myself up to the Lord while remaining steadfast in my covenants, I found revelation and healing at the temple.

So when my friend asked what the temple meant to me, I thought upon the many healing insights I have received in the temple that have guided me to overcome personal weaknesses (a continuing process, by the way). I thought upon a sacred spiritual experience I had in the Chicago Illinois Temple when I was given specific instruction from my deceased grandfather to help me in that quest. I thought upon a day in the Detroit Michigan Temple when I was serving in the baptistry, performing confirmations for my own children who were proxies for our ancestors, and I felt the presence and love of these ancestors so strongly that I was overcome with emotion and could hardly speak. I thought upon the feelings of comfort and peace I have felt in several temples as I prayed about personal challenges that seemed greater than my ability to overcome them. Only occasionally did I receive direction on how to deal with them, but I always felt God's love. I know that these blessings came because I was steadfastly keeping my covenants, even when I was sometimes tempted to forsake them.

I then thought upon the many doctrinal insights I have received through nearly five decades of regular temple attendance and scripture study. Many of these insights have been included in this book and my previous one. While contemplating my first book, I was often in awe at the connections I discovered between the endowment and the writings on the small plates of Nephi. I remembered a time in the temple when I suddenly recognized some distinct parallels between the covenant admonition to avoid light-mindedness and the Book of Mormon story I had recently read talking about the rudeness of Nephi's brothers during their ocean voyage. My heart began racing, and I could hardly wait to reach the celestial room where I could share the insight with my wife. It was while performing proxy sealings that I gained many of the insights included in the first two chapters of this second book. Often after serving in the temple, I would hurry to a prayer roll credenza and help myself to the slips of paper and pencils there so I could record notes on my insights. The revelatory insights that have come to me in the temple have enlarged my understanding of the temple ordinances and covenants and have fortified my understanding of the role of Jesus Christ as the center of our worship in His holy house.

So during that temple recommend interview, I bore witness to my friend that the temple is a place of revelation and healing. Making and keeping our covenants qualifies us for these blessings. I bear this same witness to all readers of this book. Because we now have so many temples throughout the world, covenant Saints everywhere can experience what the Lord promised in 1831: "When men [and women] are endowed with power from on high and sent forth, all these [needful] things shall be gathered unto the bosom of the church. And . . . ye shall be the richest of all people, for ye shall have the riches of eternity" (D&C 38:38–39).

As members of the Church, we are indeed the richest of all people, for we have hundreds of temples throughout the earth, and the covenants and ordinances thereof bring us the riches of eternity. The quantity and grandeur of these covenant cathedrals of the Restoration reflect the fulfillment of the promise the Lord gave when He accepted the Kirtland Temple: "The fame of this house shall spread to foreign lands; and this is the beginning of the blessing which shall be poured out upon the heads of my people" (D&C 110:10).

This work is true! God lives, and Jesus is the Christ, the Savior of the world. Joseph Smith was a prophet of God who restored the fulness of the gospel to the earth. The Book of Mormon is true. And we are led today by a living prophet who possesses all the keys and authority from God necessary to administer His church and the ordinances of salvation and exaltation. Sure, there are some things I still don't understand, but I have gained enough insights to satisfy me, and I accept the rest on faith. In the meantime, I am nurtured with the Spirit as I pray, the same as when I was a boy, and I am comforted by the same spiritual feelings of love and peace whenever I attend the temple. I know that these spiritual feelings and many other blessings have come to me because I am striving to keep my covenants. I am grateful for the temple and the principles taught there that draw me closer to Jesus Christ. He is the heart of my covenants, and to Him I give my heart in return. He is the source of my joy, my healing, and my peace.

Valiant K. Jones
January 2025

About the Author

Valiant K. Jones grew up in Utah, Indiana, and Idaho, and he attended Brigham Young University where he received a BS degree, summa cum laude with honors, followed by an MS degree, both in chemical engineering. He worked for over thirty-two years in the chemical industry where he authored many research and technology reports during his career.

Brother Jones enjoys using his analytical skills in the study of Latter-day Saint scripture and doctrine. He previously authored *The Covenant Path: Finding the Temple in the Book of Mormon*. He has served in a variety of callings in The Church of Jesus Christ of Latter-day Saints, including missionary in the Argentina Cordoba Mission, temple worker, seminary teacher, branch president, and high councilor. He has also served in civic and community roles, including extensive BSA volunteer positions where he received the Silver Beaver Award.

Brother Jones resides in central Michigan where he enjoys the beautiful outdoors, camping, biking, and snow skiing. He and his wife, the former Lori Ransom, are the proud parents of five children and have a growing number of grandchildren.

Scan to visit

https://valiantjones.com/